Food, Film and Culture

ALSO BY JAMES R. KELLER

Queer (Un)Friendly Film and Television
(McFarland, 2002)

Anne Rice and Sexual Politics:
The Early Novels (McFarland, 2000)

———————————————

EDITED BY JAMES R. KELLER AND LESLIE STRATYNER

The New Queer Aesthetic on Television:
Essays on Recent Programming
(McFarland, 2006)

Almost Shakespeare: Reinventing His
Works for Cinema and Television
(McFarland, 2004)

Food, Film and Culture

A Genre Study

James R. Keller

McFarland & Company, Inc., Publishers

Jefferson, North Carolina, and London

LIBRARY OF CONGRESS CATALOGUING-IN-PUBLICATION DATA

Keller, James R., 1960–
    Food, film and culture : a genre study / James R. Keller.
        p.   cm.
    Includes bibliographical references and index.

    ISBN-13: 978-0-7864-2616-4
    ISBN-10: 0-7864-2616-0
    (softcover : 50# alkaline paper)

    1. Food in motion pictures.   I. Title.
    PN1995.9.F65K45   2006
    91.43'6559 — dc22   2006018727

British Library cataloguing data are available

On the cover: theater ©2006 Brand X pictures; baked potato ©2006
PhotoSpin.

Manufactured in the United States of America

McFarland & Company, Inc., Publishers
    Box 611, Jefferson, North Carolina 28640
    www.mcfarlandpub.com

Table of Contents

Introduction: The Cinematic Hunger Artists

The chapters in this volume sample the multiplicity of roles that culinary imagery can play in contemporary cinema, identifying what may be construed as a food film sub-genre, one in which food production, preparation, service, and or consumption play an operative and memorable role in the development of character, structure, or theme. The cinematic hunger artists manipulate gustatory imagery in order to increase the sensory response of the film audience to a medium that cannot access smell or taste, but, nevertheless, seeks to create a full sensory response to a strictly visual and auditory medium. Food cinema thus invokes the gustatory appetite in a fashion similar to the arousal of the libido through romantic and sexual imagery, accessing the full sensory experience of the actor and, subsequently and vicariously, of the audience. Rarely does the producer of food cinema seek, however, to evoke sensory response only via culinary imagery; in most cases the filmmaker simultaneously links visual and sensual responses to ideas peripheral to food and its consumption. The culinary is highly suggestive of abstract cultural processes, such as class, race, gender, ethnicity, history, politics, geography, aesthetics, spirituality, and nationality, as well as more subjective conditions, such as obsession, indifference, depression, elation, rage, meditation, neurosis, psychosis, mental illness, mystical ecstasy, carnal desire, and love. The present work seeks to explore the abstract links between food and idea and to trace the recurring thematic nexus of food, film, and culture, as well as the metaphor of the filmmaker as chef and or artist.

The term "palette" signifies simultaneously both the board on which an artist mixes paints before applying them to a canvas and the range of colors that s/he will utilize in the composition. Thus an artist's palette may be said to include both substance and potential, color having no materiality but the paint itself a mixture of pigments with oil, water, or chemicals.

Color and, consequently, shape and design in painting are evoked by a trick of the light, by a reflection of light on pigment. The range of the artist's palette is multiplied through the mixture of a limited number of primary hues from which are derived the entire spectrum of color and all the potential within painting The successful application of color to canvas remains an alliance of mental acuity or creativity and physical dexterity or training. However, the apprehension of the artist's success lies outside of his control, the audience filtering the reflection of light and evaluating the resulting imagery. The perception of a painting is the physical act of processing light while the reception of a composition is a physical process rooted in the chemistry of the brain. In this sense, the mental image itself is a painting, the union of light and chemistry, and the success of this composition is dialectic, the image evaluated in connection to other images and ideas preserved within the brain's vast collection of memories. The concept may be pleasurable, satisfying, disturbing, or revolting when processed in relation to an entire history of images that have previously made an impression. Thus while the painter's work remains evocative of a mental process in the audience, the appreciation of his work lies entirely with that audience; nevertheless, the apprehension of art necessitates a collective experience, even in exclusion of the artists.

"Palette" is a homophone for the term "palate," signifying both the roof of the mouth and the sense of taste. While the palette is both the board on which the artistic medium is placed and the medium itself, the palate is only juxtaposed to the canvas for gustatory compositions, unless one considers that the palate — as in the sense of taste — is the tongue which generates flavor by crushing the food mass and the taste buds on to the hard roof of the mouth, a rich analogue to the application of paint to canvas. Specific patches of receptor cells, discretely arranged on the tongue, are responsible for sensing particular flavors, the primary ones being bitter, sweet, salt, and sour. The stimuli from these cells in combination with saliva and the olfactory sense generate taste. Just as the primary hues generate all others in the color spectrum, the four taste sensors blend to create all flavors. Thus the palate is the palette for the chef's creative endeavors. Crushing the tongue against the roof of the mouth drives the food mass into the taste buds, and this clamping or sucking motion intensifies and prolongs the flavor. However, taste also requires the intervention of the brain which must recognize, evaluate, and categorize the stimuli from the mouth and nasal passages. The evaluative quality of taste or the recognition and judgment of flavor can be processed only in the brain, and, as with the visual imagery of painting, the quality of taste is assessed in relationship to a history of tastes, and the pleasure or revulsion generated relates in large part to the familiarity of the flavor. The tasting subject frequently judges the outcome of the experience in opposition to or alliance with previous experiences of the same or similar tastes. This process might be defined as the "syntax" or "semiotics" of taste. A chef or diner may rate a dish as "better" or "worse" than the last time the gustatory composition was prepared, or describe a new taste combination in relation to one that is familiar: "It tastes like chicken."

The experience of taste is also social or collective (Amerine 104-120). The eater may make an evaluation of his dining experience in accordance with the perception of others, perhaps a restaurant critic or a dinner companion. The individual diner will certainly be predisposed to favor a new taste if s/he has been told in advance that the experience is enjoyable. Even a sense of social position can influence an individual's reception of flavor. One may sample a new or a formerly reviled taste in socially elevated company and find the experience more appealing than when consuming the same alone. Some may overcome a revulsion to a particular food, such as oysters or brie, because they consumed it in the company of those whom they desire to emulate socially. I, for example, overcame my childhood reticence to eat salmon by consuming it in a collective setting where I had to pretend to enjoy it. As in the audience's apprehension of art, the success or failure of a dish is determined by the eater, and that evaluation is culturally constituted, defined by social, geographic, and biological categories as diverse as class, race, ethnicity, nationality, and gender. What one group savors, another spurns and often such conclusions are based largely upon consideration of the collective or upon conformity.

The filmmakers addressed herein engage the palate as a principal medium in their compositions. One might say, as with the chef, that the director's palate is his or her pallette. However, the filmmaker faces a unique challenge in the creation of onscreen culinary experiences. S/he has no access to the audience's palates, but can only invoke appetite and desire in a strictly visual and auditory medium, the most important ingredients in the gustatory experience — smell and taste — remaining inaccessible to the audience. Thus food can only ever be metaphor in film as it can never be consumed by the audience, save in a visual or auditory sense. The pleasure of dining and the quality of food must be made evident in light, color, and sound. The filmmaker's pallette is, therefore, remarkably similar to that of the painter, both designs being evidenced by the play of light and color on a flat surface. Cinema is thus an effect rather than an object; however, the effect resides partially in the object that is celluloid tape and partially in the audience's own cognitive processes, as each member must recognize and interpret the visual and auditory stimuli. Yet, as with the previously cited artistic media, filmmaking and film viewing maintain an additional social dimension.

Filmmaking is rarely ever a solitary practice save in home videos and some student compositions. The director, of course, requires a large staff to complete his compositions, and not just the writers and actors but an army of trained professionals whose acknowledgments are routinely ignored by American audiences at the conclusion of theatrical presentations. Many of these ancillary filmmakers play a very important role in producing the unique appearance of a project. In the instance of cinematic food imagery, the staff would include chefs and food photographers as well as artistic designers whose efforts concentrate on making the gustatory image alluring, uninspiring, or revolting as the need may be. Thus the film crew and director are telling the audience how to enjoy the celluloid feast. Food that appears onscreen is in many cases not even edible since even the most appealing foods often include unpalatable ingredients intended to improve the appearance of the dish on camera. Nor is the food in film intended to be substantive in the rare cases where the actors actually consume it. In all probability the actors do not consider the stage food a source of sustenance, and even if they were inclined to glut themselves on the dishes, they would be consuming stage props, and one can assume that the set managers would have an objection to creating a new dish each time the director wished to reshoot a scene.

The audience members know that they cannot have a taste of onscreen food, and they must suspend disbelief in order to convince themselves that the film sustenance is actually substantive for anyone, even the actors. Herein lies another of the social dimensions of cinematic cuisine. The facial expressions of actors as they consume stage food evaluate the quality of the culinary experience, coding the food as delicious, unfamiliar, or revolting. The cinematic dining experience thus reveals the binary or dialectical quality of taste, and not only in that one taste is evaluated in opposition to another, but also in that the acting diner impacts the reaction of the imaginary/imaginative diners in the theater seats who have no further access to gustatory sensation. The onscreen eaters teach their viewers to enjoy, ignore, or revile their food. There is little chance that the audience would imagine an appealing gustatory experience if the images of consumption were coded as unpleasant. The same dialectic is operative outside of the theater where the individual is conditioned by the collective culture to enjoy or despise particular tastes. Accounts of gustatory pleasure either verbal or visual offer instruction to subsequent diners, encouraging and in some cases determining whether those who come later enjoy their food. Restaurant critics have made a profession of this practice, and certainly many patrons who dine at a well reviewed establishment will enjoy the experience as much because they were told they would as because the tastes and service reached expectations within an abstract standard. Dining in the company of others results in a similar effect, in which facial and verbal expressions make other diners apprehensive of their impending first taste. Diners who register shock or disgust over a sample of the available dishes will increase the reticence of table companions. In another situation, a diner may be unwilling or even unable to enjoy a particular food because the social context in which it is consumed would deem that enjoyment vulgar. For example, one may not want to protest one's longing for hotdogs and hamburgers at a Palm Beach garden party, nor would one want to lament the absence of caviar and paté at the company BBQ.

Nowhere is the manipulation of appetite and desire more blatant than in food cinema. The director mobilizes the audience's appetites, steering the resulting energies into contexts extraneous to the pursuit of nourishment. The inclusion of culinary imagery in film creates a tension within the viewer, exciting the appetite but refusing fulfillment, drawing out desire and attaching it to objects unconnected to the slaking of one's thirst or the glutting of one's appetite. The experience of gustatory pleasure on screen is not unlike the frozen figures on Keats' Grecian Urn; the imagery of life's pleasures and beauties are depicted on the side of the urn, capturing the moment just prior to fulfillment and suspending that heightened sensibility indefinitely. Moreover, the idyllic environment painted on the urn exceeds reality. Since the urn's perfect melodies, beauties, tastes, and passions can only be imagined, the life depicted must transcend reality. Similarly, the taste, smell, and texture of onscreen food can only be imagined by the film audience, and this supplementation of the visual and auditory experience may exceed the actual consumption of a dish, which would certainly be less than perfect if for no other reason than that the delight in eating is limited by the size of the portion and the diner's appetite.

The expression "food pornography," as defined by Frank Chin, refers to the practice of "making a living by exploiting the 'exotic' aspects of one's ethnic foodways" (qtd. in Ty 62), and it is certainly true that the most engaging food scenes onscreen are those that include exotic or unfamiliar dishes, whose preparation generates a sense of wonder in the audience, as well as a fascination with the culture that produced the peculiar dishes. The cinematic hunger artists exploit the audience's visceral response to the imagery of food in a fashion similar to the manipulation of sex onscreen. The film industry cliché that a script needs romance and flesh in order to be financially successful may be only partially true. The respective representations of violence and food can sometimes be equally engaging and,

The Man in a White Suit emphasizes the meta-cinematic trope of Juzo Itami's *Tampopo* (1985) when he directly addresses the camera after arriving at a movie theater with his lady, setting up a table of food, and warning another audience member about making noise.

interestingly, these three ingredients frequently stand in for each other in the visual imagery. The connection between sex and the consumption of food is a virtual cliché in film narrative. Peter Greenaway's *The Cook, the Thief, His Wife, and Her Lover* juxtaposes depictions of fine dining with the amorous dalliance of the wife and lover; indeed, the multiplicity of sex scenes take place within the various pantries of the restaurant kitchen, the lovers surrounded at varying times by fowl, bread, fruit, and even rotting meat. And, of course, one cannot forget the sex scene in front of the open refrigerator in *9½ Weeks*. While the scenes equating the gustatory and the carnal appetites abound in contemporary film, food can also signify more broadly.

One of the recurring motifs in food film narrative is meta-cinematic in that the preparation and consumption of elaborate meals and dishes signifies the material process of producing a film. The meticulous attention to appearances and ambiance, the careful consideration of ingredients, and the scrupulous adherence to complicated procedures — not to mention the obsession with customer satisfaction — are shared by both the chef and

An old man (Ryutaro Otomo) teaches Gun (Ken Watanabe) to savor his ramen soup in Juzo Itami's *Tampopo* (1985).

the filmmaker. The spectacle of food onscreen constitutes a self-conscious effort on the part of the director to invoke the sensory and sensual appetites in his visual imagery, allegorizing the heavy-handed exploitation of the desires. Itami Juzo's *Tampopo* (1985), the story of a failing noodle stand rescued by an itinerant trucker, subtly equates both the production and the enjoyment of a perfect noodle soup to the montage structure of postmodern film and the "pattern of consumption" within the consumer market (Iles 232). The trucker Goro assists Tampopo in selecting each of the appropriate ingredients for her improved ramen noodle soup, concentrating on the appropriate processes for ensuring that the broth remains clear, the pork is thinly shaved, the noodles are not over cooked, and the vegetables are artfully selected, chopped, and placed within the bowl. The close attention to each stage of soup production mirrors the construction of cinematic art, which, in process, resembles a pastiche of disjointed scenes, seemingly filmed haphazardly and only constructing a coherent narrative after the editors have reassembled the disparate cinematic fragments. Itami's film, even in its completed form, resembles the seemingly random selection of scenes in film production, his whimsical camera pursuing subjects that bear only a peripheral or thematic relationship to the central narrative, each communicating people's varying preoccupations and even obsessions with food (Inouye 136-138). Itami's film also samples various cinematic genres, a rich metaphor for Goro and Tampopo's odyssey through Japan's noodle stand industry, searching for the best ingredients and recipes. The film samples the Hollywood western, the gangster film, the family melodrama, and the productions of the silent age, to name only a few. These are drawn out along the narrative (or suspended within the broth, if you will) of Tampopo's noodle stand, ingredients in the soup that is the film. The effort to create a perfect noodle soup culminates, predictably, just as the film is reaching its conclusion, once again suggesting that the composition of the soup is coterminous with the composition of the story line, and the satisfaction of her co-workers and customers parallels the film audience's delight in the resolution of the narrative.

The cinematic hunger artist plies his or her craft for a variety of reasons, and the reductive assumption that food in film always signifies desire reveals a very limited scrutiny of the body of works in this sub-genre. Certainly, onscreen food can stand in for many kinds of appetite; however, it can mean much more. The films that have been selected for this volume maintain a fairly continuous focus on food or food related activities, such as agriculture, consumption, and restaurant or kitchen management. Some chapters concentrate on the representation of a single food while others may observe the organizational and structural attributes of the formal dinner.

The first chapter in the volume, "The Allegory of Intemperance: Spenser and Greenaway's *The Cook, the Thief, His Wife, and Her Lover*," offers a detailed comparison between Greenaway's controversial film and Book II, Canto ix of Edmund Spenser's *The Faerie Queene* in which the knight of temperance tours Alma's castle, an allegorical representation of the moderate and salubrious human body that repels the assaults of the sickness and the seven deadly sins. In ironic contrast, the restaurant Les Hollandais of Greenaway's *CTW&L* constitutes the intemperate body infiltrated by sickness and sin. The various rooms of the restaurant roughly correspond to the chambers of Alma's castle and, thereby, to the human anatomy. In addition, the Spenserian analogue adds a new dimension to the film's oft cited political satire on Thatcherite Britain of the 1980's.

Chapter 2, "Itzam Revealed: *Chocolat* and Mayan Mythology," addresses meaningful changes that were developed in the cinematic production of Joanne Harris' novel of the same name. The Celeste Pranile, Vianne's chocolate shop in Harris' narrative, is transformed into the Chocolaterie Maya in the film. This chapter examines the importance of Mayan culture and mythology within the narrative. Vianne's Mayan chocolate shop serves as a pagan counterpoint to the lenten season of the film, the chocolate signifying the redemptive qualities of pleasures forbidden within the Catholic period of abstinence. The confectioner offers an alternative redemption to the town's misfits and succeeds in exposing the hypocrisies of the church and the city government.

"*Scotland, PA:* Macbeth, McMeat and McMurder" examines Billy Morrissette's cinematic satire of the fast food industry, in which fast food innovations such as the french fry and the drive through window are equated to high tragedy. Based upon Shakespeare's Macbeth, the protagonist disturbs the universe through his professional ambition, and his precipitous behavior parallels the tragic hero's overweening pride, the same that precedes his inevitable fall. The narrative equates the development of the fast food industry to Macbeth's tragic mistake, which placed the health of an entire nation in jeopardy. Finally, the film's effort to expose young people to Shakespearean narratives through popular entertainments in order to construct culturally literate adults who can appreciate the classics is reminiscent of accusations against the fast food industry that strives to get children hooked on their cuisine at an early age in order to create lifelong brand loyalty.

"Four Little Caligulas: *La Grande Bouffe,* Consumption, and Male Masochism" addresses the construction of male gender roles in Ferreri's *La Grande Bouffe.* Masculinity is fashioned not only through the male's ability to inflict harm but also through his ability to endure great suffering. The four middle aged protagonists of Ferreri's film decide to commit suicide through culinary over-indulgence, their efforts a metaphor for the excess of the privileged classes and the desperate need of men to demonstrate their masculine prowess even at the expense of their own well-being. The men encourage each other's masculine performance serving as witnesses to their supposedly courageous dissipation.

"*What's Cooking?:* Multiculturalism and Holiday Histrionics or a Banquet of Shouting" focuses on the most American of holidays—Thanksgiving. Gurinder Chadra's *What's Cooking* strives to define American multiculturalism by observing the holiday celebration of four separate ethnicities living on the respective corners of a single intersection in Los Angeles. The four households constitute varying levels of assimilation into the mainstream culture, but despite their differing backgrounds, the four families wrestle with similar problems that in origin are generational, sexual, political, and racial. However, for these denizens of L.A., the single unifying concern is violence. The plurality of the California neighborhood becomes a microcosm for the nation as a whole. Made up of immigrants from all over the world, the American populace remains unified in its pursuit of happiness and material success. The holiday fare that is featured at each of the four Thanksgiving celebrations signifies American diversity, each household preparing the traditional turkey, but each also adding its own ethnic flare to the feast, thus maintaining a unique cultural identity within the overarching American context.

"*Mostly Martha:* Appe/type and Stereo/tite" examines the clash of national temperaments in Sandra Nettelbeck's 2001 film about a moody and uncompromising German chef. Martha, reclusive, disciplined, and orderly, a stereotype of the Germanic temperament, must learn to cope with interruptions and disturbances in her life when her niece comes to live with her and a rival chef, an Italian, whose lighthearted philosophy of life and cooking is antithetical to her own, is hired to replace her during Martha's family crisis. The recipes that Martha prepares in her work are metaphors for a simple and disciplined lifestyle in which the ingredients and procedures are rigidly controlled and ritualized. Martha must come to appreciate excitement, companionship, and disorder in order to live more fully. Her eventual transformation generates a synthesis of the traditional Germanic and Mediterranean dispositions.

"Culinizing" the Female Form: *Felicia's Journey,* Predation, and Cultural Imperialism" investigates the culinary motif in Atom Egoyan's *Felicia's Journey,* a thematic that compares food preparation and consumption to a serial killer's predation and exploitation of his female victims. The elaborate dinners prepared by Joseph Hilditch suggest the ritual and compulsion of the serial murderer who methodically follows the same steps with each of his crimes, slowly perfecting the process. On a broader level, the interaction between Hilditch and his final victim, Felicia, signifies the historic hostilities between the England and Ireland. The sumptuous feasts upon which only Hilditch dines reveal the economic discrepancy between the two regions. Felicia, who travels to England in search of her lover, is destitute, lost, and homeless when she is befriended by the predacious gentleman.

"Dreaming of the Pure Vegetable Kingdom: Ecofeminism and Agriculture in *A Thousand Acres* and *Antonia's Line*" addresses the ecofeminist equation between the female body and the environment, distinguishing between the exploitation of women on *A Thousand Acres'* Iowa farm and the feminist agrarian utopia of *Antonia's Line* where male rapaciousness toward women and exploitation of the environment are consistently curtailed. Jane Smiley's Cook family, despite their agrarian lifestyle, are out of sync or at odds with the rhythms of nature and the seasons, poisoning the environment to optimize the yield of their land. In contrast, Antonia lives in harmony with nature, following the cycle of the seasons, the rhythms of life and death, without ambition to control more and more land and produce larger and larger crops.

"The Kitchen Panopticon: Indeterminacy and the Myth of Objective Surveillance" examines Bent Hamer's film *Kitchen Stories*, a prolonged interrogation of the integrity of scientific or objective analysis, implying that a researcher cannot observe a subject without affecting the behavior or perception of that same subject. Through surveillance and acquired knowledge, the observer exerts power over the observed, the subject retaining the look of a subject that is looked at. The narrative involves a Swedish study of the kitchen habits of single Norwegian males, which is ostensibly intended to help the Swedes create a paradigm for the ideal Norwegian kitchen, one that serves the individual needs of the targeted population, but while the study aims to be disinterested in the outcome of those observations, it is simultaneously fraught with preconceptions about the proprieties of modern living, and in effect, it imposes more than it observes. The subject of the film is broadened to encompass political relations between Norway and Sweden in the wake of the Nazi occupation of the former, the cultural politics of scrutiny alluding to the insidious Nazi surveillance network.

The films *Big Night* and *Dinner Rush* are examined in the chapter entitled "Filming and Eating Italian." Each of the narratives depicts a transitional moments in the evolution of Italian American cuisine and culture. *Big Night* addresses the struggle of recent immigrants to create a successful restaurant without making concessions to the vulgarizing American mass market, and *Dinner Rush* depicts the repudiation of the Italian mafia narrative, even at the same time that it constitutes yet another example of the same. Both films address the conflicts that arise when the culinary artist is asked to compromise his aesthetic and cultural integrity for the purposes of financial success.

Nana Djordjadze's *A Chef in Love* allegorizes the cultural and culinary influences on the former Soviet Republic of Georgia. Depicting a love affair between a Georgian princess and a successful French chef, the film laments the interruption of western cultural influence following the soviet domination of the region and, simultaneously, celebrates the brief years of the Georgian Republic that flourished between the periods of Turkish and the Soviet control. In "*A Chef in Love:* The Fable of a Communist and Culinary Re-Evolution" I argue that the cultural dearth of communism is represented in the progressive degradation of the French chef Pascal and the increasing vulgarity of the cuisine consumed by the Georgian populace, and the frame of the film signals the reawakening of Georgia's cultural heritage following the collapse of communism in eastern Europe.

Gabriel Axel's cinematic version of Isak Dinesen's short story *Babette's Feast* transfers the narrative from an isolated Norwegian fjord to the coast of Jutland in Denmark where the exiled French gourmet lives among a Lutheran sect who have forsaken the pleasures and luxuries of life to embrace instead a strict asceticism that brings them closer to their God. Babette must teach her employers that spiritual and physical (or culinary) ecstasy can co-exist. The concluding feast in the narrative reveals that the gustatory artist has the capacity to manipulate the emotions and desires of even the most provincial and reticent people. "The Artist in Exile: Babette's and 'Alexander's Feast'" discusses the parallel between the artist's sleights in John Dryden's St. Cecilia poems (particularly "Alexander's Feast") and Babette's ability to manipulate and inspire her uncultivated diners.

"Family Suppers and the Social Syntax of Dissimilation" addresses three films—*Soul Food, Eat Drink Man Woman,* and *Tortilla Soup*—all of which attempt to address the problem of social and familial cohesion through the ritual of the weekly family dinner. The chapter argues that the defining attribute of social cohesion is not inclusion, but exclusion. The meaning or the unifying principle of familial identity is determined by those social forces which are excepted. In all three films, it is the ubiquitous and engulfing American materialist culture that threatens to annihilate the unique cultural identity of racial and ethnic family unit.

Finally, "Food Fights: The Martial Chefs and Magical Arts of Asian Cinema" analyzes the curious melding of the martial with the culinary arts in several Asian films—*The God of Cookery, Chinese Feast,* and *The Magic Kitchen.* Each features chefs whose skills are so prodigious that they can only be represented by the magical proficiencies of the cinematic martial arts master. The respective protagonists follow a character development modeled on that of the epic hero who suffers a degradation but is eventually rehabilitated to triumph over h/er rivals within a competitive context. The magical and martial qualities of the gustatory master reinforce the objective of Asian food cinema which seeks to reveal the long, exotic, and even mystical legacy of Asian cuisine, not to mention the prodigious knowledge and herculean skill requisite to mastering its secrets.

1

The Allegory of Intemperance: Spenser and Greenaway's *The Cook, the Thief, His Wife and Her Lover*

Filmmaker Peter Greenaway has been very explicit in identifying his scandalous avant garde film *The Cook, the Thief, His Wife, and Her Lover* (1989) with sixteenth century revenge tragedy, even citing John Ford's *Tis Pity She's a Whore* as an analogue (Siegel 69), and his familiarity with the period is further confirmed by his Shakespearean adaptation, *Prospero's Books* (1991). However, the filmmaker's knowledge of early modern literature may be more comprehensive than has thus far been acknowledged. *CTW&L* shares very few similarities with Ford's tragedy, save for an abusively misogynist ambiance and a collection of vicious thugs as its dramatis personae. Conversely, a compelling number of parallels exist with the second book of Spenser's *Faerie Queene*, particularly Canto ix in which Guyon visits the House of Alma. This sixteenth century text serves as an effective cipher to many portions of the film even enhancing its oft touted political allegory.

The second book of Spenser's epic addresses the quest of the Knight of Temperance, Guyon, as he makes his way across Faerie land to destroy the witch Acrasia and her Bower of Bliss. His task is to prosecute excess in many varied forms, including lust, greed, wrath etc. Following a successful yet exhausting trek through the Cave of Mammon and a subsequent fainting spell, Guyon approaches the House of Temperance for a much need recuperation before his final battle. In the tradition of the medieval morality play, the *Castle of Perseverance*, Spencer's edifice is actually the human body. Accompanied by Arthur, the allegorical representation of grace and magnificence, Guyon tours the various chambers of that structure/organism.

The hostess and owner of the house, Alma, the body's soul, leads the knights through the stomach, heart, and mind. Guyon's presence in the structure can be construed in at least two separate ways: either his visitation is a learning experience in which he is taught moderation through the example of Alma's tenants, an episode parallel to Redcrosse's visit to the House of Holiness in Book I, or his presence actually brings temperance into Alma's house which is not always so well-balanced. After all, the castle is under attack when Guyon and Arthur arrive, and the subsequent respite lasts only so long as they are in the body, resuming upon their departure. Yet another aspect of Spenser's allegory pertinent to this discussion is the political dimension. The body that is Alma's castle is England, and predictably, Alma herself is its Elizabeth I.

Greenaway's film shares a metaphorical geography and architecture with Spenser's epic. Film critics have previously recognized the metaphor of digestion represented in scatological imagery of the dialogue and the labyrinthine the rooms of Le Hallandais, the restaurant where most of the action of the film takes place (Kilb 63; Siegel 85; Phillips 99). The business has been appropriated by mobster Albert Spica, his wife Georgina, and his band of seven thugs. They hold court in the main dining area each night, indulging their gluttonous appetites and abusing each other, as well as the regular patrons. The essence of the action involves the infidelity of the thief's wife with another diner, Michael, the discovery of this impropriety, and the subsequent revenge. The action is presided over by the master chef and owner of the restaurant Richard Borst, whose labors include the facilitation of infidelity and cannibalism.

The kitchen of Alma's house is the stomach, which is vault-like, lined with "many raunges" and "one great chimney, whose tonnell thence/ The smoke forth threw." In the middle of the room was a boiling cauldron, attended by many cooks with "hookes and ladles, who "did about their businesse sweat and sorely toyld." The stomach includes two ports of egress for "all the rest that noyous was." The excess fluids were conveyed through a "conduit pipe" and the additional waste was transported to the "back-gate" where "[i]t was avoided quite, and throwne out privily." The boiling and burning of the cauldron in Alma's kitchen is, of course, an allusion to stomach acids and digestion. The cooks who "remove the scum," "bear the same away," and "use" the rest "according to his kind," are also part of the process of digestion, gathering the waste and absorbing the nutritional remains. The main chimney refers to the esophagus, and the "two bellowes" that cool the fires are, of course, the lungs. The two portals for disposal are the colon and urinary tract (Book II, Canto ix, Stanzas 29–32).

The set of Greenaway's kitchen resembles Spenser's in many compelling ways. The room is cavernous, reminiscent of the "aircraft industry of the 1940's"; "The ceilings are very high and — for the most part — lost in dark shadow" (Greenaway 14), the room "echoic and resonant ... like a cathedral" (Greenaway 15). On the ceiling are placed "eight large revolving extractor-fans" intended to remove the heat and smoke; these, of course, are reminiscent of the "bellowes" that cool the cauldron in Alma's cookery. In the center of the room is a large and complicated stove apparatus over which many cooks hover, and above the stove are two large hoods to extract heat and odor from the room. This structure could be indicative of the lungs as the tubes lead down to triangular stainless steel vents, but it seems more suggestive of Alma's chimney, the esophagus. The steaming and burning of Spenser's kitchen is echoed in the "lazy trails of steam that drift up and disappear under the dark ceiling" (Greenaway 15). In some scenes of the films, the kitchen becomes completely engulfed in smoke. One particular shot from the dining room captures the huge doors to the kitchen thrown open to reveal a thick smoke that obscures the structures of the latter room. The central stove is attended by a sweating, shirtless fat man named Troy, who toils over "a dozen saucepans of various sizes–all bubbling with sauces and gravies and bristling with spoons and ladles" (Greenaway 16), his demeanor evocative of the cooks with ladles toiling and sweating over Alma's cauldron. Spenser's emphasis on waste disposal and digestion is also prominent in Greenaway's kitchen. Richard is shown discarding unworthy foods at the back door, and trash receptacles can be seen lining the back wall of the building's exterior. The labyrinth of adjoining rooms — "pantries, larders, cold stores, and sculleries" (Greenaway 15) — is suggestive of the convoluted digestive tract where nutrition is absorbed.

Greenaway's dining area is similar to Spenser's, the latter described as

> ... a stately Hall
> Wherein were many tables faire dispred,
> And ready dight with drapets festiuall,
> Against the viaundes should be ministered.
> At th'upper end there sate, yclad in red
> Downe to the ground, a comely personage,
> That in his hand a white rod menaged,
> He steward was hight *Diet;* rype of age,
> And in demeanure sober, and in counsell sage.
> [Book II, Canto ix, Stanza 27]

The above description is suggestive of Greenaway's restaurant in which the dining area is very formal, even palatial, with thick red drapes on all of the walls and tables decorated with huge candelabras, crystal vases, sterling silver vessels, and elaborate floral centerpieces. While the dining room of Le Hollandais is not nearly as empty as Spenser's, Albert Spica, the gangster, maintains a domineering position within the room and is certainly the center of the wait staff's attention. Like "Diet" Spica is literally draped in red. While he wears a black suit throughout the film, his scarf and sash change colors as he moves from one area of the restaurant to another. In the dining area, his sartorial accents are blood red, alluding to the similarly draped walls of the room. Moreover, he rules over this environment with verbal and physical abuse, an allusion to Diet's "white rod," the symbol of royal power and the parliamentary body (Nelson 198). Diet's sober and sage demeanor is, of course, ironically reversed in the person of Spica, who constitutes the antithesis of both of these qualities. He is not representative of the temperate life, but its converse, the embodiment of intemperance in appetite, wrath, lust, avarice, pride, etc. In Alma's house, the dining area signifies the mouth where sustenance is introduced, and Diet may suggest the tongue, hence his red hue. Similarly, Spica's name and his predominant behavior — speech — suggest that he may be an allegorical personification of the tongue (Lawrence 175). His speech predominates throughout the film; indeed, at times, the soundtrack is virtually a monologue of his ravings.

Albert Spica (Michael Gambon, center), Georgina (Helen Mirren, left) and Grace (Liz Smith, right) Dine in the main room of Les Hollandais Restaurant in Peter Greenaway's *The Cook, the Thief, His Wife, and Her Lover* (1989).

Spenser's Diet is attended by "Appetite" who walks "through the Hall ... to and fro":

> ... he did bestow
> Both guestes and meate, when euer in they came,
> And knew them how to order without blame. (II, ix, 28)

Appetite's function is to monitor consumption in the temperate body. Ordering "without blame" suggests his proficiency at this task as well as the moderate and salubrious outcome of his efforts. Diet only receives those viands conducive to health and to his disposition. The cook, Richard Borst, constitutes the analogue to appetite, partially revealed in his iteration of the expression "bon appetit," but more importantly in his judicious distribution of food portions to the various guests. The menu is determined by Richard not by the individual guests, and he serves particular foods based upon his assessment of the diner's palate. In one instance, he brings a small complimentary dish to Georgina at the thief's table. When Albert protests that he should receive the same, Richard reminds him that Georgina has an "excellent palate," while he has only a "serviceable" one. He adds that Albert is a "conservative eater." In another exchange, Richard refuses to serve Albert sole because the quality is not sufficient, even for him, and in the penultimate scene of the film, Richard discusses his pricing philosophy, arguing that particular types of food deserve to be taxed. He charges extra for vegetarian dishes and diet foods, but most importantly, he taxes all black foods because they comfort the diner with the illusion of consuming his or her own death. Richard also charges extra to the old and the beautiful because good food is wasted on them. Finally, he maintains that Michael, Georgina's dead lover, was the perfect guest because he could dine almost for free. This last confession is the most meaningful because Michael is described as a "modest man" throughout the script (Lawrence 178), and Richard's facilitation of his appetite is indicative of his endeavor to promote moderation.

Perhaps the most Spenserian aspect of *CTW&L* is the book depository, to which Michael and Georgina flee when Albert discovers their infidelity. This location resembles the "stately Turret" in Alma's House. Alma leads Guyon and Arthur up a set of stairs to the brain, composed of three rooms, each occupied by a wise man. The three compartments account for three aspects of consciousness—future, present, and past or foresight, intelligence, and memory. In the first room, the occupant is a scientist and artist, imagining the future, in the second, a politician preoccupied by current affairs, and in the last, a librarian, ordering and surveying the historical record of England. Greenaway's set is based largely on the latter of these three rooms.

When Alma leads the two knights upstairs to the brain, they observe the structure's windows or eyes, which are described as "Two goodly beacons, set in watches stead,/Therein gave light and flamed continually" (II, ix, 46). The turret and eyes were "lifted high aboue the earthly masse,/which it suruew'd, as hils doen lower ground" (II, ix, 45). The book depository is similarly elevated, occupying "the fifth floor of a 19th Century building" (Greenaway 68). The window above the lovers' bed "looks out over the city roof tops–a wide urban panorama," and the arched window itself suggests an eye through which the movements of the sun and moon are displayed prominently, dominating the center of each scene and serving as the principal light source. While the lovers are sleeping, the camera briefly captures a side window that is partially covered by a semicircular drape resembling an eyelid (Greenaway 69).

The third room in Alma's brain is a library, a chamber "hangd about with rolles,/And old records from ancient times deriu'd,/Some made in books, some in long parchment scrolles" (II, ix, 57). The resident of the room is Eumnestes (Good Memory), an "old oldman half blind, " and he is attended by a boy Anamnestes (Reminder) who moves back and forth between the old man and the book shelves retrieving the scrolls. Eumenstes is charged with remembering

> ... things forgone through many ages held,
> Which he recorded still as they did pas,
> Ne sufferd them to perish through long eld,
> As all things else, the which this world does weld,
> But laid them up in his immortal scrine,
> Where they forever uncorrupted dweld... [II, ix, 56]

Both Guyon and Arthur select a book from Eumentes' shelf and begin to read, Arthur concentrating on "An ancient booke, hight *Briton moniments*" and Guyon on a related subject, "*Antiquitie of Faerie lond*" (II.ix.59–60), both works chronicling English history, the subject of Canto x.

The parallels with Greenaway's film are striking here. Michael indicates that when his job in the bookshop is slow, he spends his time "cataloguing French History." He carries at least one book throughout the film, except, of course, when he is making love to Georgina. His habit of reading at the table while he eats is the activity that first brings him to the attention of the disapproving Albert. When Georgina remarks about the book depository that one could "spend a lifetime reading in here," he agrees: "Two lifetimes—yours and mine" (Greenaway 69). Like Eumnestes, Michael devotes his life to reading; he literally lives in a library which contains a bed, a kitchenette, and a bathroom (that last two only in the script).

When he is murdered by Albert and his cronies, the task is completed by stuffing the pages of *The History of the French Revolution* down his throat with a wooden spoon. While Michael is not old like Eumenstes, he is "half blind," wearing reading glasses that are the inverted shape of the windows in the depository. In age and demeanor, Michael resembles the occupant of the second room in Alma's house more than the third:

> There sate a man of ripe and perfect age,
> Who did them meditate all his life long,
> That through continuall practice and usage,
> He now was growne right wise, and wondrous sage.
> Great pleasure had those stranger Knights, to see
> His goodly reason, and grave personage... [II, ix, 54]

Michael is described throughout the script as the "modest man," and he too is of "ripe and perfect age," Spenser's reference to middle age, the mean between Phantases in the first room, "a man of yeares yet fresh" (II, ix, 52), and Eumnestes in the third, an "old oldman." Michael's wisdom and reason are revealed in his demeanor, particularly in those instances where he was forced to endure Albert's bullying. Michael maintains a sober and even amused expression, seeming completely unflappable.

The exterior of Alma's castle is a wasteland where sickness and sin mount continual assaults upon the body. Indeed, the House of Temperance is under siege until Arthur and Guyon enter, at which time the structure enjoys a brief respite from the harangue. The marauders signify mortality, the many temptations to excess and intemperance that limit the length of one's life. Upon the departure of the knights from the house in Canto xi, the combatants resume their onslaught. They are twelve: the seven deadly sins that attack the gate of the castle and the five vices that harry the five senses. Interestingly, all of the principal combatants are associated with sin, thus equating sickness and mortality to the state of one's soul. Moreover, the text explicitly cites their objective as the capture of Alma or the damnation of the soul, the destruction of the body merely a means to that end. The leader of the group, Maleger, the embodiment of sickness, keeps the company of two hags: Impotence and Impatience, the first indicative of unruliness and intemperance and the latter intolerance.

Spenser's exterior also has an analogue in Greenaway's film. The car park that is the setting of the first scene of *CTW&L* is a dark and desolate region behind the restaurant populated by scavenging, mangy dogs, impatient for a handout and eager to leap on any available morsel. The area is associated with excrement and rotting meat. The action of the first scene takes place between two vans, one filled with meat, the other with fish and

sea food. As the drama progresses, the neglected food in the vans deterio-
rates, as revealed when the discovered lovers are thrust into the van full of
filthy and rotted carcasses to be taken to the safety of the book depository.
The car park becomes associated with raw sewage and obscene violence as
Albert and his gangsters torture Roy, the owner of a small pie shop, by
force-feeding him dog excrement and smearing it all over his body. Roy's
offense is his refusal to comply with Albert's extortion.

Albert and his six companions are indicative of the enemies outside
of Alma's House. The descriptions of his cronies plainly reveal a pageant of
the seven deadly sins. Spangler is a "heavy," "thick-set man" and a "greedy
eater," an appropriate cognate for gluttony. Harris, who is "greatly concerned
with his clothes," wears much "wrist and finger jewelry," and considers himself a lady's man, suggesting pride and vanity. The unambitious Cory, who
has no illusions about himself and who would like to settle down, reveals
sloth. Mitchel who is a "dangerous, erratic, psychopathic innocent," is actually the embodiment of lust to whom Albert is drawn by "sexual attraction"
and whom Albert will later refer to as a "sex maniac." Albert himself is indicative of the wrath, a "sadistic" and "foul obnoxious bully" (Greenaway 11). Perhaps the most ingenious representation is revealed in the pairing of Mews and
Turpin, who resemble Avarice and Envy, who occasionally ride alongside
each other in the traditional pageant of the seven deadly sins, Envy keeping
a jealous watch over Avarice's gold. This is true in Spenser's own parade of
sin in Book I, Canto iv of the *Faerie Queene* where Envy is quite unsettled
through his close proximity to greed: "Still as he rode, he gnasht his teeth,
to see/Those heapes of gold with griple Couetyse" (31). Similarly, Mews
and Turpin are "closely linked. They could be cousins." Turpin, a "failed
accountant — good with cooked figures," personifies greed and covetousness, while the description of Mews emphasizes his closeness to Turpin and
his eyesight as he constantly shifts his glasses back on his nose (Greenaway 11).

The movement of Albert and his companions into the back door of
the restaurant following their torture of Roy suggests — in Spenserian
imagery — that sin, sickness, and intemperance have taken the castle. Albert
is the new part owner of Le Hollandais; he is running a protection racket
and has extorted a portion of the business from Richard. This detail is, of
course, an ironic inversion of Guyon and Arthur's defense of Alma's house;
the irony lies in Albert's confession that the restaurant is being protected
from his own associates. There is no doubt that the mobsters have a negative impact upon the function of the restaurant. When they enter at the
beginning of the film, they cause a power outage and then prove demanding and disruptive in the dining room throughout their nightly visits. In
other instances, they fight amongst themselves and bully the paying guests.

The advent of the thieves into the body is also accompanied by Pup's singing of *The Miserere* by Michael Nyman, a plaintive song that pleads for the purging of iniquity: "Wash me thoroughly from my iniquity, and cleanse me from my sin.... Create in me a clean heart: and renew a right spirit within me" (Greenaway 9). Appropriately, Pup washes the dishes. His shrill and increasingly insistent song is a supplication for assistance in cleansing the filth and pollution from the restaurant and the body. The song is so inapplicable to the spiritual condition of a small boy that the plaintive lyrics must allude to the collective body of the restaurant, corrupted by the presence of Albert and his polluted crew. Pup seems to signify innocence, the body's soul. His small stature and his cringing demeanor suggest that the soul is embattled and fearful, and he is periodically harried and tortured by Albert. In one particularly meaningful exchange, the thief ridicules the boy's innocence and tries to grab his testicles. The boy, using a frying pan as a shield from the groping, invokes Albert's response: "My God! Armor plating! You protect yourself son, you might need it. I was like you till Georgie came along—wasn't I, Georgie? Innocent" (Greenaway 40). The armor is, of course, an allusion to the incorruptible nature of the soul, and consistent with the Spenserian imagery, the armor plating suggests the medieval romance. After the discovery of his wife's infidelity, Albert tortures Pup, digging out the boy's navel, in order to discover the whereabouts of Georgina. Symbolically, the injury suggests the cutting of the proverbial umbilical cord between the boy (the soul) and the restaurant (the body). Ironically, however, the act does not establish Spica's sole dominion over and total corruption of the restaurant/body, but instead initiates his expulsion.

The title of the film invites an allegorical reading of the characters, identifying them as types. The individuals form an allegory of the intemperate body. In Spenserian terms, Michael is the personification of the mind. His association with the books and his intellectual inclinations are sufficient to corroborate this explanation. Georgina can be understood as the embodiment of the heart. While the script refers to her as an "untouchable whore," she, nevertheless, is the single individual who seems most capable of compassion, most memorably revealed in her visit to the hospital to console the wounded Pup. In addition, she is the principal manifestation of love in the film, and not entirely through her lovemaking, but also through the devotion that she demonstrates to Michael before and after his murder. The manifestation of the stomach is Richard, an assumption that requires no leap of faith considering his gastronomic enterprise. Moreover, his task of feeding the rest of the body and his actions as a facilitator for the activities of the other guests, particularly Michael and Georgina, suggest the prerequisite nutrition in the adequate functioning of the other portions of the mortal coil.

While the temptation might be to understand Albert as the stomach out of control, since his chief activity is to feast, he, in spite of his part ownership of the restaurant, remains the individual most alien to the environment. The activities of the others are largely unobtrusive even when they include behaviors uncommon within a restaurant, such as lovemaking or reading. Albert, on the other hand, is intrusive, disrupting the normal functioning of the body, and he must be purged at the conclusion of the film. His persona suggests the intemperate appetite, the same that leads to obesity and ill-health. In Spenserian terms, he is the "anti–Guyon." He keeps the company of a woman named Grace (Georgina's mother), this, of course, reminiscent of Arthur, Guyon's companion as he enters Alma's castle and the embodiment of Grace and magnificence. He invites all manner of seedy characters to dine with him and have the run of the building. He chases away the well-behaved, paying customers; however, in the end, all of those whom he has injured revolt and drive him away. Perhaps their newfound courage in the expulsion is literalized in Georgina's primary role. Since courage is mythically situated in the heart, she is the appropriate person to face down Albert, force-feeding him the mind (Michael's body) and, significantly, shooting him in the head.

Albert Spica's consumption of Michael's well-cooked body in the resolution of the drama invites a host of metaphorical readings. The image is a literalization of the activities he has been engaged in since the beginning of the film. He has been destroying and consuming the body with disease and immodest appetite. The implication of the conclusion is that upon his death, the body will resume its modest functioning. It is here that the Spenserian reading of the film dovetails with the often noted political allegory of the film. There is a wide consensus among critics that the film's content allegorizes contemporary political complaints in Britain during the 1980s. It is widely perceived as a diatribe against Margaret Thatcher and her conservative government that was accused of being insensitive and destructive in the extreme. Greenaway describes the political thematic in several interviews:

> CTW&L is a passionate and angry dissertation for me on the rich, vulgarian, Philistine, anti-intellectual stance of the present cultural situation in Great Britain, supported by that wretched woman who is raping the country, destroying the welfare state, the health system, mucking up the educational system, and creating havoc everywhere [Siegel 81; Kilb 64].

In the political allegory of the film, Albert Spica and his gangsters are emblematic of the culture of self-interest created by a political leadership indifferent to social programs and education, that only valued money and power, generating a political climate of "avarice and crass materialism" (D'Arcy 120). Spica signifies the moralizing, misogynistic, anti-intellectual, insensitive, and pretentious elite who were encouraged to pursue their own interests and self-gratification at the expense of the poor and disadvantaged. Albert is a lewd puritan, a paradoxical combination of crudity and prudishness. He can make vulgar jokes about sex and excrement at the table but becomes incensed and embarrassed when Georgina mentions her gynecologist in the dinner conversation. He can coach his associates in proper table manners but then pour wine in Georgina's food, stab another guest with a fork, and pour soup on the head of a diner who refuses to move to accommodate Spica's entertainment. He ruins other people's food and fun. Figuratively, he consumes more than his share of the banquet and shoves away the "worthy bidden guests." His boorish anti-intellectual bias is revealed in his contemptuous treatment of Michael's dinnertime reading. He informs Michael that he is in a restaurant not a library and later scornfully inquires whether books can make money, thus alluding to one of the most bitter complaints of the British populace regarding the Thatcherite government, that she had weakened the educational system by reducing its funding. From this perspective, Albert's consumption of the Michael's body constitutes a very specific social satire on the destruction of the educational system. In addition, the cannibalizing of Michael's body, forced on Albert by his former victims, is a literalization of the exploitation that previously had been only implicit in his selfish actions. The rich are feeding off of the poor, the country devouring itself. The intemperate appetite of the wealthy and powerful can only be glutted at the expense of the lower classes. Albert's cannibalism signifies the greedy and intemperate appetite consuming the body politic.

The Spenserian allegory contributes substantially to the political commentary. Alma's House in the second book of *The Faerie Queene* represents the English state, and Alma is its Elizabeth I. The temperate body is healthy, all parts cooperating in the modest behavior requisite to a salubrious outcome. In contrast, Le Hallandais, as a representation of England, reveals the body politic gone mad, infiltrated and polluted by excess, by the intemperance embodied in Albert. In Spenser's House of Temperance, the mind is a repository for wisdom, knowledge, and particularly England's proud history. Conversely, Greenaway's book depository is destroyed and the keeper of its history killed, an event that lampoons the contemporary disregard for tradition, intellect, and social justice. Spica neglects to learn from the very history that he destroys. The book that his cronies ignorantly force-feed Michael addresses the French Revolution, a historical event that constitutes an object lesson for those governments that have become callous and insensitive to the suffering and concerns of the commoners (D'Arcy 121).

2

Itzam Revealed: *Chocolat* and the Mayan Cosmology

In the film adaptation of Joanne Harris' novel *Chocolat*, screenwriter Robert Nelson Jacobs and director Lasse Hallstrom make some significant departures from the text, including the alteration in the chronological context of the novel, the transformation of Reynaud (Alfred Molina), the principal antagonist, from a priest to a politician, and the shift in ethnicity of the lady confectioner Vianne (Juliette Binoche) and the transfiguration of her shop from *La Celeste Praline* to the *Chocolaterie Maya*. It is from the last of these alterations that the content of this chapter is derived. The introduction of the Mayan motif into the film creates an important new dimension which generates a mythical subtext for both the narrative and the chocolate imagery and acts as a meaningful polarity to the Catholic Lenten calender of the text.

In her novel, Harris does acknowledge the Central American origins of chocolate preparation and consumption; however, her discussion is limited to a few short paragraphs that focus on the Aztecs' use of chocolate in their sacred rituals. Vianne is not of Mayan ethnicity as in the film; she is European. However, the pagan and magical element of her character remains intact as she comes from a line of European witches. Screenwriter Robert Jacobs elects to emphasize the New World pagan origins, the Mayan mythology of chocolate. The revision of this portion of the text has an eloquent impact on the events of the narrative. In many ways, the Mayan myths of ecstasy, death, and resurrection parallel those of Lent and Easter, acting as a counterpoint to the Christian postulate that one only accesses the divine through abstinence, deprivation, austerity, and meditation. The Mayan wisdom of the film suggests that a portal to the sacred can also be opened through indulgence in sensual and worldly pleasures, represented by the consumption of chocolate.

Several reviewers of Hallstrom's film have accused the filmmakers and the novelist of an anti–Catholic bias, arguing that there has never been a Catholic prohibition against the consumption of chocolate. Melanie McDonagh reminds us that it was the Catholic Conquistadors who introduced chocolate to Europe following their sojourn in the New World, and she cites the commonplace use of chocolate in the celebration of Easter (23). The reviewer does acknowledge that chocolate is a metaphor for pleasure in the film, for all sensual and sensory indulgence. Similarly, Bee Wilson refers to the premise that a Catholic priest would oppose the consumption of Chocolate as "implausible" (48). However, the history of Catholicism and chocolate is not as simple as reviewers have suggested. In their book *The True History of Chocolate*, Sophie and Michael Coe delineate the controversy that chocolate ignited within the church. For 250 years, church officials debated whether it was acceptable to consume chocolate during the ecclesiastical fast or during the forty days of Lent. If chocolate was merely a drink and not a form of nourishment, then the faithful could consume it during these periods. However, there was no consensus as to the nutritional value of the drink (150–51). It is important to remember that the events of the film and the novel take place during Lent and the objections of Reynaud to the confection shop are at first explicitly related to timing, to Vianne's decision to open such a shop when the faithful were obliged to practice temperance. He regarded it as an unnecessary temptation. Furthermore, the anti-chocolate bias in the film can hardly be attributed to church policy since there is only a single person (Reynaud) who is obsessed with closing the shop, and he is not a priest in the film, but a politician. Moreover, he is more vexed by the shop owner's apparent atheism and independence than by the confections.

Reynaud's hostility toward the chocolate shop increases as the narrative progresses and the ostensible reason is that he perceives a growing number of people are patronizing the shop and recognizes that he is losing control of his town. The challenge that he faces includes an alternative path to spiritual salvation. The townspeople, particularly those who have been marginalized, find acceptance, belonging, and rebirth at the Chocolaterie Maya. The people's fervor for traditional religion and its emphasis on self-denial diminishes. Vianne Rocher constitutes an alternative spiritual leader who encourages her followers to seek their salvation through pleasure and indulgence. She brazenly opens her shop across the square from Lansquenet's church and receives most of her business on Sunday morning after Mass. She is no priest but a Mayan shaman, her craft devoted to the technology of ecstasy.

"Shamanism is a visionary tradition, utilizing altered states of consciousness to contact gods and spirits of the natural world" (Drury 1). The term "ecstasy," as it is employed in the shamanic craft, refers not only to intense pleasure (the signification in the contemporary vernacular), but also to the archaic revelatory tradition in which the souls of the faithful leave their bodies and commune with the spirits of gods and ancestors in order to receive insight into the divine mysteries. The primary duty of the shaman was spiritual healing, and the principal catalyst for his/her intervention was "soul loss." The sick have been deprived of their souls because the spirit has either wandered away or been stolen. In an ecstasy, the shaman searches for the lost soul to capture and return it to the body (Eliade 215).

Vianne Rocher is a shamanic legacy, her powers having been received through hereditary transmission, the most common means of succession in that vocation (Eliade 13). Her mother, also a healer, a native of Central America, met Vianne's French father while he was visiting the region to study medicinal plants. Chitza, the mother, was from a family whose members, notorious for their inability to settle down, wandered, distributing cacao (the Mayan term for chocolate) remedies to those in need. The father married Chitza but was soon disappointed when she and her daughter abandoned him to pursue their healing vocation. Vianne spent her youth following her mother from town to town apprenticed to her other craft. Even as an adult she carries her mother's ashes in a traditional Mayan crematory vessel, conversing with the spirit contained therein, the same that urges Vianne to continue her perambulations. The hereditary delivery of the shamanic evocation has been passed to the third generation in the person of Anouk, who like her mother before her, follows her parent on her healing quest and learns the secrets of their family trade.

The ecstatic techniques of the shaman include divination and clairvoyance (Eliade 184), traits that are not difficult to recognize in Vianne's behavior. Her knack for guessing people's favorite chocolate is a light hearted example of the latter. Since each of the confections addresses a different spiritual ailment, the lady's guesses are diagnostic, based upon a recognition of the individual's spiritual and physical needs. She is an insightful observer of the troubled townsfolk, progressively invigorating each of her patrons. The shaman's search for lost souls is modernized in the film, made metaphorical. Each of the people she heals has lost his/her lust for life, his/her vitality, and in each case she draws the ailing person out of isolation and self-loathing. She rescues Josephine Muscat (Lena Olin) from an abusive marriage, transforming her from a mute and cringing kleptomaniac into a confident, beautiful, and expressive woman. In Josephine's case, Vianne's cure involves teaching her the craft of chocolate production. Vianne rescues Armande Voizin (Judy Dench) from a life of isolation and bitterness by reuniting her with her grandson Luc, a solitary and melancholy boy.

They meet over a cup of hot chocolate and a piece of cake, becoming reacquainted in spite of the mother's prohibition against the relationship. The confectioner transforms the sex life of one married couple when the passion of the husband is renewed by a bag of chocolate beans and inspires love between a woman who has been mourning her dead husband for forty years and a man who has no meaningful friendship with anyone save his dog.

The role of chocolate in the spiritual rebirth of the townsfolk alludes to yet another tradition particularly associated with Central and South American shamanism: the use of psychoactive plants to induce altered states of consciousness. In the Amazon, the shaman drinks a hallucinogenic brew created from the vine Ayahuasca; the Toltecs were known for the consumption of peyote buttons for religious rituals as early as eighteen hundred years ago; and some indigenous North Americans would induce altered states through the consumption of peyote buttons and psilocybin mushrooms or even through heavy doses of tobacco. Most relevantly, the Maya's Ahau (shaman king) would engage in a multiplicity of techniques to achieve spiritual insight. The most notorious of these is bloodletting, the piercing of the tongue, hand, or foreskin. While it has also been suggested that the Maya may have consumed peyote like their northern counterparts among the Toltecs, the practice most relevant to the current discussion is the consumption of cacao, unrefined chocolate, a drink to which the Maya attributed great power. In the past twenty years, Mayan scholars have successfully decoded many of the mysterious hieroglyphics that adorn central American temples. The writing was determined to be a combination of word and phonetic signs (Coe, *Code* 233–34). The Mayan scribe could capture an idea either by utilizing a pictorial glyph or by spelling the word phonetically. One of the glyphs that recurs on cylindrical Mayan drinking vessels used by the Ahau includes a fish and a comb, images that spell "cacao" phonetically. Moreover, there is a recurring phrase that describes the drink consumed therein: "tree fresh cacao." From the twentieth century perspective, it is difficult to think of chocolate as a mind-altering substance, yet the Maya may have. There is evidence as well that they insinuated more powerful hallucinogens into their chocolate drinks to aid in their ecstatic rituals. Whether or not the Maya believed that the consumption of chocolate was a significant visionary and life-altering experience is actually immaterial to this discussion since it is clear that the screenwriter of Hallstrom's film chooses to portray it as such. The transformative quality of the ecstatic experience is the recovery and healing of the soul, and in the film *Chocolat*, the shaman's techniques are limited to the capacity to recover the parishioners' appreciation for life through the enhancement of pleasure. The chocolate mythology within the film suggests that pleasures are interrelated and that the enhancement of one leads to the appreciation of others. Vianne's Mayan chocolate shop retains an additional relationship to the ecstatic traditions of Meso-America, one that is particularly appropriate to the Lenten chronology emphasized in the film narrative. I refer to the blood rites of the Mayan nobility and priests, and particularly to the Ahau, the shaman king, whose task it was in the archaic rituals of the society to monitor the portal between the physical and the spiritual realm. It was the shedding of blood, either self-inflicted or sacrificial, that opened the aperture between the two plains of existence and summoned gods and ancestors to a communion and consultation with the living. Blood sent through the portal was "itz," the cosmic sap, believed to contain "ch'ul," the soul or spirit, and this substance spoke to and nourished the attendant gods and animated and invigorated the world (Freidel, et al *Cosmos* 201–202). The sacrificial priests sent human blood through the opened portal, and the gods returned maize which nourished humanity, the same substance from which the gods created the human form (Schele and Freidel, *Forest* 87–95). Those who worked with "the cosmic sap" were Itzam, the Mayan shaman and technician of ecstasy (Freidel, et. al. *Cosmos* 210). The name "Itzam" derived from "Itzamna," the first and most powerful shaman who assists others in their rituals by opening the cosmic portal from the far side.

The connection between sacrificial blood and chocolate in the Meso-American consciousness was strong, as was the link between chocolate and spiritual ecstasy. The former symbolic association remains most blatant among the Aztecs whose priests used the phrase "yollotl eztli," meaning "heart blood," to refer to chocolate, a correlation that may have its origin in the shape of the cacao bean, which vaguely resembles a heart. However, an additional analogue may be that "both [are] repositories of precious liquids— blood and chocolate" (Coe and Coe, *Chocolate* 101). There is also evidence of the inclusion of chocolate in Aztec sacrificial rituals involving heart extraction. In one account of the sacrificial ceremonies, a European observer noted that the priests created a chocolate drink for the reluctant victim so that he would forget his plight and participate willingly. The drink was stirred by obsidian knives bloodied by previous killings. The liquid was called "Itzpacalatl" or "water from the washing of obsidian blades." The drink was believed to intoxicate the victim and make him/her embrace death (Coe and Coe, *Chocolate* 102). The combination of blood and chocolate and the inclusion of the term "Itz" in the expression "Itzpacalatl" create a strong connection between chocolate and the cosmic sap that imbues and enlivens nature.

The role that chocolate plays within the Mayan ritual may be para-doxically stronger yet more vague to the modern world, perhaps because the Classic Maya predated the European conquest by many centuries. Some of the most powerful evidence for the use of cacao in Mayan blood rituals can be found on the surface of their vessels, many of which display the pho-netic glyph for cacao (a fish head and fin), indicating that the vessels were used for the consumption of a chocolate drink. Chemical analysis of some of these vessels has indeed revealed the presence of chocolate residue (Coe and Coe, *Chocolate* 49). The imagery painted on the surface of the vessels, as well as the presence of this pottery in the tombs of their nobility, clearly connects chocolate with their sacrificial rituals, their spiritual lives, and by association, their blood requisite to the invocation of that portal which offers egress to the realm of ecstasy and death. One chocolate cup found among the burial artifacts of a Mayan Ahau from Calakmul depicts the shaman king at the moment when he pierces the veil between this world and the next. The conduit between the earth and Xibalba is a serpent with a head and gaping mouth at each end of its form. One mouth is opened in this world and the other in the spirit realm. The king of Calakmul is depicted emerging from the serpent's mouth into a realm of monsters (Brennan 206–7). Another chocolate cup depicts a shaman manipulating the same threshold, this time the opening decorated with images of the sacred "itz," represented as beads or bubbles. There is a strong suggestion here that the itz signifies the chocolate once contained in the vessel (Brennan 221).

Still other chocolate vessels reveal images from Mayan mythology, par-ticularly the events narrated in the *The Popal Vuh* where the adventures of the Hero Twins— Hunter and Little Jaguar Sun (or Jaguar Deer)— are delin-eated, the Mayan myth of origin which includes the brothers' battle with and defeat of the Lords of Xibalba, or the Lords of Death. The Hero Twins res-urrect their father the maize god, once destroyed by the denizens of Xibalba, and his rebirth signifies the creation of humanity from corn. The brothers are the mythical progenitors of the shaman, and their struggle against the Lords of Death mirrors the priests' endeavor to open and close the gateway to Xibalba and manipulate the spirits and gods therein. The inscription on one vessel associates the Hero Twins and their task of controlling the under-world with the consumption of cacao: "It came to being, was presented, its surface, their drinking vase for fresh from the tree cacao, the hero twins, portal gods" (Brennan 170–71). In one episode of *The Popol Vuh*, the hero twins, in their struggle with Lords of Xibalba, are killed, their bones are ground up and thrown in a river. However, returning, their heads replaced with fish heads, they now have the capacity to sacrifice and resurrect each other. They trick the Lords of Death into self-sacrifice by promising to bring them back, but then refusing to resurrect them; thus the twins triumph in the prolonged ordeal (Freidel et. al. *Cosmos* 108–110). This episode may have importance in the mythology of chocolate since the Mayan hieroglyph for cacao is a fish head and cacao a symbol of rejuvenation.

Still other allusions to cacao in Mayan iconography suggest its connection with blood, death, spirituality, and resurrection. In one depiction of the Mayan myth of origins, the head of the dead and soon to be resurrected maize god hangs like a bean in a cacao tree. Traditionally, that maize god's head is hung in a calabash tree, but here the artist takes creative and meaningful license with the religious tradition. In a depiction from the Madrid Codex (an illustrated manuscript dating from the post-classic Mayan period), the gods sprinkle their own blood on cacao beans, and in still another image, two Mayan gods are presenting cacao beans as a sacrificial offering (Coe and Coe, *Chocolate* 41–45).

The above catalog of Meso-American allusions to chocolate and blood are pertinent to the narrative of Hallstrom's film, particularly in light of the redemptive qualities of Christ's blood as implicated in the Lenten/Easter setting of the film's chronology. The salvation and symbolic resurrection of the faithful through the redemptive qualities of Christ's blood corresponds to the same in Mayan myths that act as a subtext for the film. The blood of the sacrificial victim sustains the world. The Aztecs believed that the sun would not rise if sacrificial blood was not offered (Coe and Coe, *Chocolate* 74). By extension, chocolate retained a vivifying quality, a capacity to redeem, a manifestation of the Itz, the life-giving balm that imbues all of creation and retains the capacity for spiritual restoration. Of course, in Hallstrom's film, this quality is metaphorical, but in fairness, the same qualities of Christ's blood are, to the materialist and the pragmatist, nothing more. We only know that Christ's blood symbolizes the triumph over death. The director and screen writer of *Chocolat* are cognizant of this analogue. They develop an equation within the cinematic imagery between the Eucharist and chocolate. The parallel editing equates placement of communion wafers on the tongue with the consumption of chocolate (Cooper 1). Moreover, the conversation in the Chocolaterie is compared to the confessional with the exception that the patrons of Vianne's shop actually appear to be restored and rehabilitated by their experience while those who employ the traditional confessional continue to be trapped in their repressed meaningless lives. Indeed, frequently the confessions address the life altering experiences that have been facilitated by the consumption of chocolate. The widow who has been in mourning for her husband for forty years confesses that the chocolate melts on her tongue and "tortures her with pleasure." Armande draws the parallel with the confession most clearly through her repudiation of the idea, complaining "Is this a chocolaterie or a confessional?" Perhaps the efficacious nature of the chocolate confessional lies in the fact that the chocolate sacrament urges parishioners to enjoy rather than regret their lives. Moreover, the divulgences in the chocolate shop are received in the spirit of compassion and understanding rather than that of judgment and penance.

The rivalry between the restorative qualities of pleasure and privation are played out most fully in the "holy war" over the rehabilitation of the Muscats. Reynaud and Vianne labor to transform Serge and Josephine respectively, a married couple who have split over spousal abuse. Serge is a hostile and unrefined bully, while Josephine is a mute and frightened kleptomaniac who cannot stand up to her husband's abuse until she has Vianne's loving support. She flees into the chocolate shop. When Reynaud tries to retrieve her, he discovers the abuse and embarks upon the reformation of Serge, including confession, catechism, and finishing school. While the transformation in Serge is substantial, it cannot endure his wife's continued rebuff. After his effort to win her back by showing up at her door dressed in a suit and bearing flowers is unsuccessful, he returns one night trying to break into the shop and take her by force. After his rebuff, he is shown passed out from drink, lying in the doorway of a public building.

While the effort to reform Serge is abortive, Josephine flourishes under Vianne's tutelage. She begins with an impromptu confession of her thievery, and her rehabilitation is not conducted through coercion, as with Serge and Reynaud, but is carried out in a spirit of mutual assistance. Josephine learns a trade and discipline through her apprenticeship in the chocolate shop. She gains self-respect, finally able to look people in the eye and offer her personal views on the matters at hand. Most importantly, she no longer passively accepts her husband's domination, even when he approaches her respectfully. While Serge becomes an embarrassing failure of the Comte's efforts, particularly after he sets fire to one of the river gypsies' boats, and is subsequently driven out of town, Josephine's transformation is permanent. She is even able to return Vianne's favor when the confectioner is compelled to flee from the town's apparent hostility. Vianne taught Josephine that she belonged to a growing group of supportive outsiders who, through their alliance and their mutual enjoyment of chocolate, were able to withstand the coercive pressure of authority—the husband, the mayor, and the church. Josephine reminds Vianne of the same lesson when the latter tries to flee following the dangerous incident on the river boat. Vianne discovers Josephine and others quietly producing chocolate for Vianne's Easter carnival. The show of support is sufficient to remind the confectioner that she too has supportive friends and a place in Lansquenet.

The tribalism implicit in the conclusions relates to the shaman's role as a consolidator of shared cultural values; the shaman's ecstasies are a reminder of the tribe's collective identity.

Armande's death near the conclusion of *Chocolat* offers insight in to the film's appropriation of an uniquely Mayan perspective. Her death teaches the other characters how to live, not because she reminds them that they have little time in "this mortal coil," but because they must feed their own longings and embrace their own destructions. One of the principal lessons of the shaman is that "only those that embrace the dark-bright ecstasy of their own deaths can live full earthly lives. Only those who live full earthly lives can choose to die, rush at the Void, and exult in their return to God. And only they can live again" (Gillette 193).

Armande continues to live independently, scoffing at the sanctimonious bombast of Reynaud and the salubrious yet self-serving admonitions of her daughter Caroline that she admit herself to a nursing home. However, despite her diabetes and general poor health, Armande continues to enjoy chocolate and live independently. Her response to warnings is to live still more recklessly. She hires Vianne to cater a birthday party for her that features a variety of chocolates, including the Central American recipe molé, and she concludes the celebration with drink and dancing with the river gypsies. Of course, this indulgence is fatal to her. She returns home on her own two feet and dies in her chair. While her perilous behavior is reviled in the subsequent church service, she nevertheless becomes a model for emulation. The townsfolk embrace Armande's example. Even her harshest critic, her own daughter, is rehabilitated by her mother's sacrifice. Indeed, Armande's death more than the Easer rituals teaches the parishioners how to face their own mortality, not with regret and fear, but with vigor and celebration. It is clear that after Armande's death, the forces of restraint that have sought to deter the pagan vitality and momentum of the chocolate shop are in retreat.

Armande's defiant dance of death corresponds to the iconography of Mayan ritual, particularly those associated with the coronation of the Mayan king, who engages in a bloodletting ritual and a symbolic death from which he emerges dancing the jig of life, celebrating his triumph over the lords of death just as the Hero Twins. A well known tablet from Palenque depicts Chan-Bahlum dancing in celebration after he has overcome Xibalba. His mother, Lady Ahpo-Hel, who also participates in the bloodletting, kneels before him offering a symbol of the Mayan kingship (Braziller 272). In another image, Kan-Xul dances out of the abyss of Xibalba carrying an ax and a vase. He is flanked by Lord Pacal and Lady Ahpo-Hel (Braziller 275).

Reynaud's metamorphosis is the final step in the ongoing transformation of the town. He becomes an object lesson in the psychology of deprivation. Stirred by the discovery that his most devoted admirer, Caroline, has joined with the chocolate cohorts, he embarks upon a desperate course, to destroy the confection shop and the preparations for the chocolate carnival on Easter Sunday. The Comte's rigidity and self-denial are emphasized repeatedly. First his wife has left him for an unspecified reason, and he lies to people, maintaining that she is traveling in Venice and will return shortly. In addition to the stifled sexual energy, Reynaud has been depriving himself of adequate nourishment. Repeatedly, he is served food which he leaves untouched, but not unwanted. In one case, he moves a picture in front of plate of food in order to remove distraction and temptation.

His self-denial makes him increasingly irritable. At the beginning of the film, he was disapproving yet courteous, but he progressively loses his charm and patience. In a final desperate act to put the Chocolaterie Maya out of business and end the irreligious carnival planned for Easter morning, Reynaud breaks into the shop to destroy the window display and the festival merchandise. However, once he enters the shop, his destructive intentions are rapidly replaced by an orgy of chocolate consumption, and when he has eaten his fill, he passes out at the scene of the crime, only to be discovered in the morning by Vianne and the priest. His self-indulgent episode reveals the extent to which he has reluctantly bourne the privations of Lent and would have preferred to glut his appetites like many others. His discovery by Vianne is not revealed to parishioners but remains a secret of the chocolate confessional, yet the experience has a lasting effect on his disposition. He experiences a *felix culpa*; the breaking of his sanctimonious will and his humiliation have beneficial effects on his personality as well as the entire town who can now enjoy there festival without condemnation and remorse. Like the townspeople, he embraces the chocolate carnival, enjoying the vendors and street performers along with his townsfolk.

Reynaud's ecstasy, of course, constitutes a reenactment of the religious mythology of Easter. His symbolic death and resurrection has a transformative effect on him. However, Reynaud undergoes an entirely different kind of rejuvenation as well. His actions have analogues within the rituals and iconography of the classic Maya. Some of the elaborate confections that he destroys in the shop window are reproductions of Mayan and other Meso-American art. Using a small golden knife, perhaps reminiscent of the sacrificial tools of the Mayan and Aztec priests, Reynaud begins his rampage by gouging the display, including a chocolate replica of El Castillo, the elaborate pyramid at the center of the ancient city of Chichen Itza. The pyramid was potentially the place of sacrifice and is notable for its usage during the rites of the spring equinox when a shadow effect at dawn suggests that the Mayan god Kukulkan (the feathered serpent) and the god of eternal return is crawling out of the temple and down the banister (Freidel et. al 34–35). A reverse effect occurs at the fall equinox. Reynaud then gluts his ravenous appetite on the candies occupying what appear to be offering bowls and passes out next to a chocolate replica of the mask of the laughing shaman, artifacts referred to as the "Remojadas Dancer" and commonly found in the area of present day Veracruz. In this scene the ecstatic disposition revealed on the mask visage comments on Reynaud's orgy of self-indulgence. When he is found by his rival Vianne, he is steeped in the colors of her trade, chocolate smeared all over his face. The image could be reminiscent of Spaniards' observations of Aztec priests who had been consuming chocolate and whose lips had been turned so red they appeared to have been drinking blood (Coe and Coe *Chocolate* 109–10), with perhaps a parallel allusion to the Eucharist.

Resurrection is an important article of faith within the ancient Mayan religious ideology, and Reynaud's episode within the chocolate shop is as evocative of the rebirth of the maize god as it is of the Easter mythology. As indicated earlier, the Hero Twins Hunahpu and Xbalanke were killed and resurrected during their ordeal with the Lords of Death; however, their triumph was calculated to facilitate a still more important resurrection, that of their father, One Maize Revealed, or the maize god. The first father and his brother battled the lords of Xibalba initially and lost. The first father's head was severed and fixed in a gourd tree where it was observed by the daughter of a Xibalban lord. The head spat into the palm of her hand, and she became pregnant with the Hero Twins whose fate would be to redeem their father's loss and resurrect his body in the ball court where he would become the object of worship, the maize god of the ancient Maya.

His resurrection corresponds to the fourth creation of humanity, this time out of maize, and the enduring Mayan ritual in which the Shaman king raises the world tree ("Raised up Sky" or "Wakahchan") and opens the portal to the divine directly associated with the resurrection of the maize god. Frequently, the world tree is an animated corn plant with the face of the god emerging at its center. The power of the shaman king was measured by his ability to resurrect the maize god and bring about a flourishing harvest of this most important plant for the denizens of Meso-America. In a familiar image from the Temple of the Foliated Cross at Palenque, Lord Pacal, perhaps the most famous of all Mayan kings to the contemporary world, along with his son Chan-Bahlum (Jaguar Sky), is depicted resurrecting the world tree in the form of the maize god. The image is a political piece intended to legitimize Chan-Bahlum's weak claim to the throne (Schele and Freidel, *Forest* 239–242). The dynastic shamans appropriate the power of the Hero Twins, resurrecting the maize god, [re]creating and sustaining humanity.

The pagan analogues for Reynaud's fall and recovery on Easter morning are more extensive than those associated with the maize god. The Hero Twins also battle with Itzam-Yeh (Seven-Macaw) in preparation for the resurrection of their father. He is a beautiful but vainglorious bird who believed that he was the sun and demanded worship. The Hero Twins found him intolerable, so they knocked out his shining tooth with their blow guns, and he was subsequently revealed as a fraud (Freidel et. al., *Cosmos* 110). They allow him to remain perched atop the world tree, a symbol of the false sun and the powers of nature. His humiliation paved the way for the awakening of the maize god and the creation/rejuvenation of humanity (Gillette 11–12). Reynaud's humiliation is compelling in its parallel to the fate of Seven-Macaw. He too is vainglorious, and his abasement requisite to the redemption and assuaging of the physical and spiritual appetites of the townspeople through pleasure. Like the mythic bird, he is allowed to maintain his place atop the political and spiritual hierarchy of Lansquenet, but the moral authority that he exerted over the people has been broken because he is exposed as a fraud. Perhaps the most compelling association between Reynaud and Itzam-Yeh is visual. The chocolate mask of the Remojadas Dancer that he lies next to in the storefront window wears the headdress signifying the mythical bird, its avian head extending from the front of the chocolate hat.

Hallstrom's *Chocolat* makes a major alteration of Harris' novel, and one that has a direct relevance to the content of this discussion. While the novel has a contemporary setting, the screenplay places the events in the context of the late 1950s so that the apotheosis experienced by the town can become a metaphor for the awakening that occurred on an international level. The spiritual metamorphosis of the town signals the period of revolution and social experimentation that would transform western culture from repression and rigidity to liberty and hedonism, the 1960's (Ansen 77). The screenwriter's decision to change Reynaud's occupation from priest to politician of aristocratic background produces a subtle allegory that is not a denunciation of the Church, as some have suggested, but a critique of the spiritual, political, and economic control that the nobility have exercised over the townspeople's lives (Bernier 12–13). The revolution is then a populist uprising, a restoration of social and political power to the average people. Reynaud signifies the means by which power attempts to control the populace through the regulation of pleasure, the church merely an instrument in this process, one that teaches the parishioner that the conditions of heaven and ecstasy are contingent upon the ascetic practice of self-denial.

Vianne's chocolate shop reveals that ecstasy and revelation can be achieved through indulgence and physical delight, that heaven can be situated in this mortal coil. Her magical Mayan recipes become the fountainhead of dramatic social change, a resurrection and unveiling of ancient wisdom long dead. Like the Mayan shaman, she unites the physical and the spiritual worlds, creating a place for the corporeal in the metaphysical and a place for rapture and bliss in the body.

3

Scotland, PA: Macbeth, McMeat, and McMurder

In 2003, a federal judge dismissed a lawsuit initiated by Caesar Barber, a maintenance worker from New York, who sought damages against the fast food giant McDonald's for contributing to his obesity. The litigation was attempting to capitalize on successful lawsuits against tobacco companies who have been forced to pay large settlements, not to individual smokers, but to states whose healthcare systems have been overburdened by the medical costs of cancer and emphysema patients. Barber's suit sought to make fast food companies take responsibility for the unwholesome diets of their customers. The dismissal of the suit was applauded by Steven Anderson, CEO of the National Restaurant Association, who accused the plaintiff of trying to "capitalize on the recent publicity and news stories on the growing rates of obesity." He added that "The important thing to remember is that there is a certain amount of personal responsibility we all have.... The issues of obesity and nutrition are much more complicated than this and involve factors such as genetics, medical conditions and the level of physical activity" ("NY Man Sues"). Despite the unfavorable ruling, Barber's lawsuit is a manifestation of the increasing tendency to blame fast food restaurants for the unhealthiness of American diets, the same trend that motivated such restaurants to add fruit, salads, salad bars, and other low fat meals to their menus.

On my first trip to Great Britain, I met a Russian woman in the dormitory at Kings College, and following my usual patterns, I began complaining, in this case about the cost of food in London. She reminded me, with no small amount of sarcasm, that I would have no trouble finding a McDonald's in the city. I was irritated at her assumption that my idea of good food was McDonald's. Being polite, I said nothing, but subsequently I wished I had availed myself of this opportunity to dispel some misinformation about Americans that provoked this particular instance of European imperiousness. I have always fantasized about telling her "I don't eat McDonald's at home, so why would I eat such food in London at twice the price?" I also thought of making a generalization about who actually eats at McDonald's in the U.S., a comment that would have appropriated her imperiousness and imposed it on families with small children, the poor, and the ill-educated, but I realized that I do not actually know who eats at McDonald's and that the group is certainly too large and diverse to characterize in one pithy quip. One cannot blame the anonymous Russian either for her assumption that Americans consider fast food good food. After all, McDonald's and Coca-Cola may be the chief ambassadors of American culture to the world (Schlosser 229). It is worth considering the role it plays in the political witticism that "America has never gone to war with a country that has a McDonald's." Here McDonald's signifies the stability brought by international, interconnected economies. In the late 1980's, when the Soviet Bloc was breaking up, the Western press heralded the transformation as it was manifest in the opening of the first McDonald's in Moscow, offering extended coverage of the people lined up to get their first taste of American burgers and fries. The event signified the end of the Cold War, the triumph of private enterprise, and the self-perceived supremacy of western culture. The media showcased American ingenuity by revealing the need to teach the Russians to raise appropriately lean cattle for their burgers (Schlosser 230), an item intended to repudiate the Soviet system for its ineffectiveness. The overly "fat cows" may have even been a metaphor for the bloated socialist system that now required American intervention and streamlining, an ironic reversal of the usual characterization of capitalism as fat and excessive.

What was even more jarring to me than the Russian lady's disdain was my own desperation to disassociate myself from this icon of American imperialism. The incident reminded me that I have a class bias associated with McDonald's and with most fast food. To be sure, I stop at the drive-through for an Egg McMuffin and a coffee when I am traveling, but eating dinner at McDonald's, Burger King, or Wendy's is a guilty pleasure that I seldom allow myself, and the reasons are fat, calories, and cholesterol. If it is true that fast food restaurants are responsible for the unhealthful diets and early deaths of Americans and that fast food chains such as McDonald's are one of America's principal exports, then perhaps we have earned the scorn of that Russian woman and all those countries with whom we would never go to war. We are exporting to their shores our unhealthy lifestyles; we are exporting obesity, arterial sclerosis, heart disease, and premature death. Thus the creation and proliferation of the burger and fries, not to mention the fast food model itself, can be construed as a crime against humanity, a tragic flaw in the classical sense.

It is this latter assumption that is the punchline of Billy Morrissette's film *Scotland, PA* (2002), which unites Shakespeare's *Macbeth* with the politics of a fast food restaurant. Obviously playing upon the names McDonald's and Burger King, Morrissette conceives McBeth (played by James LeGros) as the king of burgers and fries. The playful revised spelling of "Macbeth" as "McBeth" in the film alludes to the name of the fast food giant as well as its ubiquitous use of the "Mc" prefix. McBeth's nickname, "Mac," alludes to the founders of the fast food chain — Richard and Maurice "Mac" McDonald, brothers who opened the first McDonald's in San Bernardino, California (Schlosser 19). The film narrative portrays the unappreciated McBeth usurping Duncan's restaurant through murder and struggling to maintain it in spite of growing suspicion of his guilt. The invention of the "drive thru" and the streamlining of burger production represent McBeth's tragic offense.

In traditional tragedy, the violation perpetrated by the hero produces universal suffering that is often portrayed (in, e.g. Sophocles' *Oedipus Rex* and Shakespeare's *Hamlet* and *Macbeth*) as a diseased or sterile land. To reveal the broad ramifications of Macbeth's crime, Shakespeare utilizes the language of suffering and disease, personifying Scotland as an ailing patient who requires medical attention and whose condition is lamentable:

> Each new morn
> New widows howl, new orphans cry, new sorrows
> strike heaven on the face, that it resounds
> As if it felt with Scotland and yell'd out
> Like a syllable of dolor [IV. iii. 4–7].

And

> Alas, poor country
> Almost afraid to know myself. It cannot
> Be call'd our mother, but our grave; where nothing,
> But who knows nothing, is once seen to smile;
> Where sighs and groans and shrieks that rend the air
> Are made, not mark'd; where violent sorrow seems
> A modern ecstasy. The dead man's knell
> Is there scarce ask'd for who, and good men's lives
> Expire before the flowers in their caps,
> Dying or ere they sicken [IV. iii. 164–173].

The complaints continue throughout IV. iii: "Bleed, bleed, poor country" (Line 31); "What's the disease he means?" (Line 145); "What's the newest grief?" (Line 174). However, the lamentations are intermingled with three

images of healing: a doctor, the holy king Edward who "leaves/The healing bendiction" (Lines 155–156), and McDuff, whose vengeful rage will
deliver Scotland from distress.

Morrissette's film similarly captures the clash between the purveyors
of sickness and health. While McBeth's initial crime is a murder, his actions
have a broad ranging impact on the world around him, and part of that effect
is the circulation of agents of ill-health — easy public access to greasy food.
The most enduring image of the Macbeths' guilty consciences is of course
Lady Macbeth's inability to wash her blood soaked hands. Morrissette clev-
erly appropriates this detail adapting it for the fast food scenario and the
particular crime of his cinematic heroes. Pat McBeth (Maura Tierney) has
a grease burn on her hand that resulted from the murder of Duncan when
she and her husband pushed his head into the fryer, and even after the burn
has long been healed, she continues to obsess over the unsightly lesion that
only she can see. The resolution of the McBeths' crime spree is equally
appropriate to the contemporary setting. The introduction of Lt. McDuff
(Christopher Walken) constitutes a dietary as well as a legal intervention.
McDuff is a vegetarian and is playfully disdainful of the food that McBeth
serves, and the latter becomes progressively defensive about his work,
resenting McDuff's culinary pretenses.

McBeth and Lt. McDuff meet for the first time at Duncan's funeral
when the police officer begins his investigation of the murder. He announces
that he has brought a bowl of his wife's Babagnoush and explains that his
entire family is vegetarian. Despite the fact that his livelihood is based upon
the consumption of animals, McBeth is not initially offended by the detective's culinary habits, even after McDuff offers a quasi-insulting joke about
fast food which alarms McBeth and his wife because it seems to reveal his
suspicion that they killed Duncan: "I envy you; by the time I get to my customers, they are already dead. At least you get a chance to kill them [pause]
with that fast food."

McBeth's growing resentment toward McDuff's dietary habits results
not only from the restaurateur's progressive paranoia, but also from McDuff's
refusal to eat meat, which constitutes a denial of the burger king's growing
influence. McDuff is unwilling to pay appropriate homage to McBeth's
success— to the ascendancy of fast food — and it is indeed such health conscious progressives who eventually begin the backlash (in the 1980's) against
the fast food industry's callous disregard for public health and the environment, one early manifestation being the battle with McDonald's over the use
of Styrofoam containers which have an adverse effect on the ozone layer.
McDuff's denial of meat is tantamount to a refusal to fall under McBeth's
charms. He cannot be dazzled by restaurateur's ingenuity and success; he,

like Shakespeare's Macduff, penetrates McBeth's secrecy. Director and writer Morrissette evidently derived this aspect of his characterization from III, iv of Shakespeare's play in which Macbeth is alerted to Macduff's desertion to the English forces by the latter's failure to attend Macbeth's great banquet, the same that is disrupted by the visitation of Banquo's ghost. Thus Shakespeare's Macduff refuses to eat at Macbeth's table: "How say'st thou, that Macduff denies his person/At our great bidding?" (III. Iv. 129–130).

McDuff's disdain for McBeth's food is further revealed during the detective's first opportunity to question the restaurant employees about the murder of the former owner. McDuff inquires into McBeth's plans for a french fry truck in which the restaurateur will give away his fries for free with the assumption that anyone who tastes them will be likely to further patronize his restaurant. McDuff recognizes the parallel between McBeth's entrepreneurial genius and the sale of illicit drugs to children: "They need 'em. Get 'em hooked. Kids on drugs. It's wonderful." The insult is lost on McBeth who is either too dumb or too intimidated to protest, or perhaps his silence acknowledges the validity of the analogy. The characterization of McBeth's marketing strategy is analogous to the fast food industry's practice of marketing its insalubrious fare to children, assuming that they will pressure their parents into taking them to the "happiest place on earth" (Schlosser 40–42).

The connection between McBeth and the consumption of meat is comically heavy-handed. He is portrayed as a threat to mammals everywhere, a characteristic that is consistent with Shakespeare's tragic hero who is repeatedly equated to a nocturnal predatory creature, most frequently an owl. Perhaps the most revealing analogue with Shakespeare's anti-hero is with the murder of MacDuff's helpless family. Lady MacDuff complains of her husband's cowardice in fleeing to the English forces and leaving his family and his castle undefended:

> He loves us not,
> He wants the natural touch; for the poor wren,
> The most diminutive of birds, will fight,
> Her young ones in her nest, against the owl.
> [IV. ii. 8–11]

MacDuff laments the massacre of his family in similar terms, equating Macbeth to a hawk and his family to a hen and chicks:

> All my pretty ones?
> Did you say all? O hell-kite! All?
> What, all my pretty chickens and their dam
> At one fell swoop? [IV. iii. 216–219].

The contrast between hawks and chickens in the above passage also captures the carnivore/herbivore dialectic found in the standoff between Morrissette's McBeth and McDuff. Chickens are herbivores largely consuming grains, while hawks and owls feed upon flesh.

Mac's appetite, hobbies, decorating taste, and profession are all predicated upon the slaughter of animals. He is repeatedly depicted consuming meat, most memorably in the scene where his wife Pat angrily serves his buddies and him by throwing a slab of charred meat on the table, stabbing it with a knife, and announcing "Dinner is served." She then explains what a fork looks like to McBeth's obnoxious friend, Jimmy McMann (David Wike), who inspires Pat's rage with his lurid sexist overtures. McBeth's car and his garage are also adorned with steer horns, and the walls of his house are decorated with trophy heads, particularly his dark basement den where he plots at least one of his murders and where his transformation from a man with a conscience to a paranoid and remorseless sociopath becomes increasingly evident. Dead animals adorn the walls of McBeth's house as well as his table. He is a successful hunter. Indeed, Shakespeare's murder of Banquo is translated into a hunting party in the film; however, while Banko (Kevin Corrigan) is a target, he is not murdered during the hunt because there are too many witnesses. His drunken unconscious body is carried into McBeth's house, and McBeth's wife, for a brief time, believes that he has been killed on the hunting trip. The imagery of this scene succeeds in equating McBeth's love of hunting animals with his stalking of humanity; his massacre, preparation, and consumption of cattle does not constitute the limit of his blood lust.

McBeth may be slow to recognize McDuff's contempt for his profession and his carnivorous appetite, but eventually his own hatred of the detective will manifest itself as a disdain for vegetarianism. In questioning McDuff's moronic assistant Ed, McBeth openly ridicules McDuff's lifestyle: "You don't think he's a little pushy, always pushing people around? Have you noticed how he is always going around in that little German car, always avoiding meat?" When McDuff visits McBeth's home to inform him of Banquo's murder, McBeth's hostility has been drawn into the open:

> What brings you here? Let me guess. You are gracing our humble little home with a vegetable tidbit to show how the other half lives.... I meant better half. No, you don't think that. That would be mean, and you don't think mean thoughts, just us vicious carnivores. I could make you a martini because that has a nice vegetable in it.... I'm not going to have one because I wanna be just like big daddy McDuff and all the little McDuff's, and I'm going to start right now. "Eat Healthy," that's my motto.

McBeth's vituperative declamation exposes his hidden guilt, acknowledging that he is a violent and disreputable person, a predatory carnivore, and he recognizes that McDuff's lifestyle is a repudiation and indictment of his own. By the time McDuff reveals that his reason for visiting McBeth's home is to tell him about "Mr. Banconi's murder," he has confirmed his suspicions of McBeth's involvement in the crime. The uncertainty of his explanation is replaced by recognition.

McBeth's propensity for self-revelation is consistent with the Shakespearean analogue. Lady Macbeth repeatedly chastises her husband for his lack of subtlety. She advises,

> Your face, my thane, is as a book where men
> May read strange matters. To beguile the time,
> Look like the time; Bear welcome in your eye,
> Your hand, your tongue. Look like the innocent flower,
> But be the serpent under it [I. V. 62–66].

However, while Shakespeare's tragic hero becomes better at hiding his guilt, Morrissette's does not. In addition, the blood guilt felt by Mcbeth for the murder of Duncan, Banquo, and Macduff's family manifests itself in the film as a guilt over the peddling and consumption of unhealthy food in addition to the overt murders.

Having successfully eliminated Duncan and Banko, McBeth redirects his hostility toward a new antagonist, this time McDuff. Shakespeare's Macbeth becomes progressively more paranoid. With the elimination of each perceived rival, he is unable to find peace and must focus on a new danger. The irony of Macbeth's psychology is that he is trying to gain peace of mind through murder. Morrissette's McBeth experiences a similar descent, moving from one antagonist to another, all perceived to stand between himself and the "golden round" or in his case the golden arches. In the film's denouement, McDuff recognizes the absurdity of McBeth's fears: "After me, you'll have to go after Malcolm and then Donald because Donald is coming after you." McBeth, nevertheless, tries to kill McDuff by shoving a burger and fries down his throat, but McDuff retaliates by biting McBeth on the hand, thus exposing him to the reality of meat eating. McBeth's destruction is equally emblematic. McDuff impales him on the hood ornament of McBeth's car, steer horns. Thus McBeth is eliminated by the same creatures that he exploited in his crimes against bovines and humanity.

Following McBeth's destruction, McDuff opens a vegetarian restaurant at the same location. In the final shot of the film, he is eating a carrot stick and standing in front of his newly refurbished building. The grand opening banner says "Home of the Veggie Burger," but the parking lot is empty. The image suggests that the public does not want to eat healthy, that like McBeth, the majority are self-destructive or indifferent in their eating habits. The irony of McDuff's struggle is that although he had the law and good health on his side, McBeth still represented the tastes of Americans. Perhaps Morrissette's point is to satirize the sanctimonious demeanor of activist vegetarians who would alter America's eating habits whether the public likes it or not.

McDuff signifies the advent of the 1980's backlash against the fast food industry and the evolution of the New Age movement. Most of the complaints that McBeth lodges against his antagonist are the manifestation of those alterations in American taste that will take place when the 1970's gave way to the 1980's. After two decades of dissipation, Americans became more health conscious as researchers produced more reliable information about the consequences of eating greasy and unhealthy food. In 1990, McDonald's switched to all vegetable oil in their fried foods in order to address public complaints about saturated fat and cholesterol in animal oils (Schlosser 120). Moreover, McDuff drives a foreign car, a trend that has devastated the American economy and particularly the automotive industry since the 1970's. Still another sign of the emerging decade is McDuff's entertainment. As he drives around in his foreign car, he listens to New Age self-help tapes in which a calming male voice offers serenity and self-affirmation. Clearly the antagonism between McBeth and McDuff has a cultural component; it is a standoff between what Raymond Williams defined as "dominant" and "emergent" cultures. McDuff's overthrow of McBeth is a prelude to the social milieu of the 1980's.

Despite his success, McDuff is not immune to the filmmaker's satire, and it is particularly his masculinity that becomes the object of ridicule. As I have already noted, McBeth mocks McDuff's unwillingness to support an industry that exploits animals and reviles his politeness toward other people. Indeed the film is constructed around the antithetical masculinities of McBeth and McDuff with the ancillary characters aligned along the opposing sides of this dichotomy. Similarly, the construction of masculinity is an important thematic in Shakespeare's play as well (Waith 265–268). Macbeth is torn between two antithetical ideals of the masculine. He evolves from a compassionate and emotional individual into a remorseless killer. Nevertheless, the paradigm of male compassion remains central to the play, embodied in Macduff, King Duncan, and King Edward, and it is this feminized masculinity that prevails at the end of the play. Macduff weeps for his slaughtered family despite the admonishment of his comrades; in contrast, Macbeth does not allow himself to mourn for his dead wife, asserting that she has died at an inconvenient time. However, the opposition of Macduff and Macbeth is not defined by the binary gender analogue female/male, but by the contrast of human and animal or man and monster. Because Macbeth loses his humanity, he loses his support and his throne.

The respective culinary proclivities of the two principal protagonists in Morrissette's film are indicative of their gender distinctions. Because men were traditionally responsible for providing meat for their families through hunting and women were charged with gathering fruits and vegetables, these particular food categories have come to signify gender. Meat is a masculine food associated with "strength and aggression" (Fiddes 146, 11), while vegetation retains a more feminine signification. The particular behaviors of carnivores and herbivores reinforce this gender distinction: carnivores associated with violence and predation and herbivores with docility. Thus the diets of McBeth and McDuff are coded masculine and feminine. McDuff is the more cultivated male with a sensitivity uncharacteristic of the masculinity performed by McBeth and his friends.

Morrissette's McBeth degenerates from a compassionate and loving individual into a brooding and paranoid killer. This transformation is evident in his interaction with his wife, Pat. He progresses from weak, submissive, and overly romantic to suspicious, devious, violent, and uncommunicative. McBeth becomes a stranger to his own wife. In contrast, McDuff remains unaltered, a humane and compassionate individual, a family man who hugs his interviewees, listens to New Age self-help tapes, opposes killing — both human and animal — and maintains a health conscious lifestyle. Mac's friends, Jimmy McMann, Kevin "Tanman" McKane, and Anthony "Banko" Banconi, share his view of masculinity. They are vulgar womanizers, who drink to excess, hunt, and lead lives of dissipation. In McDuff's camp are Malcolm and Donald, the sons of the murdered Duncan. The film includes a variety of indications that Donald is gay. He hates football, but idealizes the masculine form through the posters on his bedroom walls. He is member of the drama club; he is defensive about his sexuality; and early one morning, he and a male classmate are discovered in bathrobes by Malcolm and McDuff. While Malcolm is not gay, he is portrayed as supportive and open-minded. He is a hippie and a creative individual — a rock musician; he defends his brother against his father's masculine presumptions that all boys like football; and he is playfully tolerant of his brother's effete "drama-geek" friends.

The director's use of Shakespeare's tragedy in his tale of a disgruntled and ambitious restaurant employee creates a biting satire on the business practices of the fast food industry. On the most superficial level, the film comments on the cutthroat business practices that are the trademark of the industry, particularly in its employee relations. Eric Schlosser has documented the now infamous behavior of the restaurant industry in his best-selling, non-fiction study *Fast Food Nation*. He exposes the industry's underhanded efforts to maintain an underpaid and untrained workforce. The fast food giants pay their employees minimum wage, offer no job training, fight unionization by closing restaurants and purging activist employees, lobby Congress in opposition to raises in the minimum wage, occasionally use coercive tactics in the effort to undermine employee organizations, and perpetrate all of these tactics on workers composed almost entirely of adolescents. The result of this exploitation is a highly dissatisfied workforce and a high attrition rate among employees (59–88).

In *Scotland, PA*, the conflict between Mac and Duncan is indicative of the complaints of fast food employees. McBeth has been a hard working, dedicated, and self-motivating laborer who is ambitious and has many valuable ideas for the improvement of the restaurant. While Duncan is fixated on promoting his son Malcolm, who is not interested in the restaurant and is not a good employee, he ignores McBeth's contributions. When the restaurateur finally decides to use some of Mac's ideas, he promotes him to assistant manager rather than manager, an act that ensures Duncan's destruction. The robbery and murder of the fast food owner is indicative of a trend within the fast food industry that is frequently targeted for theft and violence by its own employees. There are approximately five murders a month of fast food employees, most of which are perpetrated during the course of a robbery, and two thirds of the robberies of these establishments are carried out by (ex)employees (Schlosser 83). The murder of Duncan is indicative of this trend since McBeth and his wife are disgruntled over his unwillingness to reward their contributions adequately and are determined to get the combination to the safe before they kill him so that they can steal the money that they have not been given through legitimate salaries. Pat McBeth explains that she and her husband are not "bad people"; they are "just underachievers who have to make up for lost time."

Once Mac and Pat have gained control of the restaurant, however, they do not prove any more sensitive toward their employers than Duncan had been. The screenwriter repeats some of the early incidents in which the McBeths were patronized by their supervisors. In these latter scenes, Pat McBeth forgets the names of her adolescent employees and subjects them to the same aggravating training sessions at the ice cream dispenser as she had formerly endured. The employer's inability to remember her employees' names is indicative of the high rate of labor turnover in fast food restaurants (Schlosser 88). The new hires do not remain employed long enough for their bosses to memorize their names. Moreover, the tiresome training session in front of the ice cream dispenser is indicative of the fast food industry's obsession with routine in food production processes and its failure to teach employees any skills that will aid them in their future endeavors (Schlosser 72).

When the McBeths take over Duncan's burger joint, they give the building a flashy makeover that is reminiscent of the architectural choices of the fast food giants who design their building to attract attention and to emphasize the sanitary condition of the kitchen and the dining areas (Schlosser 17). Duncan's restaurant is transformed from a cluttered, dingy diner with filthy dark corners into a clean environment with bright lighting, streamlined food productions, and smooth chrome and tile surfaces. The changes in the restaurant constitute the birth of the standard fast food restaurant. Of course, historically the film is inaccurate since the creation of the recognizable design for fast food occurred in the 1940's and '50's, but the industry did expand nationwide between 1962 and 1973 (Schlosser 24). However, just as the clean surfaces of fast food restaurants are intended to draw attention away from the cutthroat business practices, the unhealthy food, and the mass slaughter of animals that is requisite to their functioning, the clean and brightly lit interiors of McBeth's restaurant hide an insidious secret as well — the murder of Duncan that made the restaurant possible. The sanitary surfaces are a mask obscuring the secret lives of Mac and Pat McBeth. The upstanding businessman is actually a murderer, and as he grows more paranoid, he is compelled to perpetrate still more murders in order to maintain his mask of respectability. The false smiling faces and the insincere greeting of the fast food employees suggest the hypocrisy in Shakespearean tragedy where one can "smile and smile and be a villain" (*Hamlet*, I. v.109).

Morrissette's decision to transport Shakespeare's late tragedy into a restaurant setting, circa 1975, becomes a commentary on more than the exploitative business practices of the fast food industry. The film also critiques the role of Shakespeare in contemporary popular culture and particularly in film adaptations. Traditional Shakespearean critics have denigrated the practice of adapting the Bard's dramas to contemporary settings, particularly to contemporary adolescent locales, such as high schools, and recently there has been a spate of such films: *10 Things I Hate About You*, *O*, *Never Been Kissed*, and *Get Over It*. Some critics have accused these movies of the "dumbing down" of Shakespeare (Boose and Burt 2) and various disparaging terms have been coined for the phenomenon: "Shakespop," "Shakesteenflix" and "Shakespawn." Yet apologists for the industry suggest that the creation of such films exposes children and adolescents to classic Shakespearean drama early in life, encouraging them to become culturally literate, to appreciate Shakespeare, and to become lifelong learners (Lanier 108). These motivations are oddly reminiscent of the fast food industry's targeting of children in its advertising campaigns, creating brand loyalty or lifelong consumers of their product. The targeting of a young audience in both the film and fast food reveals an additional parallel. The restaurant association targets children who will then compel their parents to dine at McDonald's, Burger King, Wendy's etc.; thus the industry lures the adults with the money into the store by manipulating the desires of the children. Similarly, the genius of "Shakesteenpix" is that they will bring in the adolescents and the adults. Culturally literate adults will pay to see the newest transmogrification of Shakespeare into cinema, and the adolescents will view the film because it reflects their needs, desires, and experiences. In this case, the parallel between the fast food and the film industries would be ironic since the two groups occupy opposite ends of the cultural spectrum. The purveyors of fast food are encouraging the public's longing for a product that is potentially destructive and physically unhealthy while filmmakers are inspiring audiences with a commodity that is potentially life enhancing or intellectually stimulating. Of course, the ultimate objective of both industries is to make money.

The metaphor of the fast food restaurant in Morrissette's film also suggests the streamlining of Shakespeare in popular culture. The shiny surfaces and brightly lit interiors of the restaurant signify the process of adapting the Shakespearean text for an audience that is not culturally literate. These films paraphrase the early modern English in the script and update the set so that it is more familiar (or palatable) to the audience. The assembly line production of burgers and fries suggests the mechanical regularity of new Shakespearean adaptations and allusions in film. The metaphor even includes a potential critique of this practice insofar as it creates an analogue that is a universal symbol of trash culture — "the happy meal," the cultural artifact that has no lasting or ennobling virtue, but is merely a quick and easy distraction for a population on the move.

4

Four Little Caligulas:
La Grande Bouffe, Consumption, and Male Masochism

In former public debates over the inclusion of women and gay men into traditionally male exclusive societies such as the military, athletics, and the police force, those who opposed integration periodically argued that they needed to be able to rely on their partners who would be engaged with them in dangerous and competitive activities. The implication was that they preferred a partner of parallel or greater physical strength, whom they never failed to envision as a heterosexual male, as well as a person from the working or middle classes. Even credible demonstrations of women's and gay men's physical strength or capacity for violence did little to allay these presumptions. Male bonding and the social construction of manhood in western culture requires constant displays of masculine prowess both in the capacity to endure and inflict pain and injury (Horrocks 42), and the presumption of male exclusive cultures is that those who lie outside of the narrow profile of hegemonic masculinity will be unable to demonstrate their physical prowess in a fashion sufficient to inspire confidence in their skittish partners.

In the socialization of young men, one of the premier venues for the construction of masculine gender performance is athletic competition. Here, young men exhibit their physical prowess, their willingness to endure strain and injury, their capacity to inflict pain on their competitors, their compliance with rule governed action and violence, and their commitment to group goals and identity. The public nature of athletic activity is a particularly central feature in the performance of masculinity which requires an audience. Men demonstrate their compliance with hegemonic gender categories for the benefit of others as well as themselves, and the trial process is never complete. In the words of Timothy Beneke, men are "only as masculine as ... [their] last demonstration" (43). Masculinity is an ideal that is very easily tarnished, unbalanced by an action as simple as the inappropriate crossing of one's legs. However, through the credible and sustained display of masculinity, men earn each other's trust and companionship. Those who are unable to conform to acceptable standards of masculine performance are marginalized, either socially or psychically.

The process of proving one's manhood is perpetual. Recently, I held the door for a ninety-something man with a walker and an uncertain gait as he attempted to exit the YMCA. When I arrived at the front desk, the clerk expressed incredulity that the elderly gentleman had allowed me to assist him; evidently, even in his geriatric decrepitude, the man had never been known to permit such support. Of course, I was never sure if the affront to his pride was related to my gender or my belief that he was too feeble for the task. However, the incident demonstrated that there is no expiration date on masculine pride of performance, although the challenges may diminish significantly. The fact that someone in his condition would refuse assistance reveals that there is a deeply masochistic quality to masculine gender performance, an unwillingness to be defeated by suffering or circumstance. The general assumption is that men reveal their compliance with gender constructs through their domination of others and their capacity to inflict pain on other men; however, just as often men display their resolution through silent acquiescence to suffering.

Director Marco Ferreri's 1973 film La Grande Bouffe parodies many of the conventions associated with masculine performance. The film depicts four middle-aged men who have decided to kill themselves through culinary over-indulgence, not over the course of fifty years as is commonplace in Western culture, resulting in obesity, high blood pressure, and clogged arteries, but through a single sustained period of gluttony. They retire to the ancestral estate belonging to one of the participants and unload an obscene amount food, thereafter beginning an orgy of culinary and erotic consumption. The opening scenes create a paradoxical contrast with the chaos that grows throughout the film. The men meticulously, deliberately, and cheerfully plot their own deaths, a behavior replete with careful rule governed activities such as the following of complicated recipes for preparation of the comestibles. They have no intention of eating themselves to death on the common fare, but only the most refined gourmet cuisine. While the excess immediately seems obscene, the anarchic and self-destructive objectives of their appetites only gradually become discernible to the audience.

The cinematic event constitutes a parody of competitive sports. The men agree to remain within the bounds of a limited space for a designated period; they comply with specific rules of engagement in the preparation and consumption of food; they monitor each other's performances, searching for signs of weakness; they nurture a fraternal and perhaps at times even a quasi-romantic affection through mutual suffering; and they remain resolute in the attainment of their predetermined goals even into death. The banquet serves as a commentary on the nature of men's gender construction through athletics. Athletes are commonly regarded as the apogee of physical health; however, the very activities for which they have honed their skills and conditioned their bodies are notoriously unhealthy, frequently resulting in sustained injury and even early deaths (Messner 71). In *Male Impersonators: Men Performing Masculinity*, Mark Simpson discusses the paradoxical outcome of hypermasculinity in the culture of body building. The very processes in which the bodybuilders engage in their effort to create the ideal male physical specimen rely upon the continued degradation of the same through steroid use and the "'blood, sweat, and tears of pumping iron'" (21–42). The athlete's willingness to endure these physical abuses for the sake of masculine performance reveals one of the masochistic attributes of male gender construction. Men are encouraged

Michel Piccoli plays a television executive who, along with three friends, decides to kill himself by binging on gourmet cuisine in Marco Ferreri's *La Grande Bouffe* (1973).

to suffer for masculinity. They wear their old football injuries like a badge of honor.

La Grande Bouffe portrays an athletic engagement that, like many other sports, involves a pleasure/pain dynamic. The activity of eating fine cuisine is both agreeable and salubrious, yet the objectives of the consumption are ultimately destructive. Just as athletics are intended to promote performance and good health, immoderate indulgence in the same engages physical prowess in the pursuit of infirmity and debilitation. Physical strength can only be demonstrated through those activities that threaten its integrity. Similarly, the gourmand's undue excess achieves enjoyment through physical torment. The men continue to eat long after the experience is pleasurable and the appetites are sated. In several instances, the participants are force fed when their own lethargy and fragility no longer permit the simple strain of eating. Philippe feeds Ugo paté while the cook is lying prostrate on the kitchen table, and Marcello feeds Michel puree while the latter is incapacitated by a bowel obstruction. As with the demonstration of masculinity through physical exertion, the men continue to endure intolerable discomfort in order to avoid losing face among their peers. Even after his friends are dead, Philippe continues to eat still motivated by the concern that his friends would find any abatement of his resolution a cowardly betrayal.

The unusual fashion with which these four Frenchmen have decided to prove their manhood has a correlation to class difference. Participation in contact and competitive sports is generally associated with the lower and middle classes and with adolescence and early adulthood. In contrast, the four middle-aged men are all professionals at the height of their careers: Philippe is a judge: Ugo, a chef; Marcello, an airline pilot; and Michel, a television executive. The manner of competition and death that the protagonists have chosen is indicative of their class status; it is an exhibition of their lofty affectations. They are not common men, so they select an uncommon suicide, one emblematic of the lives they lead. The pretentious competition is parallel to the sophistication of their other pursuits. The dialogue is replete with references to art and literature. Michel recites Shakespeare — "to be or not to be" — as he dances around carrying a cow's head. Later he comments on a "splendid drawing" by Galle, even offering the date of its completion — 1890. While eating oysters, the men view vintage pornographic slides and pause to comment on the "artistic lighting" of the images. Michel offers an ongoing philosophical commentary, cataloging the epiphenomena of their experiences. The gentlemen consistently refer to the 17th century nature poet Richard Boileau who is in some way associated with the property on which the residence stands. The participants' preoccupation with high art is matched by the sophistication of their cuisine and the dining milieu. The food is refined gourmet cuisine presented as works of art in an environment that is tastefully decorated. The table is always elaborately set, including fine china, floral centerpieces, and silver candelabra. The men dress for dinner and frequently address each other with a formality inappropriate to their activities. The food preparation includes an emphasis on elegant presentation. Most memorably, for his final meal, Ugo creates a goose, chicken, and duck paté shaped like an ornate architectural structure. He calls it "poetry" and remarks that he "could be a millionaire in one month making these dishes for people."

The diners' appetite for food is echoed in their other yearnings. While their appreciation of gourmet cuisine and fine art defines them as cultured elite, their baser hungers distinguish them as sensualists. Indeed, the story of their gluttony allegorizes their lifestyles as aristocratic consumers, and not simply as materialists, but also as sophisticated hedonists. Hegemonic masculinity is often constructed as brutish and rapacious. Western culture retains many stereotypes of the unattached male whose life is an endless round of parties and one night stands, whose apartment is a wasteland of beer cans, condom wrappers, pizza boxes, and dirty laundry, whose notion of high culture is Monday night football, *Sports Illustrated*'s swimsuit edition, and monster truck shows, and whose appetite for fine cuisine includes tacos, buffalo chicken wings, and Subway sandwiches. The taming of the unrestrained male occurs with the intervention of a woman, who civilizes the male. A portion of the prohibition against life-long bachelorhood is related to the fear of the unattached male's uncontrolled appetites. Nevertheless, even while our culture ostensibly condemns such profligacy, we privately acquiesce and even sanction and admire it. Young males are expected to experiment with sex and to break hearts. The expression "lady killer" is not a derogation among men even though it refers to males who insensitively use and abandon women. Secretly, men envy the freedom and opportunity that such behavior affords. When Wilt Chamberlain confessed to having slept with thousands of women in the 1970's, the public response was a mixture of incredulity, jealousy, and respect. One critic remarked that no woman could ever make such a revelation without being universally denounced.

The events of *La Grande Bouffe* dramatize the release of male inhibition, exposing his voracious animal appetite. The director/screenwriter has chosen four genteel middle-aged men to demonstrate that the propensity for indiscretion and dissolution is latent even in those males with a credible claim to civility. While they begin their suicidal binge with order and formality, it gradually descends into orgiastic turmoil. They become increasingly indifferent to or incapable of maintaining further pretenses to sophistication. Indeed the film suggests that the cultured affectations may be no more than a charade for the seduction of unsuspecting women. As the men contemplate including prostitutes in their endless repast, Marcello satirically characterizes their pretension by submitting the following inscription for invitations: "A dinner offered by four Burgundian gentlemen to three nice Canterbury whores." The legend reveals the contempt with which the men regard women and the extent to which women will become not only participants in the feast, but also one of the main dishes. The cinematic imagery is loaded with somewhat cliché equations between food and sex or between food and the female body, both of which the men devour with great relish. At the aforementioned dinner party on the first evening, the men consume oysters (a sensual food that traditionally alludes to the female genitalia and is a mythical aphrodisiac) while they view pornography. Andrea, the only woman who remains with the men during the entire banquet, is privy to several erotic dishes. Ugo creates an imprint of her butt on a pastry, punning on the slang "tart" — slut and pastry — and she presents Philippe with a gelatin shaped like women's breasts, the same dish that will finally kill him. There are a significant number of culinary allusions to male genitalia as well. The participants consume ziti pasta during the sex act, and the dish that Ugo prepares for the formal dining experience with the prostitutes includes skewered meats propped up at 45 degree angles on the serving dish. In a more subtle allusion, Philippe and Andre butcher turkeys in the garden; Philippe exposes their necks on a chopping block while Andrea lops off their heads.

The equation between sex and meat is broadened within the film to include a glib satiric commentary on masculinity and human mortality. The film creates a correlation between the reverent and meticulous unloading of the meat truck at the beginning of the men's sojourn in the banquet house and the arrival of the prostitutes on the second night. The women are a substantial portion of the meat that the men will consume. However, there is an ironic reversal of the meat metaphor that becomes apparent in the final scene. Just as Philippe begins to expire, a previously purchased delivery of meat arrives in the garden. Philippe orders the multiple carcasses to be spread around the garden. The final image of the film depicts the delivery men roguishly attempting to balance a side of beef in the branches of a small tree. As they depart, dogs consume the meat strewn about the garden. This, of course, is a heavy handed allusion to the corpses of the diners littering the house and a commentary on the hedonistic masculinity that brought them to that state. If manhood is measured by the unfettered indulgence of one's sensual and sensory appetites, then the

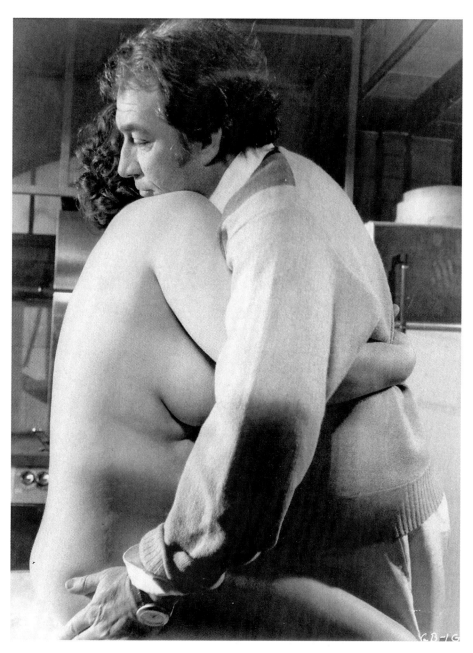

Ugo Tognazzi creates the culinary masterpieces on which the four suicidal gourmands of Ferreri's *La Grande Bouffe* (1973) overindulge. In this scene, the chef puns on the word "tart" by making a pastry in the shape of Andrea Ferreol's posterior.

construction of masculinity is self-destructive, and this idea lies at the center of *La Grande Bouffe*. In the process of proving manhood, the protagonists accomplish their deaths. Marcello, after his death, is placed in a walk-in meat locker where he gazes through the window, presiding over the remainder of the feast like a memento mori. The subtext of the meat imagery is one familiar to the hedonist. Meat becomes an absurdist metaphor for futility in the film. The indifference with which the diners threw away their lives on gustative indulgences—the same process whereby they became meat themselves—becomes reasonable in a world view that recognizes no spiritual objective for humanity. If "the paths of glory lead but to the grave," then one should be certain that path is dotted with as many appetizing dishes as can be managed.

The exploitation of women during the feast is counter to the role that they play in the men's personal lives, a role that the director succinctly dramatizes in the opening scenes of the film. All of the men are, in a manner of speaking, managed by women. In the opening scenes of the film, Ugo is interrogated by a woman who may be his maitre d' or perhaps the restaurant owner as he packs his recipes and cooking knives for his holiday. He falsely reassures her that he will return after his excursion, but the items that he has chosen to take with him do not ease her suspicions. Michel is shown in conference with his assistant, reminding her that he has taped four weeks of shows and that he needs rest and relaxation. She regards his plans with trepidation. He then turns to his daughter, leaving her the keys to his apartment and asking about his estranged wife. Marcello lands the plane on his final commercial flight and orders the obliging stewardesses around that cabin to collect his belongings. Interestingly, Marcello is the most unfettered of the men; none of the women express any concern about his intentions. His profession is perhaps representative of the freedom in his life. Finally, Philippe is mothered by his childhood nurse who still attends him in middle age. She awakens him at 10:00 AM and begs him not to go to the prostitutes who are evidently permanent features in the judge's life. She offers herself as a surrogate lover reminding him that she has filled that office before, but he indulgently declines the offer. The effect of this montage of brief scenes is to emphasize a paradox at the heart of gender relations. While masculinity is constructed through performances of domination, self-assurance, independence, and skill, men unattached to women are domestically helpless. Masculinity has been described as a withdrawing from multiple areas of life, a process of restriction defined negatively by those activities in which men cannot engage and remain men (Horrocks 25).

The vacation from women is short-lived. Within one day, the men discover that they need prostitutes to slake their libidinous appetites, to save them from boredom, to mediate their internal relations, and to witness their heroic expression of masculine self-destruction. Women are the bridle on men's galloping desires; they bring an end to the orgy of self-indulgence that characterizes male adolescence and bachelorhood. The men's release from women's control has the expected result. Emancipated from the constraints posed by civilized living, the men very rapidly self-destruct in their sensual and gustatory binge. Even those women whose profession it is to pander to men's base desires—"the three nice Canterbury whores"— have no stomach for the gastronomic gallantry; they are driven out of the house by the binging, but not before they offer repudiations of the diners' behavior. Anna remarks, "You're grotesque and disgusting. Why do you eat when you are not hungry?" Another adds her own condemnation: "They're crazy. All four of them are imbeciles, idiots, moral defectives." She offers her criticism as she brushes her hair, a healthy sign of her own self care. The prostitutes were selected for the gathering not only because they were easy to enlist, but also because their own loose living would guarantee their indifference to the men's suicidal agenda.

The prostitutes try to convince Andrea, the school teacher, to leave with them, but she expresses her indifference to the course the men have chosen: "If they want to commit suicide, let them." Because masculinity needs an audience (Simpson 39), Andrea must remain in the house as a witness to the activities there. The gentlemen's displays of masculine prowess would be futile if there were no women for whom to perform and whose admiration they hope to achieve. Gender is a binary construction. Masculinity only has meaning in relation to femininity, and masculine bravado is partially motivated by the desire to prove one's worthiness of women. However, there is a more subtle necessity for the woman's presence. Andrea articulates the relationship between the men themselves. Masculine performance with women (particularly men's willingness to exploit women sexually) negotiates the interaction of males and serves as the term of admission into exclusive male societies. As pioneering queer theorist Eve Sedgewick observed, the relations between men are arbitrated by the intervention of women. Sedgwick observed love triangles represented in western literature and recognized that the important relationship within each of the narratives was the one negotiated between the men, over the body of the disputed female (21–27). Andrea plays a very similar role in *La Grande Bouffe* where she is passed around between the men, and she actually facilitates an intimacy that did not previously seem to exist. Before the arrival of Andrea, the men kept to their own beds; however, as the gastronomic carnival progresses and the men become increasingly loose, they begin to share the same bed. This progress is facilitated by Andrea's presence. The men sleep together in order to be near her. Yet it becomes clear that their evolving familiarity is also related to their need to comfort each other under the distress of their suicidal binge.

The occasionally dangerous course of manhood is worthwhile because it convinces men that they are worthy of women's affection. Andrea is privy to each man's individual drama. She is called upon to comfort them, to muster their courage in the face of death, but mostly she is called upon to witness their dauntless heroism. As Ugo ingests his fatal paté, Andrea is invited to masturbate him, bolstering the last bit of courage requisite to going all the way. She accompanies Marcello in his sports car, allowing him to flaunt his athletic interests, and makes out with him in the garden; however, when Marcello tries to copulate with her in the bed, he becomes exceedingly distressed by his impotence and tries to abandon the party. In the morning, he is found frozen to death in his auto. His demise is indicative of his inability to break the rules of the game and lose face with the other men, to be shown a coward as well as a "eunuch," an appellation that he uses to insult the other men before he leaves the house. He would have survived the night had he the courage to open the property gates and leave or return to the house and face his own impotence and death. Andrea is enlisted to accompany Michel to his bed while he suffers from intestinal disturbance. She agrees, "If it is for your health." Of course, the health she promotes is only masculine vanity. Michel weeps and experiences severe flatulence as she makes love to him. Finally, Andrea is present at Philippe's passing; she serves the fatal dish, holds his head during his death throes, and walks away indifferently leaving him on the garden bench.

The function of Andrea is related to another attribute of masculine pride that motivates the men's action. The suicidal drama these four gentlemen have embarked upon constitutes a literalization of their respective middle-age crises. Each of the men is perhaps mid to late forties in age. As is commonly known, this type of psychological distress frequently results from a fear that an individual may no longer be attractive to the opposite sex. The crisis may be particularly acute in these cases because the men are all lifelong bachelors. Their desire to remain unfettered to a wife and to avoid the sexual frustration of old age has resulted in desperate measures. They would rather be dead sensualists than living, aging "eunuchs." Andrea's fidelity throughout the ordeal confirms that they are still desirable to women. If they kill themselves because they fear aging and the rejection of future love interests, then the compulsion to prove that they are still appealing upon their deaths would be great.

The self-destructive odyssey of the four diners may be understood as a cynical commentary on the role of genteel white males in the growing pluralism of Western cultures. Their binging signifies the decadence of genteel white males and the progressive decline of that social group's political and financial affluence. The gustatory enterprise carnivalizes the excess and covetousness of the bourgeoisie male, revealing the shameless materialism and hedonism of this dominant social class. The banquet house becomes a microcosm for France in advance of dramatic social change. The four diners are indicative of a divided consciousness, each male representative of specific masculine virtue: Philippe, reason; Ugo, craftsmanship; Michel, creativity; and Marcello, athleticism. The growing chaos of their enterprise parallels the decline of their unchallenged dominion; the grounds of their estate may suggest either the ever shrinking sphere of their influence or the contested region of France upon which they have performed the pageant of masculine excess for too long.

5

What's Cooking?: Multiculturalism and Holiday Histrionics or a Banquet of Shouting

The first Thanksgiving is a uniquely American myth, celebrating survival, as well as harvest, abundance, and concord. Those individuals willing to face great challenges and adversities to settle in an unknown continent, far from their origins and fraught with dangers, permitted themselves one day of feasting and celebrating before settling in to endure the often harsh North American winter. The myth also suggests that the settlers included in their feast those with whom they were in competition the remainder of the year — the indigenous people of the continent. The celebration emphasizes sharing and tolerance, an effort to live amicably with one's neighbors, each participant contributing a dish to the feast. While Thanksgiving has evolved to focus primarily on the gathering of the extended family who may be separated by great distances the remainder of the year, the idea of Thanksgiving as it is taught to American school children is less insular than contemporary practice. It was a celebration of inclusiveness, an overcoming of differences to acknowledge the mutual struggle for survival in the wilderness and the imagined intervention of the divine.

Of course, in a more cynical age such as our own, the holiday has often become a punchline associated with disharmony, the occasion for familial upheaval, as was so hilariously portrayed in *Home for the Holidays* (1995). Yet the Thanksgiving myth is perhaps more reflective of American society today than it has ever been in the past, having become a powerful metaphor for our increasingly prosperous, tolerant, and multicultural society. Each ethnic and racial group contributes its own unique flavor to the great banquet that is American democracy and plurality, thus diversity nourishes and sustains the country. It is just this idea that serves as the inspiration for Gurinder Chadha's film *What's Cooking?* (2000) in which four families living on the four corners of a single intersection in Los Angeles celebrate a Thanksgiving fraught with reunion, feasting, and upheaval. The director is developing a paradox: that Americans are separated by great distances (ethnically and ideologically) even when living across the street from each other, but are nevertheless united by common rituals and concerns.

Despite allusions to the national identity, the film is mostly an L.A. story which begins with a children's Thanksgiving play, involving members of three of the four households and emphasizing diversity and tolerance. The play involves children of multiple races and ethnicities. The final and definitive piece of dialogue comes from Joey Nguyen, a Vietnamese-American boy, who paraphrases Rodney King in his articulation of the values of the holiday: "for our prosperity, future progress, harmony, and so we can all get along." The inclusion of King's call for calm during the L.A. riots informs the film audience that the narrative will address Southern California's oft contentious race relations. Thus, the film invokes the problems of the "American family" in order to discuss social relations at several levels. The American family signifies the nuclear as well as the metropolitan and national families—the populace of L.A. and the U.S.A.

What's Cooking? is two hours of parallel editing, a pastiche of the holiday rituals, narrating the Thanksgiving process of each household: the Avilas, a Latino family; the Nguyens, a Vietnamese family; the Williamses, an African American family, and the Seeligs, a Jewish family. Each celebration begins with goodwill, proceeds to upheaval, and ends in forgiveness. Central to each narrative is the food that they prepare and consume. Each household cooks the obligatory Thanksgiving turkey and potatoes, but each family embellishes on the meal in a fashion that is consistent with its own racial or ethnic heritage. For example, in the Avila household, the women prepare tortillas and tamales to supplement the standard Thanksgiving fare while the turkey itself is baked with fruit and vegetables. The Nguyens prepare two dinners, one for the children and one for the grandparents: the former includes a turkey, half covered in chili paste, but eventually replaced by Kentucky Fried Chicken after the bird burns in the oven, and the latter is composed of traditional Asian dishes: rice noodles, stir fried vegetables etc. Audrey Williams tries to create a gourmet Thanksgiving dinner that is reflective of the family's prosperity. The dinner features oyster and shiitake mushroom dressing, fruit compote, and steamed asparagus, but her mother-in-law insists on including macaroni and cheese because Audrey's food is unfamiliar and because her son enjoyed it as a child. The Jewish family prepares the most traditional meal; the only deviation seems to be the inclusion of polenta, which Ruth Seelig does not know how to prepare.

Chadha documents the main food preparation by a series of rapid cuts between the four kitchens. The musical score is a medley of four renditions of "Wipe Out." As the camera switches from one home to another, the music alters to celebrate the traditional sounds of each respective ethnicity. In the Williamses' kitchen, blues and jazz tones are prevalent; in the Avilas', the music has a Latin flare. The particular music may have been chosen because its title predicts the crises that will engulf each holiday feast or because it is a distinctly L.A. music associated with the surfing community of the mid-twentieth century, a choice also manifest in the use of Beach Boy songs and reflective of the social cohesion of a bygone age in Southern California.

Preparations for the holiday emphasize differences in similarities. While the food may vary in each household, there is still a core of holiday dishes that signify the traditional Thanksgiving. While each household has its own fashion for executing the holiday festivities, the objective is nevertheless the same, to honor family and prosperity. There is a parallel sequence of events that transpires in each house. On the day before Thanksgiving, a member of each household shops for groceries in a local market, contacts absent family members to determine their travel intentions and or picks up people at the airport. The matriarch of each house makes initial food preparations such as thawing and preparing of the turkey and laying out dishes for the meal. On Thanksgiving day, the preparations begin early with the placing of the turkey in the oven. As the guests arrive, the women work in the kitchen while the men watch football and drink. When each family sits down to dinner, there is a ritualistic presentation of the turkey, replete with complimentary remarks followed by a prayer of thanksgiving. Consumption of the food proceeds without incident. It is after the meal is done or during dessert that the harmony of each table is disrupted, and in each case, the disturbance is created by the arrival of an unexpected guest. The interruptions divide family loyalties, resulting in a breech of the harmony signified by the holiday feast.

On its surface, the intrusion of the unexpected company seems to undermine the spirit of Thanksgiving, not only because the respective celebrations degenerate into shouting, but also because the holiday is intended to honor inclusiveness. However, in each case, the resolution of the argument leads to openness and stronger family ties, a parallel objective of the holiday. In the Williams household the arrival of son Michael (Eric George) delights the mother Audrey (Alfre Woodard) and grandmother Grace (Ann Weldon) and aggravates his disapproving father Ronald (Dennis Haysbert) who is the only member of the household who knows that the son threw white paint on the Governor the previous day, the same politician for whom

Ronald works. When the father informs the entire family of the incident, the son counters by revealing the father's adultery with a co-worker. As it turns out, the white family, the Moores, who had been invited were actually the intruders, both physically and symbolically. After the order of the table is broken by the revelations and the Moores depart, the family airs its grievances through shouting and is reconciled. The Moores signified the racial infidelity that accompanied Ronald's sexual indiscretions. He works for a racist politician whom Michael accuses of having "sold out affirmative action" in California. The inclusion of the Moores in the Thanksgiving dinner signifies Ronald's assimilationist tendencies, his desire to live the traditional white bourgeois life, replete with a rugged individualist philosophy. In several subtle shots, Ronald and his white co-worker, James Moore (Gregory Itzin) exchange irritated glances, provoking the father into asking Michael what he intends to do with a degree in African American Studies and why he wants to isolate himself in D.C. at an all black school. When the Moores are routed from the house by the shouting, the father, at least visually, returns his loyalty to his families, both nuclear and racial.

The disruption in the Williams household is reiterated throughout the neighborhood. In the Nguyen home, the relative peace is interrupted by a knock at the door. The visitors are three friends of the middle son Gary (Jimmy Pham), the same who are responsible for giving him the gun that his sister had found in his room, a fact that she had thus far been concealing. She chooses this moment to reveal her discovery to the family in order to keep her brother from leaving with his friends. The subsequent shouting involves a variety of accusations and some very bad acting, but perhaps the most important statement is the grandmother's reminder that the family came to America from Vietnam to escape guns, an interesting irony considering L.A.'s reputation for violence. Here, as in the other households, the issues that arise are related to the family's gradual assimilation into American culture over the three generations represented at the feast. The Nguyen mother, Trinh (Joan Chen), prepares two dinners to accommodate the respective levels of social integration represented by the three generations in the house. When the mother and grandmother spread chili paste on one half of the turkey the daughter, Jenny (Kristy Wu) asks why they have to make the turkey taste like everything else they eat, to which the grandmother responds, "Why everything has to taste like McDonald's?" Earlier, Trinh remarked that she did not know her children anymore since the family had moved to America. The true crisis comes when the youngest son, Joey (Brennan Louie), picks up the gun and fires it while the rest of the family is preoccupied with its loud disagreements. The camera allows the audience to believe that he may have shot himself, since it shows him pointing the gun at his face just before the image breaks away and the shot is heard. The close call shocks the family into better behavior, revealed in their renewed openness to outsiders. Jimmy brings his Latino girlfriend to the house for dessert, and she is greeted with compliments, a visual contrast to the earlier episodes in which Jenny's caucasian boyfriend is routed from the video store. The process of assimilation is most visible in the Nguyen house where the grandparents still speak Vietnamese, and the parents speak English with an accent, but the children are completely Americanized in their dress, their romantic choices, and their ability to speak English without an accent.

The principal conflict in the Avila household is a battle of the sexes, and the interruption in the celebration is twofold. Elizabeth, the family matriarch, played by Mercedes Ruehl, is irritated when she finds that her son has invited Javier (Victor Rivers), her estranged husband, to Thanksgiving without asking her. When he arrives in spite of her efforts to uninvite him, she is nevertheless cordial because the family is happy to see him. The dinner proceeds without incident for a time. When Javier tries to win back his wife by reminiscing about their courtship and her forbidding father, Grandma Avila (Ellen Lopez) reminds him that if Elizabeth's father were still alive, Javier never would have messed with Rosa, Elizabeth's cousin, the event that led to the couple's split. The shouting does not begin until Elizabeth's new boyfriend arrives for dessert, startling and infuriating all of the males in the house. The subsequent histrionics divide the family in half along gender lines, the males siding with Javier and the females with Elizabeth, but it is Javier who is forced to leave when Elizabeth tells him that there is no chance of their being reunited and reminds him that she did not invite him and did not expect him.

The food consumed in the Avila house is indicative of the events that transpire there. The hot and spicy dishes reflect the sensual passions expressed among the family members. The Avila house is charged with sensuality and lovemaking, more so than the other houses. The only sex scenes in the film occur within the context of the Avila family. Elizabeth makes love to her boyfriend Daniel (A. Martinez) at the beginning of the film, and the daughter Gina (Isidra Vega) has sex with Jimmy Nguyen (Will Yun Lee) in the shower before dinner. Moreover, the context of the family dispute involves adultery and the conversation at the table gravitates toward the passionate. The level of assimilation within the Avila house is substantial, reflecting the lengthy period that Latinos have been in southern California, of course, predating all other ethnicities, save those of pure native American ancestry. Nevertheless, the Avilas have maintained their distinct cultural heritage, speaking both English and Spanish within the family. The generational conflict lies in the contrast between Gina's progressive interracial match and Grandmas Avila's reminder of the traditionally strict rules for courtship.

The Seeligs prepare a number of dishes that are sweet, including cookies, candies, and yams with marshmallows. The dishes are indicative of the syrupy relations between the members of the house. The complication begins when Rachael Seelig (Kyra Sedgwick) brings her lesbian life-partner, Carla (Julianna Margulies), home for the Thanksgiving. Carla is not, however, the unexpected guest, nor is this the first time she has met Ruth (Lainie Kazan) and Herb (Maury Chaykin), the parents. Nevertheless, the Seeligs are only ostensibly comfortable with Rachael's orientation. They are sweet to the lovers in person and disturbed in private. However, their disapproval manifests itself in guilt and passive aggressiveness. Ruth breaks down into tears during the dinner preparation, protesting that all she ever wanted for Rachael was that she be happy and have a family. She has no idea how her wishes will reveal themselves. Rachael reminds her that Carla makes her very happy. Even though the parents quietly endure their daughter's domestic arrangement, they are, nevertheless, embarrassed by it, instructing the couple to conceal their relationship from the other dinner guests. It is only after the couple is aggravated by a lengthy discussion of conservative politics (particularly the incident involving the paint strewn governor) that Rachael decides to announce her pregnancy to the family. Herb Seelig is the one who, in a state of shock, reveals her sexual orientation: "But you're a lesbian!" The unexpected guest at the Seelig Thanksgiving is Rachael's baby whose presence convulses the diners and provokes shouting. Herb's insistent demand to know the name of the father, at first met with dismissals, eventually leads to the revelation that another guest is the sperm donor who accommodated the couple: Rachael's sister-in-law's brother, Jerry (Andrew Heckler), who is also gay. The disclosure of the father's name brings peace to the table again and acceptance is signified by Aunt Bee's (Estelle Harris) inquiry, "Is the baby Jewish?"

As in the other households, conflict emerges from a clash of progressive and conservative perspectives as realized in the generational disparities. The Seeligs, like the other families, retain a traditional cultural memory; their assimilation into mainstream American culture has retained vestiges of European Jewish traditions. Uncle David (Ralph Manza) speaks Yiddish when referring to Jerry as a feggler (a fag), and Ruth does the same when complaining of Art's (Albie Sleznick), her son's, failure to circumcise his son. Herb's insistence that the baby have a proper father manifests the conservative assumption that families can assume only one form. Clearly, the younger generation is moving away from a strict adherence to Mosaic law which forbids homosexuality and demands circumcision.

The single event in the film that has an impact on all four households is the discharging of the handgun in the Nguyen home which echoes through every dinner party, bringing the celebrations and the arguments to an abrupt halt. Chadha chooses this particular event to bring the families together and to acknowledge for the first time that they are occupying the four houses on the corners of a single intersection. The sound of the gun blast brings every family into the street, suggesting that the prospect of violence is a universal concern among the population of that battleground L.A. and of the nation. The idea that the gun was discharged by a child emphasizes the universal concern for the safety of America's youth in the face of increasing violence. The same neighbors who did not recognize or acknowledge each other at the school their children share, at the airport, or at the grocery store are, nevertheless, drawn to the site of potential violence. Perhaps the film suggests that Americans may hotly dispute culture and politics but they form a cohesive society by deploring violence, the boundary between the civilized and the savage, between society and wilderness.

The clearest manifestation in the film of Americans' desire to settle their disputes peaceably is the dousing of the governor with white paint, a metaphor for California politics and American democracy. The perpetrators choose a symbolic rather than a violent form of protest. Chadha's film may be a response to California's recent the demographic milestone: whites are no longer a majority in California. In other words, the number of whites no longer exceeds the number of all other ethnicities combined. This population shift is manifest in the fact that there is no white Anglo-Saxon household represented in the film. The only representatives of the new minority are the Moores who are merely the guests of the Williamses'. Whites are now guests at the banquet where minorities have become the majority. However, the incident with the governor reveals that whites still wield a disproportionate amount of the political power in the state, and they do so through the cooperation of the former ethic and racial minorities. The governor's humiliation at the hands of Michael Williams and other social activists suggests that his policies favoring whites are no longer tolerable, and it is clear from the dinner conversations in the Williams home that Michael also wants to throw white paint on his father whom he implies is an "oreo" (black on the outside and white on the inside) because Ronald works for the racist politician who repealed affirmative action. The narrative suggests that the governor's policy of handing out turkeys at Thanksgiving is hypocritical since the holiday traditions commemorate inclusiveness and generosity, attributes that he evidently does not advocate.

The film is not entirely progressive in the political philosophies and policies it articulates. Discussions of politics occur at most of the celebrations, and a wide variety of views are expressed. The real divide in the political debate can be observed between generations. This could manifest the demographic reality that older people tend to become more conservative and less tolerant, and younger people tend to be more open to change. However, the petty squabbles over politics do not overwhelm the conversation at the holiday table, but are symbolically parallel to the family issues that are the real source of disturbance. The relationship between the microcosm and the macrocosm, the nuclear family and the regional and national families, is perhaps the most important point of the film. Just like the families at holiday dinner, Californians and Americans as a whole are one clan who can bicker over the more subtle points of political philosophy, but are nevertheless committed to shared ideals, such as free speech, free enterprise, equality, prosperity, the welfare of children etc. Indeed, all of the holiday celebrations are vexed by similar troubles: generational conflict, political conflict, sexual conflict, and racial and ethnic conflicts. Thus the structure of the film indicates that the true unity within American culture is the universality of disagreement, our willingness to debate heatedly but to resolve problems peacefully and maintain a fundamental commitment to American ideals.

What's Cooking? can be understood as illustration of affirmative action at work even at the same time that the program is being dismantled by the governor in the film. The interaction of the L.A. urbanites reveals the difference between multiculturalism and the now obsolete melting pot metaphor for American culture. The latter was objectionable because it described a society in which people of diverse origins discarded their cultural baggage and disappeared into a white, middle class, western European identity, the same group whose repressive cultural imperialism of the past several centuries may not make them a desirable object of emulation. In contrast, multiculturalism acknowledges the diverse cultural legacies of those who settled the North American continent and reveals that difference is not a threat but a strength. America is an ongoing banquet with 275 million participants at the table, sharing its prosperity, disputing its ideals, denouncing its inequities, and exalting its variety.

6

Mostly Martha:
Appe/type and Stereo/tite

In browsing the video stores, one could be forgiven if one mistook Sandra Nettlebeck's film *Mostly Martha* (2002) for one of the many productions of *Martha Stewart Living*. After all, the cover of the video depicts two individuals cooking and the word Martha is printed boldly across the cover. Indeed, such mistakes could have been part of the marketing strategy for the film in America. The individual who picks up the display cover to read about the content of the video or rents it without further inquiry will not be disappointed in the selection. The female protagonist of the film could be based on Martha Stewart, the woman who made a fortune elaborating the rules and procedures of comfortable living, who has a reputation for being an exacting and difficult employer and personality, and whose public persona is constructed on the presumption of her cultural refinement and superiority to her audience.

Nettlebeck's *Mostly Martha* portrays a melancholy and overly rigorous German chef, Martha Klein (Martina Gedeck), whose orderly world is disturbed by the introduction of a child and an Italian lover. The narrative traces the progressive alteration of Martha's values, particularly a growing appreciation for companionship and an acceptance of disorder. She is a chef without an appetite who eventually develops a taste for life through parenting and romance. The title of the film suggests the insularity that Martha must overcome in order to develop as a person. Her life has been focused "mostly" on herself and her work, but she must permit others to interrupt her isolation and comfortable routine. The film is also an exploration of the relationship between cooking and nationalistic stereotyping.

Martha is a chef who does not seem to understand the social meanings of food. Serving is second nature to her, but she cannot share food with others. Her profession is her armor against the social. The preparation of food allows her to remain aloof from the communal rituals of consumption.

When she cooks, she is not then obliged to sit down with others and enjoy it in an environment of social equality and harmony. The narrative is punctuated by images of the restaurant staff sharing a meal before work. Martha remains unengaged because she "never eat[s] in the afternoon." While she appears to like the people with whom she works, she makes no effort to participate in the conversation at the table; instead, she sits reading the paper and then signals the staff when it is time to resume work. Martha leaves no doubt in the kitchen and at the table that she has no peer, but is an imperious chef/artist without equals. Her frequent jaunts to the cooler where she can be alone during work reinforce her avoidance behavior.

Martha has difficulty negotiating the conflict between art and commerce. Her frequent disagreements with the restaurant owner, Frida (Sibylle Canonica), revolve around Martha's inability to compromise her culinary art for the practical necessities of business. Unlike the predicament in the film *Big Night*, where a chef's uncompromising demeanor is interfering with the success of a restaurant, *Lido*, Frida's business, is very successful, and that success is directly attributable to Martha's skill as a chef. However, Martha is very weak in the area of customer service. She has high expectations regarding the sophistication of her customers; they must be worthy of her efforts. During the dinner rush, she is willing to leave the kitchen for a brief time to accept the praise of her admiring customers, the Teinbergs, but she is more drawn to the complainers against whom she can defend her labors. In the opening scene of the film, she dismisses the Teinbergs' effusive acclaim to argue with a customer who complains that his "foie gras is undercooked." Martha's indignant efforts to defend her dish with an exacting description of the process of preparation rapidly descends into insults: "Like casting pearls before swine. Where do you think you are? At a snack bar? If you want liverwurst go someplace else.... I'll never cook for you again.... He's a barbarian." Frida insists that Martha allow her to deal with the customers, offering the argument that the customer is always right and informing her that the only reason she is not fired is because she is the second best chef in the city.

Martha's combativeness does not improve immediately. She is defensive about her cooking because her self-image is constructed around her achievements as a chef, and she has not learned to cope with those who doubt her. Her truculence masks an apparent insecurity which is evident to her boss. When Frida tells Martha that she is only "the second best chef in the city," the observation provokes Martha's incredulity and leads to speculation regarding the identity of her superior, and when a new cook, Mario, is introduced into her kitchen, Martha regards the change as an insult and a not so subtle hint that she should resign her post.

Frida forces Martha to see a shrink, and the narrative is punctuated by these sessions. Indeed the voiceover for the film is Martha's self-satisfied monologues directed at her therapist, commentary that outlines her philosophy of cooking. She moves through a series of topics relevant to her profession beginning with a detailed description of her recipe for pigeon along with all of the appropriate side dishes. In her second visit, she discusses the attributes of a "good chef" which are revealed through "the quality of his simplest dishes." In the third voiceover, she addresses the necessity of effective logistics in the kitchen, explaining that it is very difficult to "coordinate 47 customers"; this latter homily is rebuttal to the psychiatrist's suggestion that she may be "compulsive," a diagnosis that seems self-evident to everyone except Martha. She explains that she is merely "precise," that "precision is the most important ingredient in a kitchen." The psychiatrist is clearly bored by Martha's self-congratulatory dissertation on her successes. Both analyst and analysand are disengaged, prompting the former to ask why Martha comes to see him every week. She reveals that Frida has threatened to fire her if she refuses but that she does not understand why her boss thinks she needs therapy.

While she may not be able to recognize her own neuroses, the audience quickly understands that Martha is trapped by the procedures and rituals of the kitchen and the dining room. Her emphasis on order and efficiency together with her innate superiority have made it difficult for her to relate to other people. While the imagery of the film repeatedly emphasizes her loneliness outside of the restaurant, she is not able to recognize this problem even as she takes steps to address it. Her day off is very revealing. She prepares her dinner in her immaculately clean and orderly kitchen and sits down to eat, but before she takes a single bite, she decides to invite her new neighbor, Sam (Ulrich Thomsen), to dine with her. However, she is not comfortable with Sam's suggestion that she is making a romantic overture, so her invitation to companionship degenerates into an offer to bring him food, a relationship with which she is more comfortable, the one act whose repetition structures her life. This abortive effort to address her loneliness is followed by another. This time she calls her sister, Christin, offering to cook for her and Lina (Maxine Foerste), Martha's niece. Also unavailable, Christin advises Martha to enjoy her time off: "It's your day off, right? Call a friend; have a nice meal; go dancing afterward." It is evident, even in the beginning of the film, that none of these suggestions are alternatives for Martha since she has no friends, and she could never overcome her pride, inhibitions, and melancholy sufficiently to dance.

The complication in Martha's life occurs when she learns of the car accident that killed her sister and orphaned her niece, Lina. Martha must take charge of the child whose father, Guiseppe, lives somewhere in Italy and cannot be readily contacted. Obviously distraught, Lina is a distraction from the central focus of Martha's life — her work — and the child is not easy to care for. She refuses to eat, quits attending school, tries to run away from home, and develops a real resentment toward her aunt. The child's lack of appetite becomes a commentary on Martha's. Both women react to loneliness and depression by refusing sustenance. Lina stopped eating when her mother was ripped out of her life, and Martha did not eat even before the accident. Both characters are emotionally and physically starved for love and companionship, and while each is what the other needs most, it takes them a while to address their mutual desolation. Interestingly, the child is more perceptive concerning relationships than is her adult aunt. Lina needs a family to care for her, and Martha needs someone on whom to focus other than herself, someone to serve out of love rather than duty and ritual.

Lina introduces disorder into a highly structured life. Martha's "rage for order" is compulsive. Her life is dictated by rituals and procedures, the camera repeatedly emphasizing the assembly line organization in the kitchen of Frida's restaurant. The cooks are shown passing plates from one work station to another, each adding a single ingredient to the dinner. Martha is creator, overseer, and participant in this process. In addition to a highly sequential process of preparation, Martha maintains an immaculately clean working environment even during the dinner rush. She is shown patiently lecturing the assistant cooks in the correct procedures for preparing the food, and from their facial expressions it is evident that they are frequently schooled thus. Martha's kitchen at home parallels the Lido environment in its orderliness. It is a space that emphasizes ease of access, efficiency, and cleanliness.

The controlling metaphor in the film is the recipe. When she coaches the customers or the staff on the appropriate procedures for preparing a dish, she is also revealing her philosophy of life and labor. She reminds her psychiatrist that a "good chef" is revealed through the quality of his or her simplest dishes:

> One knows a good chef by the quality of his simplest dishes. Take for instance salmon in a light basil sauce. Most people think it is no big deal and put it on the menu. But frying or steaming the salmon just right and putting the right amount of salt and spices in the sauce is very difficult. In this recipe, there is nothing to distract you. No design. No exotic ingredient. There is only the fish and the sauce.

The above description emphasizes Martha's attention to detail and her appreciation for the uncomplicated. She dismisses the exotic and the elaborate as a distraction from the fundamentals of cooking. She also reveals a faith in the reliability of systematic behavior. If one follows a recipe exactly, then the results will be gratifying. When she defends the quality of her foie gras, she articulates the process of preparation in exacting detail with the assumption that the revelation will bring satisfaction. There is no place for diverse appetites in Martha's philosophy; the recipe is the final word on taste and propriety. Most importantly the above recipe reveals Martha's appreciation for the routine; she desires no distractions in her simple existence.

The monologues that Martha delivers in her analyst's office reveal cooking as a metaphor for the development of her character through the various stages of contentment, grief, and resolution. Her first voiceover, articulating the appropriate side foods for her signature dish, pigeon with truffles, is also an allegorical commentary on her need to be selective in her choice of companions. The second monologue, which addresses the quality of simple dishes, is an elaboration on the first, revealing her need to keep her life simple and unencumbered. In her third session with the psychiatrist, she discusses the logistics of the kitchen and the importance of timing. These comments coincide with the progressive disintegration of order that occurs when her sister dies and her niece comes to live with her. Martha, who had previously been very punctual, becomes less reliable, missing work and forgetting to retrieve Lina from school. The fourth monologue is an allegory of grief, addressing the selection and preparation of lobsters, which she maintains eat themselves internally while sitting in the tank. The chef needs to check the lobster's weight before purchasing it to make sure it has not "been in the tank too long." This commentary reveals the beginning of Martha's insight. Like the lobsters, she and Lina, both refusing to eat, are consuming themselves from the inside; they are wasting physically and emotionally. In Martha's case, the insight can be related to her sense of entrapment in her new child-rearing obligations, her need for love and romance in her life, and her sense of loss over her sister's death. The final voiceover in the film reveals Martha's newfound wisdom regarding the necessity of companionship. She reveals that she can recognize the ingredients missing from a dish that would make it more enjoyable.

Lina's intrusion into Martha's life is troublesome, not because Martha is unwilling to make the effort to help a newly orphaned child, but because her life has left her unprepared for complicated emotional entanglements. On the occasion of her sister's death, Martha has no comfort to offer the child except a promise to cook for her. Martha naively assumes that the provision of shelter and nourishment is the only requisite for child-rearing. Following a particularly unpleasant confrontation when the child tried to run away, Martha complains, "I wish I had a recipe for you that I could follow. I know I can't replace your mother. I am just trying to be there for you the best I can. I know I am not doing a very good job, but I am trying very hard."

Martha's longing for a "recipe" for childcare reveals the extent of her reliance upon simple and methodical solutions to complex problems and interpersonal relations. However, in this case, she has to improvise, and Martha is not spontaneous enough to be comfortable with extemporization. She has a protocol for her behavior in most social situations, but intense emotional and familial entanglements are alien to her. Interestingly, when she confesses that she does not know what she is doing but, nevertheless, demonstrates a real motherly concern for her niece by scolding her for running away, the relations between the two of them begin to improve. Lina has felt unwanted and unloved.

Despite the ostensible differences, the two women share many character traits. Neither became hysterical upon the death of Christin. They both turned inward and stoically negotiated their loss. There is no evidence that either cried or attempted to discuss the tragic incident, but they both refuse to eat in silent protest of their misfortune. The two are unhappy because they have no love in their lives, and it is only when they feel needed again that they start to recover. Of course, the solution to their isolation has been at hand the entire time, but it takes them a while to recognize that they need each other. Martha needs to serve and care for someone she loves, and Lina longs for maternal loyalty and affection. Martha's life improves when she finds something to live for besides food and work, and Lina's predicament is redeemed by Martha's commitment to her.

The film emphasizes the parallels between Martha and Lina, but highlights the incongruity between the former and her rival chef Mario. While Martha attends her sister's funeral, Frida hires a chef to fill in for her, an Italian whose philosophy of cooking is radically opposed to Martha's, and the return of Martha to the kitchen, following her family business, creates tension that ensures disruption in both her domestic and her professional life. Her first confrontation with Mario occurs when she unwittingly returns to the restaurant to find him in her kitchen. The usually sober and tidy environment has been introduced to levity. Martha overhears Mario coaching her assistant, Lea, in a cooking philosophy that is retrograde to her own: "Only a well fed cook is a good cook. First you must saturate your taste buds and only then season to taste. If you're satisfied on a full stomach, then you're really a good cook."

Mario's theory of taste and satiation flies in the face of Martha's refusal to eat in the afternoon before work. It also offers a counterpoint to Martha's allegory of the lobsters in a tank. She is not a "well fed cook," and she is not "satisfied." At the same time that Mario offers his insights, he offers Lea a taste of the dish he is preparing, a breach of kitchen decorum that would not be countenanced under Martha's administration. At the same time, Italian music blares from the stereo, and Mario and Lea dance, an activity that Martha cannot endure even on her day off. Perhaps the most distinguishing contrast is Mario's habit of showing up late for work. Martha is repeatedly late for her domestic obligations to Lina, but she is not late for work. Martha upbraids Frida for introducing a madman into her orderly kitchen and reminds her that she had been guaranteed the right to choose her own staff. Frida, clearly delighted by the more uplifting environment created by Mario's antics, defends him: "...he isn't mad. He's eccentric."

Mario is not threatened by Martha's return, nor is he disrespectful. He addresses her with effusive praise for her pigeon and truffle dish, a gesture that is antithetical to Martha's own defensiveness about her work. Despite their differences Mario quickly conforms to Martha's more sober government of the kitchen, and he makes a dramatic gesture of capitulation to her will by refusing to remain in the job unless she states specifically that she wants him to stay.

The peace that ensues is negotiated by the presence of Lina in the restaurant. It is through her that Mario and Martha begin to develop a working relationship and even a rapport. Mario is successful inducing Lina to begin eating again, and Martha enlists his help in tracking down Lina's father, Guiseppe. The most significant breakthrough occurs when Lina requests that Mario cook dinner for them at home, stating that she prefers Italian to Martha's cooking. The event challenges many of Martha's patterns. When Mario arrives, he and Lina push Martha out of the kitchen, refusing to allow her to help, and later serve dinner on the floor, "family style," without plates or utensils. Martha protests, requesting that they at least eat at the table, but the most troublesome feature of the evening for Martha is shocking mess in her usually clean kitchen. She has a panic attack when she sees the disarray and begins to hyperventilate until Mario shuttles her out of the room, insisting that he and Lina clean it up. The three end the evening playing games, a telling alteration in the home environment since earlier in the film Martha confessed to a potential babysitter that there were no games in the apartment.

Martha clearly enjoys the evening despite having been forced to relinquish control and suspend order. In the middle of the night, she eats the leftovers of Mario's food — the first time that the audience has seen her eat with any enthusiasm. Her appetite and taste have altered, becoming more akin to lust and pleasure, a breakthrough which ought to lead to an alteration in her philosophy of cooking. What Martha did not understand in the beginning of the film was that taste is not a rule governed activity. She had discounted or perhaps only de-emphasized the importance of pleasure in the consumption of food. She assumed that her customers' appetites would be ruled by reason and culinary tradition, rather than the vicissitudes of the personal palate. She seems to understand that food preparation is an aesthetic activity, but does not recognize that food consumption is as well, and where there is aestheticism, there is disagreement; a flawlessly executed painting is not necessarily more pleasurable than one with a multiplicity of mistakes. These assumptions explain her overreaction to the customer's complaint about the undercooked liver. Martha assumes that her having followed the exacting dictates of a recipe should produce satisfaction in her customers, and thus she is incredulous when Frida reminds her that the customer's taste is the final word on the success of cooking; if the customer says his liver is undercooked, then it is undercooked.

The real threat to Martha's safe and tidy existence is the nuclear family. Lina's efforts to introduce Mario into their home environment is a paradoxical scheme to [re]create her own parents. Lina is the progeny of a German mother and an Italian father. Her intrigue works—Martha and Mario become romantically involved and the three of them begin to spend more time together. The film suggests that Lina understands the nature of loss and loneliness more profoundly than does Martha and that she also understands the recipe for happiness—family and companionship—a concoction that her aunt cannot create in her kitchen. Martha's life changes with the inclusion of Mario and Lina; she is clearly happy at home for the first time in the film, and despite her absenteeism at work, she becomes a better employee and perhaps even a better cook.

When the biological father, Guiseppe, arrives to claim Lina and take her to his home in Italy, Martha is faced with a life altering decision. The film offers her the option to return to her former orderly and solitary existence, and at first that is the decision that she makes, allowing Lina to leave with her father and ejecting Mario from her apartment shortly thereafter. The film does not offer any simplistic solutions for Martha. Guiseppe is not a "deadbeat dad" whose devotion to the child can be questioned; Christin never told him of the child's existence, and he did not know that Christin had been killed. He indicates that he would have come for the child sooner had he known. In addition, Guiseppe is a devoted father and husband to his family in Italy, and all indications are that the child will have a very happy, peaceful, and normal life. All of these factors require Martha to make a decision that is at least partly derived from self-interest. She is forced to acknowledge that Lina and Mario improved her life and, by extension, that her recipe for orderly living is flawed, and she must take decisive steps to alter her patterns, to include new ingredients in her recipes.

In a brief interval, she allows herself to return to her former patterns, becoming compulsive about work and melancholy at home. She, however, is able to recognize her unhappiness and take appropriate steps to address it. In an incident that reveals her regression, she argues with a customer over his undercooked meat and concludes the conflict by slamming a raw steak on the table and shouting, "Is this rare enough for you?" As she walks out, Frida warns her that she will be fired if she leaves, but the chef explains, "I know, but I have to go." The steps that she takes are for her own happiness. She enlists Mario without a word, and they travel to Italy to retrieve Lina.

The brief medley of images that conclude the film reveals the positive transformations in Martha's life. The cold, grey, urban environment of Germany is replaced by images of the sunny, verdant Italian countryside. Martha and Mario pick up Lina at her father's home where she is playing on the lawn with her half siblings, an image antithetical to the loneliness and enclosure she experienced in Martha's apartment. Martha's hunger, rigidity, and solitude are supplanted by images of her impending nuptials— dressing for the ceremony, dancing on the lawn, and feasting at her wedding banquet, a celebration set on a sunny hillside where children frolic and the guests share Italian food—family style. The new couple and their adoptive child are also shown touring and renovating an abandoned building for their new restaurant. The final voice over of the film captures the essence of Martha's new wisdom. When she allows her psychiatrist to cook for her, she is critical of the sugar that he uses. He responds with incredulity, "Are you telling me that you can taste what kind of sugar I used?" to which she responds, "Of course not, but I can taste which kind you didn't use!" She has become sensitive to absences, accepting the necessity of companionship and love, both maternal and romantic. The concoction that is her life requires a sweetening with new ingredients to suit her palate.

The development of Martha and Mario within the film is based on stereotypes of national temperaments, and while broad generalizations about ethnicity may be offensive, the film reveals that the dispositions are not represented universally within the populace and are not comprehensively negative. Indeed, the ethnic stereotyping is mitigated by compromise since *Mostly Martha* is a German language film and the nationalistic stereotyping is harshest toward the German temperament. Thus the film could be suggesting the Germans could use a little more levity, leniency, and recklessness. Moreover, the characters are capable of positive change, an alteration that does not erase their national heritage, but simply modifies it.

Martha's rage for order, her hyper-rationality, efficiency, compulsiveness, and industriousness are qualities that — right or wrong — are part of the mythology of the traditional German or northern European temperament. In addition, she can be dour, quiet, angry, unyielding, and humorless. Mario, on the other hand, embodies stereotypes of the Italian or Mediterranean humor: informal, carefree, comical, aesthetic, effusively courteous, unreliable, and messy. Each character can be both endearing and infuriating. While Mario's disposition is the more pleasant, his zaniness and unreliability could be aggravating, and Martha's pride, rigidity, and severity would be equally difficult to endure. Even her psychiatrist seems frustrated, irritated, and bored with her. Lina is the ingredient that brings these two antithetical dispositions together, and with a German mother and an Italian father she appropriately embodies both nationalities. Thus the wedding at the conclusion of the film unifies the two complexions.

Of course, the conflict of national stereotypes is revealed in the respective foods that the characters prepare as well. They constitute a clash between commercial food preparation and household cooking. Martha specializes in individual dishes prepared with exacting standards and served with the ritual of a formal dining room. Even at home, her meals remain formal, her dining orderly and ceremonial and her kitchen tidy. The dishes that she prepares are those more typical of restaurant than home dining — pigeon, lobster, salmon etc. Mario's food, on the other hand, is produced in quantity for informal consumption. The preparation is not for individual dining, but for groups — bowls full of pasta and vegetables from which each person serves him/herself. The Italian food is messy and filling. One does not glut oneself on Martha's dishes as one might with Mario's; her servings are adequate, intended to emphasize the refinement of taste and the appreciation of the aesthetics and precision of the culinary arts.

The two styles of cuisine are easily associated with the domestic and the social, and in this, the narrative reverses gender stereotypes about separate spheres for men and women. Traditionally, women were associated with the home environment and domestic cooking responsibilities, while men were consigned to public and commercial food preparation. In *Mostly Martha*, the female protagonist does not remain dedicated to the comfort and satisfaction of her spouse and children. She has little time for and even less interest in domestic responsibilities. In contrast, the male facilitates enjoyable domestic consumption and interaction. There is even reason to believe that the new matrimonial arrangements will allow Martha to focus on her restaurant while Mario continues to discharge domestic obligations. After all, Lina prefers Italian food. However, it is more probable that they will divide their duties since to do otherwise might negate Martha's personal growth.

On the issue of Martha's progress, there is some cause for concern regarding the sexual politics of the film. The plot development resembles a "taming of the shrew" narrative in which a woman is shown that her true happiness lies in her devotion to family and subjugation to male rule. However, the fact that she is not forced to give up her career or to capitulate completely to domestic responsibilities leaves room for both personal progress and political progressiveness. While there is no indication that Mario will dominate her, she does make a significant capitulation to his world view and lifestyle, an act which suggests that he is more knowledgeable or emotionally mature than she is. Moreover, Martha's odyssey resembles the questionable conclusions of studies from the 1980's and '90's in which many professional women presumably expressed disappointment in the unfulfilling corporate life and a desire to return to domestic living.

Any contextual association with Martha Stewart that the film and/or marketing campaign may nurture creates a more subtle level of misogyny. While Martha Stewart is a wildly successful business woman, she is evidently a less successful person. Her recent stock trading scandal has provoked her critics and her defenders. She has become an argument for right-wing demagogues who cite her as an example of women's emotional unsuitability for leadership, and she has been shielded by those who see her indictment as a persecution of strong women by a misogynistic culture. If the made for television movie *Martha Inc.* (2003) is accurate, one could conclude the Martha Stewart has a personality disorder not unlike Martha Klein's. Both women are perfectionists with very rigid notions of propriety; both demand sophistication and compliance from others, customers and subordinates alike; both can be unpleasant when others do not live up to their expectations; both have placed their professional success before personal fulfillment; and both need to lighten up and accept some disorder in their lives. The most important difference between the real and the reel Martha is that the latter is capable of change. Whether the same is true of the real Martha remains to be seen.

7

"Culinizing" the Female Form:
Felicia's Journey, Predation,
and Cultural Imperialism

Atom Egoyan's thriller *Felicia's Journey* (1999), based upon William Trevor's bestselling novel of the same name, may seem an unlikely choice for study as a food film, yet central to both book and film are the culinary passions of Joseph Hilditch (Bob Hoskins), a lonely, seemingly gracious catering manager who assists itinerant women and then kills them when they decide to leave. His final attempted victim is a pregnant Irish woman, Felicia (Elaine Cassidy), who has come to England to track down the father of her baby. The encounter between the homeless young woman and the wealthy middle-aged man allegorizes the nationalistic struggles between Ireland and Great Britain and comments on the parallel between imperialism and sexism. Mr. Hilditch's careful preparation of elaborate meals on which he dines alone becomes the key to Egoyan's exploration of the serial killer's interior life.

While Trevor's novel develops in detail Hilditch's professional and domestic interests in the culinary arts, Egoyan's screenplay clarifies the motivation behind the character's appetite, creating the link between food and sensual desire. In Trevor's novel, Hilditch's mother is a promiscuous women who does not try to hide her activities from her child. Although it is not clear whether she is a prostitute, it is evident that she is at least emotionally dependent upon her gentleman callers, so much so that when they stop visiting, she turns to her own child for sexual gratification. The emotional scars that incest and molestation left on Hilditch compel him to reenact the drama of his mother's life within his nefarious sexual hijinks. There is no direct evidence that Hilditch sleeps with any of the women whom he befriends and later kills although all are prostitutes desperate for cash or itinerant women in need of assistance. The reader is left with the impression that Hilditch's compulsive behavior may constitute an effort to reform his mother vicariously. He recalls picking up a prostitute and paying her only to share tea with him at a roadside restaurant where she was swiftly solicited and swept away by a lusty trucker when Hilditch excused himself to use the toilet. Hilditch's relationship with the desperate women is more paternal than amorous although he does seem to enjoy imagining that others think him sexually involved with them. It is clear that he murders his companions when they indicate that they are going to continue their peregrinations. The murders may thus be a desperate effort to keep the women near him. When he discovers that he cannot reform them (or symbolically his mother through them), he punishes them. Or perhaps his filial affection for them constitutes an effort to fill the paternal void in his own childhood, his fatherly concerns a rehabilitation of his own emptiness, and when they reject him, his violence becomes a form of vicarious self-annihilation. In his effort to kill Felicia, he explains that he is releasing her from her burdens, explaining that he understands her suffering and that her imminent murder is an act of mercy. In Trevor's narrative, Hilditch repeatedly indicates that he killed the women when he perceived a particular look in their eyes. That look may be the distant stare of those who long to continue their wanderings; however, he indicates that the glance is directed toward him. Thus it may be the eye of recognition and reproach that exposes his lies, the look of pity that fills him with self-loathing, or the eye of desire that threatens to pollute their filial bond.

Egoyan's script alters the relationship between Hilditch and his mother and creates an original impetus for childhood flashbacks of the narrative. Joseph's mother was a chef with her own television show and a line of culinary appliances and products in her name. As he prepares his dinners in his cavernous kitchen, Hilditch watches his mother's cooking show on video and recalls his childhood taking place on the periphery of the camera and the studio set. He was merely a hindrance to his mother's professional and romantic ambitions as she flirted with the camera crew. Like the mother of Trevor's novel, Egoyan's is voluptuous and potentially promiscuous, but the inclusion of the culinary dimension to her character creates an impetus for Hilditch's own fascination with food and creates an analogue for his equation of food and sex. While the film includes no clear references to the incestuous molestation of Trevor's novel, it is clear that the pubescent Hilditch desires his mother from afar. As Laura Mulvey has taught us, the eye of the camera is the eye of the objectifying amorous male that directs the audience to scrutinize, eroticize, and fetishize the female form (11–17). In those scenes that include videos of the mother's cooking show, the eye of the camera becomes Hilditch's roving gaze, and it concentrates on his mother's sensuality and voluptuousness. Carrie Zlotnick-Woldenberg has argued that the "antecedent" for Hilditch's "pathological behavior [is] rooted in his early maternal relationship" (40). The flashbacks to his childhood suggest that he was forced to "swallow" his desires for his mother, a process that is literalized in the repetition compulsions of his adult life in which the preparation and consumption of food becomes a ritualistic effort to fill the emptiness left by the absent father and the distant mother.

The process of viewing the cooking show (re)produces the experience of his childhood without bringing resolution to any of the issues that constituted his character. As a television star, she was the focus of attention and desire, both Joseph's and that of her audience and crew; thus Hilditch was relegated to the margin of his mother's life, an admirer rather than an object of admiration, an audience rather than an actor. While he watches his mother's cooking show, he is once again placed on the fringes of her actions, doomed to view, not interact. In cooking as an adult, he literally emulates her every move, preparing the same dishes about which she offers instruction. In this repetitive act, he equates food with desire. He is frequently distracted from his cooking by televisual imagery that provokes sensual reverie. Subsequently, his interaction with women (particularly his victims) constitutes the habitual resumption of the role of voyeur watching and assisting from the periphery, only attempting to become a part of the real lives through philanthropic acts. As with Eliot's Prufrock, he is not the central figure in his own life, but only "an attendant lord," his role to assist women in distress.

Because Hilditch had no paternal influence as a child, he did not experience the castration complex that redirects the child's longing for the mother toward mother replacements, but was compelled to retain, yet sublimate his desires. Now that the mother is dead, his only contact with her is through her videos, a medium that reinforces the equation between mother love, sexuality, and food. He can symbolically consume the mother's body through the emulation and consumption of her recipes. The conclusion of the film's opening credits finds the camera in the kitchen observing Hilditch as he copies his mother's cooking show. As she tastes the broth that she has prepared, Hilditch does the same, pausing for the ecstatic appreciation of his labors. The narrative suggests that Hilditch developed his refined palate through the emulation of his mother, and this is the same culinary skill that drives his professional and domestic lives. At work, his opinion regarding the quality of the factory kitchen's output is awaited with great anticipation by his subordinates who are either encouraged or crestfallen in the aftermath of his evaluation. Once the kitchen has prepared the dishes to his satisfaction, he takes samples around the installation allowing the various foremen in the shop to taste the most recent batch.

The equation between food and love (both sensual and filial) is reinforced by the imagery of mother's cooking show to which the sensuality of Hilditch's French mother is integral. She wears low cut dresses that accentuate her cleavage, and in her instruction, she teases and cajoles the audience with pouting and playful scoldings, the stereotype of a sexy French temptress. Hilditch's memory of the show's filming focuses on his mother's constant flirtation with her camera crew as well as his own activities as nuisance and voyeur. The mother embraces her child on camera, but just as frequently scolds and humiliates him for his failures and interferences. The maternal bond that remained untroubled by a father figure continues into his adult life. Hilditch's home is a living memorial to his mother. Her image presides over the diningroom, and his pantry is filled with the line of kitchen appliances marketed in her name and image. Moreover, when Felicia stays with Hilditch, he suggests that the image of his mother is actually his deceased wife, Ada, a lie that reinforces the subconscious erotic bond that he shared with his mother. The pantry that is filled with his mother's products, videos, and memorabilia also contains the secret tapes of his victims and is carefully padlocked before he allows Felicia into his house.

The proximity of the pantry (containing the mother's cooking relics as well as the serial killer's trophies) to the kitchen spatializes and literalizes Hilditch's cognitive association between food, love, and murder and draws an even more credible link between his mother's memory and his compulsion to kill. The same room that contains the videos of his mother also conceals the carefully labeled tapes of his victims as they converse with, reject, and struggle to escape their captor. The combination of these seemingly incongruous items in a single secured closet generates a clever metaphor for the mind of the serial killer. He has catalogued and stored the motivations for and the culminations of his murderous obsession, and he can retrieve and prepare them for (re)consumption whenever he chooses. The memory of his mother is embodied in the boxes filled with her cooking aids, a fact that literalizes her role as the unwitting instigator of his predatory instinct.

Mother's professional output literally taught him how to prepare and cook a "bird" (a British slang term that signifies both a woman and the victim of a con). While Trevor's novel repeatedly equates Felicia to fowl caught in a trap, Egoyan's screenplay renders that metaphor substantive by filming the preparation of a turkey, a process that parallels Hilditch's initial interaction with Felicia. His mother's instruction urges him to pinch the turkey, moving his hand under the skin to massage, soften, and season the flesh. These directions coincide with his subtle efforts to manipulate Felicia by gaining her trust through feigned philanthropic gestures. He does not abduct and murder her (or any of his victims) in a single ferocious struggle, but instead, "pinches and massages" her until he gains her trust and brings her under his power. He repeatedly meets her on the street under what appears to her to be coincidental circumstances, first while leaving his job as catering manager and later while returning home from grocery shopping, each of these incidents reinforcing the association between Felicia and that which will feed him. He "pinches" her and gets under her skin by feigning an interest in her futile search for Johnny Lysaght, the father of her baby. He takes care not to frighten her away by being overly aggressive, but lets her make her own decisions, offering only his quiet and thoughtful advice. Nevertheless, he is taking steps to ensure her dependence upon him, such as when he steals her money so that she will become desperate for his support.

From this perspective, the narrative of *Felicia's Journey* becomes a prolonged and detailed examination of his preparation for dinner, dramatizing the identification and capture of his main dish as well as the culinary processes that render it fit to eat. The landscape within which these activities takes place bespeaks his intentions. The urbanized and industrialized environment of the unnamed town just north of Birmingham where Hilditch resides offers a symbolic backdrop for the pursuit of his prey. Several of Hilditch's initial encounters with Felicia are framed by the imagery of gigantic steel structures that resemble cages, but may be the partially completed oil tanks or the unfinished shells of nuclear cooling towers. These images predictably coincide with Hilditch's efforts to win Felicia's trust, to, in a manner of speaking, capture her in a cage, one partially of her own making. As the relationship between the two principal characters becomes more intimate and the dramatic tension increases, the steel cages are replaced by actual nuclear cooling towers smoking in the distance; they appear to be huge cooking pots, suggesting not only Hilditch's simmering hostility, but also the progressive roasting of his dinner — Felicia. This particular implication is strongest when he passes the towers returning from the abortion clinic with Felicia. At that moment, she is fully prepared for his consumption, and Hilditch moves forward with his murderous designs as soon as he arrives home.

The narrative of the film is punctuated by images of Hilditch preparing dinners large enough for an extended family's holiday feast and then eating alone in his formal dining room while, through opera glasses, he watches his mother's cooking show still playing on the small television in the kitchen. In a particularly revealing dining scene, he watches the video that he secretly made of Felicia, once again drawing a parallel between his mother, his sensual desires, and his gourmandizing. The video camera that captured Felicia on the street seems to be mounted surreptitiously in the passenger side visor of Hilditch's vehicle or perhaps on the rearview mirror. The video imagery of Hilditch's multiple victims is shot from this particular angle. In the recording of Felicia, the camera is only able to capture her legs since he speaks to her while she stands on an elevated sidewalk. The effect is to accentuate and fetishize Felicia's legs, a process that has been underway since the beginning of the film. Felicia wears a particularly short skirt for a character who retains a childlike naivete, her muscular legs, her most prominent feature, a sharp contrast to the innocence of her face and the bashful simplicity of her personality. Her legs are a visual analogue to the turkey legs that Hilditch first massages, then cooks, and later consumes. Moreover, the opera glasses that Hilditch uses to view the recordings reveal an additional source for his aberrant behavior. He recalls sharing the glasses with his mother as they viewed a theatrical presentation of the execution of John the Baptist. The horrifying image of the head on a platter may be a harbinger of Hilditch's cognitive equation between murder and food and the portrait of the callous and selfish Salome alludes to Hilditch's degenerate mother and, by extension, to the wayward women whom he befriends and destroys.

The imagery of the empty chairs around the elaborately set dining table creates a fertile metaphor for Hilditch's life and obsession. In Trevor's novel, the walls of the dining room are covered with pictures of other people's relatives whom he pretends are his own, thus creating the illusion that he has a rich familial heritage. In Egoyan's movie set, the room has only one portrait — that of his dead mother — but the effect is the same. In both cases, the images emphasize Hilditch's need to amend his solitude; he desires company at the table, someone to share the elaborate meals that he prepares — a crown roast and a full turkey dinner with all of trimmings, culinary symbols of the holiday communion of family. Despite his persistent solitude, Hilditch regards food preparation and consumption as a social act. When a salesman tries to convince him to replace his factory kitchen with a line of high tech vending machines, he balks, citing the necessity that food be "served by caring hands." He adds that it "makes us feel loved." This wistful recitation of his culinary philosophy exposes Hilditch's psychic wound, the sense of emptiness, loneliness, and betrayal that he tries to fill through his gluttony. His reverie also illuminates the repetition compulsion of his murderous activities. Hilditch's approach to each of the women he kills is that of a caring father who assists them in their time of need. His violence is provoked only when they attempt to leave him. Thus the murders may be a delusional effort to compel the women to remain, to keep him company. Perhaps the table at which Hilditch dines is not empty after all, but full of ghosts. He keeps his company stored in the pantry on the ghoulish tapes that he views as he dines. A serial killer's trophies are stolen objects belonging to the victim that allow the murderer to relive the violent passion of their immolation. The objects that Hilditch steals are the stories of hardship that each of the women recounts while riding in his car and from which he derives personal gratification, not sexual, but sensual. He eats while the video in the kitchen replays the tragic stories of those women whom he perversely believes he has saved.

The juxtaposition of Hilditch's food preparation and consumption with images of his predatory erotic life serves to emphasize the similarity of the respective appetites that motivate his behavior. Indeed the repetition compulsion of the serial killer is subtly equated to a recipe much like those he prepares from his mother's cooking show. Hilditch is a middle-aged catering manager who has been familiar with his mother's cooking techniques since boyhood. In all probability, he no longer requires his mother's televised instructions to produce her well crafted dishes. However, he views the tapes because they allow him to spend time once again with the dearly departed and to reenact the circumstances that concocted his obsessional appetite. Just as the successful chef methodically follows familiar steps in the preparation of a standard recipe, making only occasional modifications for the pragmatic purposes of perfecting a pattern or altering ingredients to accommodate the vicissitudes of availability or the individual palate, the serial killer executes his crime by following methodical stipulations that he has progressively refined in a compulsive, pragmatic, and gratifying effort to render the act safer and more efficient, altering his behavior to accommodate the particular personality and circumstance of the selected victim. Thus Hilditch reviews both the tapes of his mother and those of his victims in order to indulge his rage for order, to relive the self-satisfying procedure that defines him.

Hilditch's predatory behavior is motivated by a perverse ideology, and one that once again connects the mother with his victims. As alluded to previously, Hilditch appears to be subconsciously punishing and correcting the mother through his murderous imperative. He confesses that his need to kill derives at least partially from an abandonment complex. He was unable to keep his mother all to himself, sharing her with her production staff, her audience, and others, yet he had no male role model to initiate the process of mother/child severance, no impetus for the castration complex that should have redirected his erotic appetite toward mother replacements. Thus he retained a tyrannical claim over maternal affection, one that would later legitimize a violent domination when the mother replacements begin to stray. While the emotional power differential between mother and child did not allow him to assert the kind of control over the real mother that he might have liked to exercise, her death gave him complete power to control when and where her videos tease, cajole, and instruct. Egoyan has related the killer's obsessional retention of the video evidence as an objective manifestation of his need to "control ... intimacy" (qtd. in Porton 40). Like Robert Browning's Duke of Ferrara, Hilditch can only attain the control over his women through their deaths.

Since Hilditch's victims are killed after they express a desire to discontinue their acquaintance with him, the murders reveal a pathological urge to keep their company, to fill his table with the ghosts of troubled women, the same women he fed and cared for. Even as he kills them, he does not drop the philanthropic façade that he adopted in order to win their trust, believing that his violence rescues them from painful lives: "They were always asleep when I laid them to rest." This aspect of Hilditch's psychology is easier to understand in Trevor's novel than in Egoyan's screenplay. Trevor presents the reader with a mother who has grown progressively more wretched and desperate through aging because her lovers eventually stopped visiting her, making her lonely enough to seek consolation in the arms of her own child. The image of the despondent mother is not included in the film version of Felicia's Journey, except perhaps in the portrait of Johnny Lysaght's angry, lonely, and defensive mother (but this is an individual of whom Hilditch has no knowledge and who can serve only as an exemplum of mothers who suffer when their children depart) or perhaps implicitly in the portrait of the single mother who has her own cooking show. The videos and flashbacks of Joseph's mother portray her only in her most public moments when she is in complete control of her own life and of those around her.

In the film, how can the audience read Hilditch's philanthropy as sincere at least for him? One must read between the lines in order to understand Hilditch's violent altruism in a way that is not completely cynical, assuming that because Joseph's mother regarded him as nuisance or an interference when he accidentally wandered into the shot or bungled his role on camera, she was not happy to be a single unwed mother, that she would have preferred to remain unfettered by maternal obligations. Thus in the serial killer's repetition, he seeks to save the women from the same mistake that his mother made. This is most evident in his interaction with Felicia to whom he expresses the conservative view that a child needs both a mother and a father, a statement that alludes to his own truncated social development. Ironically, his argument in favor of traditional families is one phase of his effort to convince Felicia that she should abort her pregnancy, a procedure that he helps to facilitate. When she is free of her burden, he equivocates, saying that "Ada [the fictitious wife whom he associates with the picture of his mother in his dining room] would have approved of today." The statement becomes a self-pitying indictment of his mother, who he believes would have preferred to remain childless. From this vantage point, the murders may be simultaneously understood as an effort to avert the conception of any more fatherless children as lonely and potentially dangerous as himself. Thus he creates a variation on the cliché profile of the serial killer who actually wants to be caught in order to end his career of violence.

The metaphor of predation so frequently associated with the serial killer and the sex criminal becomes particularly appropriate in the film version of *Felicia's Journey* with its ubiquitous food imagery. The voracious appetite that Hilditch reveals in his solitary feasts becomes the objective manifestation of his libidinal desires. He eats the expansive feasts because he cannot consume his victims. The subconscious association between the consumption of food and sexual desire is a common place within Western culture. Women, as objects of salacious longings, are so frequently associated with comestibles that the symbolic connection goes unacknowledged, much like the virtually invisible parallel between the language of religion and that of romance. Consider, for example, the frequently used expressions "dish" or "treat" as signifiers for a desirable woman or the expressions of a "sexual predator," who acknowledges the connection between the hunt and seduction, between coercion and consumption. The fetishizing or "culinizing" (if I may be allowed to create a cheap pun) of the female form constitutes a symbolic practice of domination, the staking of a territorial claim over the corporeal and sensual body.

Preparing, cooking, and consuming the female form constitutes a rich metaphor of patriarchal and or masculinist control. Felicia, the designated "dish," is manipulated or prepared by each of the men in her life, all of whom have a particular notion of the circumstances under which she should be consumed. Her father wanted her to save herself for a nice Irish boy who would devour her virginity within the lawful context of a matrimonial bed. However, Johnny Lysaght has a more cavalier attitude toward Felicia; she is a "treat" to be casually eaten and discarded. He woos, screws, and impregnates her; then departs to join the British army, leaving no forwarding address. Hilditch unifies both Johnny's predatory sexuality and the father's concerns and solicitations. Perhaps this is the reason he is so devastatingly successful in his manipulation of Felicia. He has concealed his rapacious intentions behind the veneer of a benevolent father, thus compensating for the inadequacies of both father and lover. While the father's moralizing drove Felicia away from home, Johnny's indifference left her "knocked up" with nowhere to go. Consequently, she is driven into the poisonous embrace of Hilditch who, from his own psychotic perspective, will both consume and preserve her or more accurately, preserve her through consumption. For Felicia, men's benevolence and malevolence prove equally destructive.

The two father figures in Felicia's life (her biological father and Hilditch) destroy even as they profess to save. The biological father claims to have Felicia's best interests at heart, yet his refusal to deal compassionately with her pregnancy leaves her no choice but to go in search of her lover. His denunciation of her as "whore" masquerades as a concern for her spiritual health, but the effect of his abandonment is a guarantee of her physical and moral destruction, since she is left with few options but those of the disenfranchised and desperate women that populate Hilditch's pantheon of victims. Hilditch, in this context, becomes a representation of the ill-effects that the father's overly moral and dismissive treatment has upon his daughter's future. Hilditch may even be viewed as the object manifestation of the father's blind annihilation of his daughter. While the biological father labels Felicia a "whore," Hilditch, the surrogate father, considers her his "special angel." Both men maintain a hyperbolic (mis)understanding of the troubled woman. She is in effect invisible to them, replaced by overly simplistic social constructs that seek to control women by forcing them into inadequate categories, and it is this process that proves so dangerous to Felicia. She is no angel but a sensual, romantic, and naive woman. Neither is she a whore, but a victim of the seductions of a cad who exploits her innocence and credulity. Yet the father's callous repudiation of Felicia leaves her with few choices but to pursue Johnny in an unfamiliar land where her desperation will contribute to the progressive degeneration of her moral character; she will become that which her father already dubbed her. On the other hand, Hilditch's idealization of her innocence creates the lunatic pretext for her murder; if she is an "angel," she is too good for a turbulent world, and, in death, her suffering will cease; her innocence will be preserved.

Visually, Felicia's appearance reinforces the virgin/whore dialectic embodied in the respective judgments of Joseph Hilditch and her father. The casting of Elaine Cassidy effectively enhanced the duality represented by this titular character. Cassidy has a voluptuous physical form but the face of a child. The camera and the costuming emphasize Felicia's sensuality. She wears a very short skirt along with platform shoes. The camera frequently captures her in long shot as she walks along the heavily industrialized streets of northern England, her muscular legs standing out as a prominent feature. Moreover, the skimpiness and gaudiness of her attire would initially reinforce the assumption that she is a prostitute. However, in closeup, Felicia is immediately recognizable as a naive and guileless young woman, very soft spoken, often looking shamefully at her feet as she is addressed by others, a sharp contrast to the confident, combative, and gregarious women of Hilditch's video collection. In addition, the filmic imagery equates Felicia with the Madonna. While searching for shelter, having been ejected from the "Gathering House," she is captured in closeup by the camera. She wears a cloak and hood, her form outlined by the soft lights of the urban night sky. Her image is immediately recognizable as tableau of the Virgin Mary; she is a pregnant woman in search of shelter in less than hospitable places, and she is eventually taken in by a man named Joseph (Hilditch) who shows her kindness regardless of her condition, only a portion of an extensive religious subtext within the film.

The virgin/whore complex has long been understood as a powerful reminder of the very narrow circuit in which women are allowed to range within a traditional morality (Abbott 47–50). An extensive collection of rules and traditions stipulate the context within which women are made available to glut men's libidinal appetites. These rules are intended to create a stable familial context for the rearing and socializing of children, to guarantee the paternity of the said children, and to protect women from exploitation. Traditionally, if the etiquette of romance is violated and the woman is prematurely sullied by carnal knowledge, she bears the full burden of responsibility. In previous centuries, this might even include rape. Shakespearean and early modern drama is populated with women who are punished for the violations against them. The complicated nexus of practices and traditions that govern romantic engagement attempt to impose order on the potentially chaotic sexual appetites of the individual. The rapist feasts without invitation; the cad leaves the table once he has consumed the main course; and the husband restrains his cravings, only consuming the desired dishes as they are made available through the designated rituals. As the reader will have already gleaned, I am suggesting a cinematic connection within *Felicia's Journey* between the rubric of seduction and romance and the etiquette of table manners. In both cases the appetite is held in check by a formal and methodical process that permits each progressive step once the former has been fully executed. Both table manners and romantic seduction constitute a semiotics, a language structure that generates social meaning once each of the cultural phonemes are coherently placed. If all of the directives governing a dinner party are carefully discharged, the hosts and guests share a sense of social coherence; the experience generates trust, respect, unity, and harmony. Table etiquette is one of the most powerful signifiers of civility, revealing the level of cultivation or the class status of each diner. Those who disrupt the syntax of social protocol, who, metaphorically speaking, consume their dessert before their salad are construed as vulgar, coarse, and uncivilized, unworthy of a place at the table among the cultivated.

Hilditch's immaculate table manners correspond to his success as a murderer, acting as an analogue of the methodical processes whereby serial killers entrap and destroy their victims and of the cliché profile in which such criminals are observed to blend easily into their environment, to follow common social customs in most aspects of their life. Because Hilditch has mastered the rules of social etiquette as obviated both in his consumption of formal dinners and his easy interaction with polite society, he is able to win the trust of his victims and figuratively devour them. To deflect attention from his unlawful hungers, he knows instinctively which fork to use with each dish as well as which comestible he is allowed to consume at the particular stage of the process. He is the portrait of a cataclysmic appetite in repose, held in check by social protocol at least until the main course is served. The well-governed appetite is key to the enjoyment of the entire dinner, each course a preparation for the next, intensifying the pleasure to come. Adherence to the syntax of the formal dinner is a metaphor for the primacy of the hunt, the predator enjoying the process because it prolongs pleasure by delaying the orgasmic apotheosis of his malignant designs.

The nexus of food, sexism, and murder is only a fragment of the most powerful tension within the cultural poetics of the film. Harte and Pettit agree that Trevor's novel is a thinly veiled "critique of the ideologies of British colonialism" (73) in Ireland and that "Hilditch's violent psychosis is thwarted imperial ambition" (74). Both screenplay and novel adopt a dialectical nationalistic structure to comment upon the protracted tensions between Ireland and Great Britain. Initially the cinematic audience is struck by the sequence of antithetical shots contrasting the pastoral and even atavistic imagery of rural Ireland with the urban industrialized environment of northern England. Each shot of Ireland is accompanied by new age Celtic music that has a plaintiff or mournful tone, implying cultural traditions in decline. Most of the physical structures within the imagery of Ireland are in an advanced state of decay and the inhabitants are angry or melancholy. The Irish parents— Felicia's father and Johnny's mother — are hostile and solitary figures, each trapped by a deep-rooted hatred of the British. Felicia's father forbids her to keep Johnny's company because it is rumored he has joined the British army, and Johnny's mother is so mortified by her son's defection to the forces of imperialism that she will not share her son's address with Felicia or even forward her letters. Most importantly for this discussion, there are no images of Irish food consumption to parallel the gluttony of Joseph Hilditch.

The images of Northern England constitute a sharp contrast to those of Mountmellick, Ireland. The unspecified town north of Birmingham where the cinematic action takes place is an industrial wasteland replete with the iconography of the modern world, manufacturing plants, nuclear cooling towers, etc. The soundtrack for the British segments replaces Celtic music with the playful, sophisticated, and satiric tones of Jazz and mid–twentieth century show tunes. The dearth that defines the Irish segments contrasts with the opulence of Hilditch's lifestyle. He lives alone in his family home amid a vast collection of antiques, curiosities, and heirlooms. The gross materialism of modern consumer culture is highlighted during one of the kitchen segments in which he is unable to operate a kitchen appliance, so he dumps it in the wastebasket and goes to the pantry to retrieve another machine just like it from his mother's collection. There is no effort to repair or even examine the broken appliance; he lives in a wealthy throwaway culture full of cheap consumer goods that render salvage unnecessary and unprofitable. The images of Hilditch's wasteful feasts — entire turkey dinners enjoyed in solitude — reinforce the images of excess that contrast with the hardships of the Irish.

Hilditch's voracious appetite and wasteful conduct become an analogue for the British imperialism in and historic colonizing of the Gaelic island. The British selfishly hoard the wealth and plenitude that results from their exploitation of other lands. The comfortable lifestyles of the British (represented by Hilditch) allow them to adopt a beneficent demeanor toward the wretched Irish, a demeanor that counters the open hostility of the Irish toward Britain in the film. Comfort and abundance have made Hilditch magnanimous, have awakened a perverse sense of social zeal, as illustrated in his philanthropic gestures toward desperate women, but the gestures are always a prelude to murder. The malignant effects of his feigned charity signify the willful blindness behind the imperialistic policies of the British, who, in what seems to be the opinion of the author and screenwriter, destroy even as they claim to save. Just as Hilditch believes that he is helping his young wards when he "lays them to rest," colonialism and cultural imperialism operate under a banner of philanthropy even as they exploit and annihilate the culture and populace toward whom they have adopted an altruistic deportment. Imperialism lies about itself, claiming to assist the underdeveloped regions of the world while merely facilitating the excessive wealth of the intruding culture through the exploitation of the indigenous people. Imperialism and colonialism bring the virtues and theories of modernity, but confiscate natural resources and material wealth and exploit the colonized as cheap labor, offered "naught but provender" for their time, muscle, and skill. Imperialism's benevolent paternalism operates to guarantee the wretchedness of its dependents while creating a pretense of goodwill. Similarly, Hilditch does not make one of his elegant feasts for Felicia; the banquet is solely for his own enjoyment. Nor does he lend her money sufficient to return to Ireland. He gives assistance to all of his beneficiaries, assistance that is insufficient to facilitate their independence from his charity, and he takes from Felicia the money that might keep her aloof.

The imagery of Ireland within the cinematic narrative is presented in retrospect, the memories of the expatriate gone in search of a historical felicity. Thus the context of her ruminations suggest the impossibility of desires that are already invalidated, her search a longing for restoration of that which was gone long before she began her journey. Ironically, Felicia hopes to construct a traditional Irish family by searching for her future husband in England, a husband who has already made the ultimate gesture of capitulation to the enemy by enlisting in the very symbol of British of domination and repression. The protagonist's inability to construct a coherent nuclear family obviates the cultural decay of Ireland, a decline, the film suggests, that results not only from meddling and exploitation by the British, but also from the intransigence of Irish nationalists— such as her father — who cannot let go of ancient grudges and embrace cultural integration. Harte and Pettit maintain that Felicia's troubles are exacerbated by a "double oppression.... In Ireland, she is a victim of patriarchal nationalism; in England, she is oppressed by the embodiment of a malign residual colonialism" (73). The failure of the Irish family is not initiated by the departure of Johnny for Britain but by the predisposition of Mountmellick's denizens against the British, which necessitate that the young Irishman Johnny conceal his professional intentions. However, the continued obstacles prohibiting the unification of potential family members are created by Hilditch, the figural embodiment of British imperialism who steals Felicia's resources, impedes her imminent reunion with Johnny in an English pub frequented by Irish lads, and encourages the destruction of her fetus, the symbol of her imagined future with Johnny as well as the restoration of unified, independent, and prosperous Ireland. The most powerful image of the violation by and against Felicia (and by extension Ireland) is her dream of a ruined church in which she encounters her father, her desired husband, and her son. Ironically, the dream occurs while she is undergoing a procedure to terminate the same pregnancy that represents her own desires and aspiration as well as those of Ireland. She suffers great trepidation before and guilt subsequent to the abortion as the procedure is a particular violation of the traditional Catholic faith of Ireland, the same that the protestant British spent centuries attempting to repress. The image of the ruined church suggests the undermining of Irish cultural coherence and harmony.

The millennial visions of "The Gathering" initiate the denouement of the cinematic action. As he is digging a grave for Felicia, Hilditch is accosted by tenacious evangelicals who remind him that "we live in a miracle," that "the healing will commence" and "the pain will wash away." The idealism of the Gatherers includes images of edenic happiness and tranquility, the tiger and wolf lying down with the lamb. The persistence of the itinerant preachers eventually shatters Hilditch's murderous resolution. He allows Felicia to escape and subsequently hangs himself, a clear analogue for the withdrawal of the British from Ireland, the change of heart that would allow the Irish to pursue their own felicity, but Felicia cannot go back to Ireland. In Trevor's novel, she becomes a bag lady, independent of all male appetites. In Egoyan's film, her future is more ambiguous. She is obviously independent of male domineering, yet she is not a homeless scavenger, but employed in public works projects, planting trees in an urban park, an appropriate metaphor for the synthesis of previous imagery of industrialized England and a pastoral Ireland. Felicia has managed to unify both cultures by escaping the ancient grudges and habitual exploitations of men whose appetites for the colonized body — both geographical and corporeal — are never sated.

The lesson of Conrad's *Heart of Darkness*, which exposes the hypocrisy of European colonialism and cultural imperialism, may be helpful in conclusion. The wealth and civility of Europe is constructed upon the horrific and brutal exploitation of the so-called uncivilized inhabitants of foreign lands. Under the pretense of altruism, the forces of European culture bring barbarism — slavery, suffering, and death — to the presumed uncultured denizens of undeveloped lands. The heart of darkness is not discovered at the end of that river in the Congo, but is imported from Europe to enthrall and rob the indigenous population and all for the harvesting of ivory, a resource that has no practical use, desired simply because it reminds the owner of his own privilege and cultivation. Similarly, the opulence and comfort of Hilditch and, by extension, the UK, is accomplished through the suppression and exploitation of the weak and the poor. The apotheosis of happiness requires that both master and slave be liberated from their respective obligations.

8

Dreaming of the
Pure Vegetable Kingdom:
Ecofeminism and Agriculture
in *A Thousand Acres*
and *Antonia's Line*

A Thousand Acres— The Patriarchal Agrarian Dystopia

Much of the scholarly attention given to Jane Smiley's novel *A Thousand Acres* and Jocelyn Moorhouse's film of the same name (1997) has focused on the story's conceptual and narrative links to the Shakespearean tragedy *King Lear,* and indeed one would be remiss not to acknowledge the heavy debt Smiley's story owes to the precedent text. However, in her speech before the 1992 National Book Critics Circle, Jane Smiley discloses the importance of pressing social and environmental concerns to her Pulitzer Prize winning novel, which constitutes a repudiation of contemporary farming techniques, including the liberal use of toxic fertilizers and pesticides to increase the quality and yield of arable lands. She contends that these chemicals are "leading us toward environmental disaster" by poisoning the earth (Bakerman 129), and the tribulations of the Cook and Clark families of the novel testify to the harmful repercussions of these practices.

The film and novel are founded upon a paradox: in order to sustain, nourish, and enhance life, one must embrace poison, destruction, and death, or in order to attain power and affluence, one must sacrifice a still more valuable possession, the health of one self and one's family. Thus *A Thousand Acres* shares with tragedy the overweening pride that overthrows the protagonist. Larry Cook, in his dynastic ambition to expand his dominion and wealth across Zebulon County, creates a toxic environment that decimates the lives of those who work it and dwell on it. The farm that should nourish and sustain paradoxically becomes a wasteland of fertility, and the farmers who should respect and safeguard the land that is their charge and livelihood are not judicious and temperate custodians, but the wasteful and avaricious agents of their own destruction.

King Lear, the tragic hero of Shakespeare's play, comes to realize his own humanity and foolhardiness, while his daughters, Goneril and Regan, devolve from the sympathetic victims of paternal capriciousness and irrationality to virtual abstractions of feminine wickedness (Keppel 106), their sibling rivalry degenerating into mortal combat over power, wealth, and desire. Inspired by Akira Kurosawa's *Ran* (another adaptation of *Lear*), particularly by the suggestion that Hidetora's sons are merely emulating their father's ambition and destructive pursuit of power and dominion, Smiley sought, in *A Thousand Acres,* to produce Goneril's point-of-view by revealing the role Larry Cook (the Lear figure) played in shaping his daughters' resentment (Bakerman 133), and the abrupt shift in the audience's sympathies from father to daughter, despite the remarkably analogous narrative, is facilitated by the introduction of a molestation and incest thematic. Ginny/Goneril and Rose/Regan are vindicated in their anger toward their father because they are both the victims of his incestuous violations. All that dwelt within the scope of Larry Cook's dominion — including people — was subject to his rapacious appetites.

Several previously published articles have focused on the representation of food in *A Thousand Acres.* In "The Polluted Quarry: Nature and Body in *A Thousand Acres,*" Barbara Mathieson argues that the narrative "repeatedly parallels the technological invasion of the landscape with the mastery and abuse of the female characters" (135), a contention that defines the subcategory of women's studies — ecofeminism:

> Uniting the approaches of feminism and ecology, ecofeminism explores the connection between anthropocentrism and patriarchy. Both Nature and women have shared a common history of objectification in the Greco-Roman intellectual tradition. Justifications for the exploitations of the natural world rest upon a conceptual hierarchy of dualisms similar to those underlying the dominion of women and men [129].

Ecofeminism further asserts that no parity between the sexes will be forthcoming until the degradation and mistreatment of the natural environment has been curtailed (130). Mathieson draws an analogy in the narrative between the rapacious farmer's contamination of the water table through the heavy use of fertilizers and pesticides and the literal and figurative poisoning of the Cook women who have been afflicted with cancers and miscarriages from the toxic water, as well as anger and resentment from their father's rapacious and incestuous appetite.

In "You Are What You Eat: Food and Power in Jane Smiley's *A Thousand Acres*," Catherine Cowen Olson suggests that the bland foods the Cooks (and midwesterners in general) consume are a metaphor for their "zestless lives" (22), for the lack of spice and flavor in their lives, and Ginny's cooking suggests both her domestic oppression and her eventual redemption. She is subjected to a rigorous schedule of food preparation for the family, but particularly for her father who insists upon specific dishes at regular intervals, which he then consumes without appropriate gratitude. However, Ginny's cooking also facilitates her escape from the oppressive farm environment when she leaves her husband and takes a job in the city waitressing in a diner. Olson spends a good deal of time analyzing the symbolic significance of the poison liver and sausages (a detail not included in Moorhouse's film) that Ginny leaves in the pantry for her sister Rose to consume. Fortunately for both women, Rose becomes a vegetarian and neglects the canned meats.

The vegetarian thematic within the narrative is addressed by Steven Kellman in "Food Fights in Iowa: The Vegetarian Stranger in Recent Midwest Fiction." Kellman identifies the production and consumption of meat as a primary metaphor within Smiley's narrative and the return of Jess, Harold Clark's draft dodging, vegetarian son, to the Midwestern setting constitutes an intrusion of west coast bohemian values into the heartland of meat production, a traitor to the values of traditional farming in the Midwest. For a time, he manages to influence the agrarian practices of both his father and Rose Cook, but the same restiveness that compelled him to return to Zebulon County from his meanderings in the Pacific Northwest drives him away again and Rose is left alone to cope with the recurrence of her cancer and the insolvency of her thousand acres.

While Jess Clark's vegetarian values amount to an indictment of modern farming and urge a return to a simpler agrarian culture, his attitude toward meat is not his only problem with his father's farm. Indeed, one could contend that the issue of meat is secondary to the interrogation of crop production. In Moorhouse's film, once Ginny and Ty obtain their share of the farm, they do attempt to convert many of their vegetable assets into porcine production, and the film includes a variety of references to and images of hogs, but the most common image and the one that any Midwesterner would recognize as ubiquitous within the heartland environment is the house high corn, which stands sentinel in the background of virtually every exterior shot of the film and even many interior images. The corn sweeps across the Midwestern plains in uniform rows of equal height like a verdant ocean interrupted only by roads, farmhouses, and small towns. It envelopes and encloses the lives of the characters, and while it signifies the vast expanse of their dominion as well as their prosperity, it is also a silent witness to and perhaps even an emblem of their family tragedy. The Cook family corn does not include the blighted stalks growing intermittently among non-agrarian people or among the organic farmers who oppose the use of pesticides and fertilizers. The sheer height and uniformity of the Cook fields constitutes a silent reminder of their own poisoning.

The Cooks and the film audience may consider the unbending corn beautiful, its height, density, and unflagging green a symbol of nature's abundance, but it is a false good and perhaps even a false god. To borrow a phrase from Tore Hogas, it is a "poisoned gift" demanding sacrifice (67), an unnatural phenomenon, a paradoxical symbol of a dangerous fertility. While there is no evidence within the dialogue that the corn itself constitutes a threat to its caretakers, its growth was nurtured by toxins, its roots irrigated by noxious waters; it is the product of poisons. In a similar sense, the Cook daughters, Ginny and Rose, by all appearances, are well-adjusted adults, seemingly unconflicted by the preoccupations of traditional agrarian life. They have husbands and are model farm wives, cooking for the field

The Cook sisters — Ginny (Jessica Lange), Rose (Michelle Pfeiffer), and Caroline (Jennifer Jason Leigh)— listen to hear their father's plan to divide his farm between them. The photo reveals the ubiquitous corn that stands as silent witness to the impending family tragedy in many shots of Jocelyn Moorhouse's cinematic adaptation of Jane Smiley's *A Thousand Acres* (1997).

hands and maintaining orderly houses. Their concerns extend to their widower father for whom they also cook and clean and whose directives they slavishly obey even into their middle age. However, just as the corn hides its noxious origins, Ginny and Rose have concealed the violations that produced their adult characters, the psychological residue of Larry Cook's violence and lust. Ginny and Rose have been nurtured with psychic poison (Bakerman 135–136), and they have dealt with the incestuous appetites of their father in antithetical fashions. As I have argued elsewhere, Rose has immersed herself in rage, constantly brooding over the trespasses. Ginny, on the other hand, has so completely repressed the memory of her father's offenses that she initially balks at Rose's efforts to remind her (Keller, "Excess" 84). Despite differences in coping techniques, each of the women was nurtured in an environment about violence and exploitation of which both have remained silent, keeping up appearances, until the narrative present.

The corn hides many secrets. On more than one occasion, the Cooks disappear into the corn when they seek to escape from unpleasant human interactions. Humiliated by Jess' failure to return her declaration of love, Ginny runs into the corn to escape her former suitor's apologia, and Larry darts into the storm-tossed fields following his savage confrontation with his daughters. In each situation, the signification of the corn shifts to embody the high sentiments of the players in the human drama. For Larry, it suggests his escape into narcissism and madness and, for Ginny, the flight from harsh reality to embalmed darkness, a hiding place for the recuperation of her newly excited passions. The corn plays an important role in the initial revelation of Rose's infidelity as well. The elder sisters sit on the side of the road facing the darkened corn as Rose voices her resentment toward her recently deceased husband and confesses her affair with Jess. In this moment lie the toxic seeds that will poison the Cook sisters' relationship; thus the corn suggests not only the tragedies past, but those that impend.

The corn that envelopes the lives of the Cooks, creating open spaces for their labors and recreations, also conceals the problems within their marriages. In an exterior scene shortly after the division of the farm, Ginny, Ty, Rose, Pete, and Jess play baseball in the yard with a hilarity that belies the growing tensions within the group. Jess' presence seems benign enough at first, yet his return to Zebulon County will be the impetus for one death, the failure of two marriages, the collapse of the Cook family corporation as well as the failure of the farm, and the estrangement of children from parents and siblings from each other. The boundaries of their game are marked by the eight foot high wall of corn that surrounds them, signifying where appearances end and reality begins. Rose and Pete have experienced marital problems following Rose's radical mastectomy because Pete is offended by her post-surgical body. There is also evidence that the marriage has been tempestuous with Rose periodically beaten by her husband, and the revelation of Rose's affair with Jess results in the drunk driving incident in which Pete is killed. The trouble between Ginny and Ty is more subtle. On the surface, they seem completely compatible; however, their relationship lacks the emotional and sensual passion of Pete and Rose's, thus making Ginny susceptible to Jess' charms.

The corn is voyeur in the Cook family tragedy, peeping through windows and appearing at the screen door of Ginny's kitchen, shuttling the characters in and out of the house and on and off of the farm. The characters must pass through miles of silent sentinels on both sides of the highway when they make for town or city, the corn permissively allowing their departure and reaching out to embrace them when they return. However, despite the multiple pathways through the verdant fields, the corn suggests a vegetable prison, a discipline and a lifestyle. It is a representation of the regimentation in the Cook family lives, of Larry's rage for order. The crop is planted in carefully spaced columns with predictable gaps between stalks and rows. Moreover, with the aid of fertilizers and insecticides, the fields grow to a uniform height and color, standing at attention in rigorous rows through the day and night, silently demanding the consideration of its warders, and posing the paradoxical question, Does the farmer grow the corn or the corn the farmer? Larry Cook exacts the same discipline from his daughters as he expects in his fields. The women know their place in Larry's cosmology, which is to serve and respect him in spite of his abuses. He demands a particular breakfast at a particular time every day, and the daughters are fearful of breaking his routine. Rose explains her acquiescence in her own incestuous rape, saying that she felt sex with her father must be right because "He was the rule maker."

For many years, the Cooks can only dream of escaping the rigidity of their vegetable prison. Rose complains that whenever she planned to flee the farm, Ginny convinced her to stay. She once dreamed of escaping with her mother and living in a "Hollywood style apartment," and even though Ginny reveals that she never wanted to live anywhere else but the farm, the events of the narrative convince her to forsake her claim to the dynastic property and seek the anonymity of city living: "I didn't know where I was going. I only knew I needed to leave." Even the family patriarch, Larry, upon his retirement and the division of the farm is unable to relinquish control of the farming to Pete and Ty. He becomes agitated and restless in his idleness, drinking and driving all over the county and litigating to reclaim his farm.

The corn is a demanding ward, the custodians of the farm fettered to the seasons and the vicissitudes of inclement weather. They cannot sit the year out or delay their labors until they are ready to plant or harvest, but they must comply with the rigorous dictates of a seasonal routine. The failure to produce a crop even in a single year would probably result in financial ruin and foreclosure. Neither are the fertilizers and pesticides that poison the denizens of the region optional as Jess's organic farming philosophy suggests. The farmer cannot risk a low yield crop that could send him into bankruptcy, nor can the non-agrarian public be fed by the half-hearted efforts and idealistic environmentalism of its agricultural industry. Corn is a staple that must be produced in as great an abundance and with as much efficiency as the industry can manage and yet much of the world will still go hungry. In *The Story of Corn*, Betty Fussell describes the economic paradox of modern farming: "Farmers who'd borrowed heavily to buy more land had to buy more machines to produce more and more crops to pay the interest, but the more they produced the more they lowered their crop prices." She goes on to quote Carl Sandburg's own characterization of the problem: "We raise more corn/to feed more hogs/ to buy more land/ to raise more corn/to feed more hogs/to buy more land/to..." ("Good Morning America" qtd. in Fussell 141–42). The farmer is driven to optimize the size of each crop and to strive to do even better in the next yield, forsaking other preoccupations. Moreover, the farmer is subject to unpredictable and often destructive weather. Just as poisonous pesticides and fertilizers are requisite to a high yield and marketable crop, moderate precipitation is necessary for fertility and growth, yet inclement weather can also destroy the production of an entire growing season in a matter of minutes.

The Cook family, particularly Larry, seems at odds with the seasonal round and, by extension, with the cycle of life, which is an inevitable and fundamental consideration for those in their profession. For all of his dynastic bluster about the three generations of Cook men who rescued the thousand acres from swamp, Larry is not at all comfortable relinquishing control of the farm to his daughters and their husbands despite having initiated the transaction himself. While he sought to unburden himself of the daunting responsibility of producing a crop with each seasonal turn, he was not so willing to surrender respect and control to the next generation. Like Shakespeare's Lear, he falsely assumed that he could retain the esteem and dignity of a king even after he had forsaken monarchical power and as Shakespeare's fool observes, the king has made mothers of his daughters. While the practice of surrendering control to the next generation — retirement — is commonplace in our culture, Shakespeare suggests that Lear's actions constitute a violation of time, nature and the cycle of life. The daughters would have their time in due course. Similarly, Larry does not want the next generation to rule in his absence; he wants them to embody his absent presence, to farm just as he would so that it will be as though he had never gone. The accusation of mismanagement in the effort to reclaim the farm implies that the only proper way to operate is the way he (Larry) would do it. There are many examples of the confusion of generational distinctions aside from the mothering of Larry by his daughters—most glaringly, the father's sexual exploitation of his own daughters, but also the failure of the Cook mother to offer Ginny and Rose a realistic perspective on their father, to teach them that he is merely a flawed man, not a god. Moreover, the hopes of a generation of Cook farmers following Ginny and Rose are truncated by the former's barrenness and the latter's deathbed efforts to make all of the dynastic wrangling over land end with her own generation. Thus she leaves the farm to Ginny and Caroline, not to her own daughters. Moreover, Rose's cancer ensures that the next generation of Cook daughters will be raised by someone other than their mother. Most importantly, from an agricultural standpoint, the Cooks' farming techniques, employed to ensure fertility and abundance, may be construed as a violation of nature or, to borrow a phrase from Hardy, "the ancient pulse of germ and birth." Their farming techniques suggest that nature's abundance is not adequate to human need but must be embellished and rectified by the shaping hand of humanity.

Increasingly, the imagery of the corn in Moorhouse's film comes to suggest a fatal abundance and not exclusively in the tragic sense where prosperity and ease creates a false sense of well-being and an inordinate pride. The corn becomes a naturalistic symbol of the inscrutable and indifferent universe. The vast expanses of stalks rolling off into the distance in every direction are calculated to make the preoccupations of the Cook family seem insignificant, to suggest that their passion play is only so much meaningless hysteria—"sound and fury signifying nothing." While the contention over the farm is conducted ostensibly with the best interests of agriculture in mind, the reality is that nature values a single stalk of corn at the same rate as ten thousand. Moorhouse's camera invites such a reading of the corn, frequently scanning the vast fields of silent unchanging stalks before she brings the eye to rest on the tribulations and preoccupations of the vexed farm family. In one particularly forceful instance, the camera rests peacefully over an unmoving field of grain and then slowly pans toward the drainage ditch where Pete has wrecked his truck and drowned himself. A visual analogue to Lear's storm tossed heath where he rages against the injustice of his daughters, the corn in Moorhouse's film seems complicit with the storm that drenches the raving and shelterless farmer. In one of the few times the corn is shown to move, the stalks wave erratically, suggesting fury and chaos, but not so much the madness to which Larry succumbed as the vindictive rage of his abused and humiliated daughters; however, the sympathies of the corn turn out to be a pathetic fallacy. The crop ultimately presides over the complete obliteration of the Cook clan. At the conclusion of the narrative, the debt burdened farm is sold to a gigantic agricultural conglomerate — the Midwestern Corporation — who bulldoze the houses to make room for more crops, so the corn obliterates the lives of its custodians, covering and concealing every trace of their lives. Here, the engulfing corn suggests fate. The farming philosophy that the Cooks practiced and advocated is the same that ultimately overwhelms them. The family's appetite for ever higher yields and incomes was only an intermediary step in the process of corporate farming that steadily drives family farms into extinction. The corn is both desolation and fertility or rather desolation via fertility. Larry's dream of owning and controlling all that he can see constitutes the same rationale that drives the rapacious greed of the Midwestern Corp., the patriarchal rage for control, conquest, exploitation, and order.

Antonia's Line — The Feminist Agrarian Utopia

Marleen Gorris's Academy Award winning film *Antonia's Line* (Best Foreign Language Film, 1996) could have been produced as a cinematic counter discourse to Moorhouse's film and or Smiley's novel. *A Thousand Acres* depicts a family at odds with each other and with nature, driven by a voracious greed and an appetite for conquest, out of sync with the rhythms of agrarian life. In contrast, Antonia and her brood are well-equipped to brook the vicissitudes of time and environment, living in harmony with the natural processes and with the numerous eccentrics who share space in their native village (Gillet 2). While both narratives share a concern over the sexual politics of the farm, *A Thousand Acres* examines the fallout of a male centered ideology, a rapaciousness that exploits land and women with equal barbarity (Carr 121; Keppel 113), creating a toxic wasteland analogous to the resentment of Larry Cook's abused family. Conversely, the return of Antonia (Willeke van Ammelrooy) and her daughter Danielle (Els Dottermans) to her ancestral farm initiates a reformation in the gendered hierarchy of the village. The women will not abide an avaricious and lascivious male deportment, permitting only the most well behaved men within the scope of their lives (Sellery 117).

When Antonia and her daughter step off the train in their native village, they are greeted by the banner "Welcome Liberators," which applauds the Allied powers that have only recently delivered the country from Nazi tyranny; however, the slogan might more appropriately prefigure the emancipating influence that the women will have upon the village, creating a communal environment that embraces misfits and non-conformists as well as the few men who are respectful of women's freedoms (Gillet 2). Antonia returns, after a twenty year absence, to care for her mother lingering near death. The dying woman has been driven insane by her husband's adulteries. Her wild eyes, her ravings, and her erratic behavior allude to demonic possession, yet the mother's perturbation is not created by a malign spirit of infernal origin, but the ghost of resentment raised by unfaithful men. She dies cursing her dead husband for his infidelities: "You two-faced, ruthless, drunken, degenerate adulterer! You wicked, wicked man." The madness that vexes Antonia's mother upon her death results from the frustration wrought by women's powerlessness within patriarchy. Perhaps, unable to make her husband honor and respect her and fettered to him by both sacred and secular law, she had no alternative but to "unpack ... [her] heart with words/And fall a-cursing." Antonia, however, will evade the relational pitfalls that destroyed her mother's peace of mind.

Antonia, like her daughters after her, refuses to marry — to make herself dependent upon a man, and thus encourage a proprietary disposition toward her. When the widower farmer Bas proposes marriage, asserting that his children need a mother, Antonia reminds him that she does not need his five boys. She does nurture a friendship with the unoffending farmer, one that, after many years, grows into romance; however, once the aging adults become amorous, Antonia skillfully dissuades any impulse toward ownership of her body by maintaining her separate residence and by insisting upon a neutral space for their love making. They even settle upon a weekly sex schedule. Within the narrative, the quality that earns Bas' admission to Antonia's bed is his willingness to wait patiently and nurture a lengthy friendship before they fall into amorous embrace. It is the other members of the male community who need to be taught respect for women. The village is split between passive males and "alpha males" (Sellery 120).

Antonia and her daughters combat and defeat the marauding male appetite whenever it impinges upon their lives. On their first visit to the village's Russian Café, Antonia and Danielle witness farmer Daan's effort to find a husband for his mentally handicapped daughter Deedee. He parades her in front of the other men like a heifer brought to market. The spectacle seems calculated more to offend the newly arrived women than to attain a partner for Deedee, who is only rescued from her humiliation by the intervention of farmer Bas, who shuttles her out of the room. Daan's disrespectful demeanor toward women is extended to his farm and his farming techniques, not to mention the socialization of his boys. Daan's farm is repeatedly constructed within the narrative as the antithesis of the ecofeminist agrarian utopia of Antonia's estate. The interconnection of agriculture and avarice, as well as the parallel exploitations of women and the environment that destroyed Larry Cook, is also predominant on Daan's farm.

The filmmaker includes several images of the farmer and his boys driving cattle across the yard, creating a visual analogue for the manipulation and abuse of the women in the house. Pitte, Daan's eldest son, beats and gropes his sister Deedee, and no one on the farm discourages him. Moreover, while searching the barn to borrow a tool, Danielle discovers Pitte raping his own sister. Horrified, she hurls a pitchfork at him, appropriately piercing him in the groin, a symbolic punishment of the male libido. Danielle rescues Deedee from her own family, bringing her to Antonia's farm where she is treated with respect and allowed to flourish. Shortly after the rape, Pitte disappears for many years only to return upon his father's death, demanding money from the estate and offending his more loyal and well-behaved brother. Pitte's return initiates another rape, this time of Danielle's pre-pubescent daughter Theresa. Once again the punishment is appropriate to the crime. Antonia reviles the man at gunpoint, and farmer Bas' boys beat him for the offense, repeatedly kicking him in the groin. Pitte's fate is even more dire when he staggers home and is drowned in a water barrel by his own brother, Janne.

Janne's murder of his brother is not, however, a punishment for the rape, but an effort to gain sole ownership of the farm. Such wrangling over family assets is conspicuously absent from Antonia's estate where the denizens live and farm communally, in harmony with nature and each other. Her farm is a vale of gentle soul making where eccentrics and social outcasts are treated with love, respect, and understanding. Antonia welcomes all those who have no other place to go. Both Deedee and her future husband Loony Lips come to live and work on the farm. Antonia also takes in Lette and her children, the same woman who helped Danielle find a man to sire her child, Therese, and Lette takes up with a defrocked priest who fathers a child with her every year for a total of twelve; these offspring too become a part of Antonia's family. All of her own progeny remain on the farm: Danielle and her female lover Lara as well as Therese and her child Sarah. Even Bas and his five boys are such frequent visitors and laborers on the farm that they too become family.

The Cook daughters of *A Thousand Acres* are offended by the family patriarchs' proprietary demeanor toward them, one which equates them with the products and processes of farming. They complain of Grandpa

Cook, who prowled around the house at night watching the sleepers as though he were checking the livestock, and of Larry, who believes that Caroline might already be "too old to breed." Conversely, Gorris' film celebrates the integration of the characters with the rhythms and processes of farming (Gillet 2). Danielle's impregnation resembles animal husbandry or, more plainly, a horse breeder's efforts to find a stallion for a prize mare. The women investigate the background of the potential father with the intention of assuring a well bred foal. Having evaluated the intended stud, Antonia, Danielle, and Letta arrange for a single encounter for coupling. While the insemination is underway in a fancy hotel, Antonia and Letta wait on the lawn sipping wine, and after conception is reasonably assured, the three women run off like pranksters leaving the stallion to his own devices. Visually, Antonia is also equated to agricultural processes, the expansion of her clan an analogue for the sowing and harvesting of the crops. Toward the beginning of the film, Antonia is several times depicted planting in a fashion reminiscent of Van Gogh's "The Sower," a basket on her ample hips, rhythmically tossing seed onto the ground as she walks the fields. The initial scattering is a solitary activity, but as her family increases along with her crops, she retains more and more sowers. The random scattering of the seeds in the field serves as a counterpoint to the systematic industrial farming of the Cook family. The regimentation of the corn rows and the subservience of the Cook daughters by the commanding farmer/father runs counter to the haphazard and non-mechanical farming of Antonia and her clan, and yet the images of prosperity and happiness on Antonia's farm abound.

The seeds that Antonia planted singlehandedly are reaped by the extended family. Gorris' film is punctuated by images of harvesting and feasting, and neither of these practices retains the formality and discipline of the Cook family rituals that were invariably dictated by a cantankerous old man. While Antonia's extended family brings in the crop through strenuous physical labor, digging in the earth with their hands, they do not maintain so rigorous a schedule that they cannot pause to enjoy each other's company. When Deedee's participation in the communal effort to bring in the harvest reveals her to be pregnant with Loony Lips' illegitimate child, the entire clan pauses for laughter and rejoicing, acknowledging the dual harvest. The images of feasting have a similarly allegorical subtext. The table that is repeatedly set in the barnyard grows over the years accommodating all of Antonia's progeny, biological, communal, and spiritual. The placement of the table in the yard near the barn suggests the expansive growth of the clan which cannot be accommodated within the confines of the house, but it also rehabilitates the offending metaphor in *A Thousand*

Acres, which involves the equation of human and animal assets. *Antonia's Line* proudly acknowledges that the most important products of the farm are people, love, and community. These, by extension, translate into the prosperity everywhere in evidence at the table, as the wealth of food items are passed equally among the diners. The prosperity of Antonia's farm is not reaped for the enrichment of a single individual but circulated equally among the denizens of the farm and their visitors. Placement at the table is a free-for-all; there is no commanding patriarch or even a matriarch who orders the ritual and demands deference. The diners place themselves along the ever expanding table. The feasts are not a visual symbol of the class structure but a celebration of life and the generous bounty of the earth.

While farmer Daan's blighted clan becomes smaller and smaller until no one remains but his aged wife, Antonia's family experiences a baby boom. The difference can be attributed to the antithetical approaches to life and farming. The patriarchal, exploitative, and avaricious environment that Daan has created (just as in Smiley's narrative) destroys its inhabitants:

Lust drove away Deedee while greed and selfish ambition killed Pitte. Daan's farm demands conformity and deference to male centered leadership. It is a place of mourning where only death and melancholy prevail. In contrast, Antonia's agrarian feminist utopia is an environment where the inhabitants are allowed to flourish, embracing their differences and eccentricities, where guilt free sexual expression is second nature, and where the restrictions of matrimonial bonds are doffed. Antonia is unapologetic about having a daughter out of wedlock, and her progeny remain similarly indifferent to social convention, each woman following her destiny without condemnation or encumbrance. When

Antonia (Willeke van Ammelrooy) enjoys one of many family feasts in the barnyard of her idyllic farm in Marleen Gorris' *Antonia's Line* (1995).

Antonia (Willeke van Ammelrooy, right) and an unidentified character (left) share a table with farmer Bas (Jan Decleir), Antonia's patient lover who waited years to consummate his love for his neighbor and who inadvertently participated in the creation of a more equitable family composed of individuals who respect each other's choices (Marleen Gorris' *Antonia's Line* 1995).

Danielle realizes she is a lesbian, her lover, Lara, is embraced by the family without even a word acknowledging the alternative union. Danielle is encouraged to pursue her painting, Theresa her mathematics, and Sarah her poetry without pressure by family or friends to conform to more practical pursuits. When Therese announces her pregnancy at dinner, the clan, including the father, wait patiently while she decides whether to have the child. After the birth of Sarah, Therese demonstrates no maternal instincts; thus the remainder of the clan takes up the responsibility of coddling the infant without trying to compel the mother to assume normative maternal duties, allowing her the freedom of her intellectual pursuits while the infant is nurtured by those more amenable to child rearing. When Antonia decides she is not ready for a relationship, Farmer Bas nevertheless remains devoted to her for years, waiting for her to change her mind. Antonia's farm is a metaphor for feminist governance — participatory, non-prescriptive, tolerant, respectful, and less rigorously ordered than traditional male centered administration.

Because Antonia's clan are willing to embrace life and pursue happiness without guilt or reticence, without obligatory conformity to the institutional controls of male government and the outmoded and sexist morality of the church, they are better able to confront death without regret and desperation (Gillet 3), which is not to say they welcome it. When Loony Lips is killed in a farming accident, Deedee is inconsolable, and when Letta dies giving birth to her twelfth child, her lover is overwrought with grief. However, Antonia's line remains stoic, continuing to enjoy life despite mortality. In one particularly allegorical scene, Antonia and Bas dance in the barnyard surrounded by the dead who have passed out of their lives. The scene is a *memento mori*, a reminder of the inevitability of death and the resulting need to live fully, to make the most of time. Dancing is a traditional representation of the celebration of life and dancing on a grave or among the dead a lighthearted defiance of fate and mortality. Antonia's decision to die even though she is not ill or melancholy illustrates the rationality that can attend death when one has lived without regret, inhibition, or constraint. Nor is she armored by a faith in an afterlife, having only recently told her great-granddaughter, Sarah, that "this is the only dance we dance." The young poetess herself has developed a curiosity about death that may seem to border on the morbid, yet she is the family member with the most sagacious perspective on mortality, regarding it as just another miracle of life and eager to witness Antonia's wondrous transition.

Antonia's Line suggests that the dread of death is a betrayal of those principles by which Antonia's family lived. Unlike the Cooks, who chafed against their own mortality, who longed to place themselves outside the seasons, the cycle of life from which they made their fortune and from which they conceived the subsequent generations, Antonio knows the same process that brought all of her joys, including the conception, birth, and growth of her children and grandchildren — both biological and spiritual — also requires her death; the love that she bears her family demands that she lie in her grave. Wallace Stevens' phrase, "Death is the mother of beauty," captures the paradox of Antonia's life and death as well as the tragedy of Larry Cook's family. Antonia has to die in order to have all of the joys that she celebrates; however, her reward does not come after death, but before. The food that sustains her family embodies the secret of her life. As one crop gives way to another, sustaining the successive waves of humanity, one generation must make a space for the next, fertilizing, both literally and figuratively, the fields that will sustain their progeny.

9

The Kitchen Panopticon:
Indeterminacy and the Myth
of Objective Surveillance

In 1927, Werner Heisenberg postulated his "Uncertainty Principle," a theory which held that the scientific observer could not determine the position or momentum of a particular particle because the process which allows access to that microscopic level necessitates the introduction of an element to facilitate perception, one that alters the behavior of the particles under observation. If the scientist strives to observe the content of an atom, for instance, s/he must introduce a photon to illuminate the area of study; however, the presence of the facilitating element alters the context and behavior of the indigenous particles. Thus the observer only sees that which s/he has instigated: the subject has the look of a subject that is looked at. Werner Heisenberg's "Uncertainty Principle" is one of the fundamental theories of quantum mechanics; however, in addition to its application to the microscopic universe, Heisenberg's work has a practical application to the social and behavioral sciences; it is a useful tool in conceptualizing the conduct of people under observation.

An argument for the theoretical difficulty of objective analysis and observation can follow a variety of trajectories. In the study of human conduct, the so-called objective observer cannot avoid impacting the subject of his study. The conditions under which the viewer views the subject can produce a multiplicity of falsifying results. For example, the individual participating in an interview or a questionnaire may be hyper-conscious of being evaluated, and even if the researcher reassures the subject that there are no correct answers to the questions, the participant, nevertheless, knows that the observer intends to arrive at conclusions based upon the study, conclusions that will encompass an implicit or explicit value system and one that may even define the subject negatively. Moreover, the subject's perception of the reviewer may impact the answers that are given. An adverse perception of the questioner may compel the subject to lean toward hyperbole or persistently negative answers. A positive perception of the observer/questioner could compel the subject of analysis to generate answers intended to impress or please. This could involve an effort either to persuade the researcher to develop a favorable attitude toward the subject or to facilitate a beneficial outcome of the study.

Even the practice of clandestine observation gives the researcher only limited access to the subject's movements and behaviors, confined mostly to the public sphere where the subject might be compelled to alter his or her behavior for any number of potential observers unrelated to the researcher's efforts. People generally do not behave in as uninhibited a manner in public sphere as within a private sphere. However, even within the private, there are differentiations. For example, a mother's interaction with her children may be considered private, yet the subject may be self-restricted in the behaviors that are permissible around the children. Moreover, the study of the individuals either through questioning or observation may falsely assume a unified, coherent, consistent and purposeful sense of self or a full self-understanding on the part of the subject, both of which seem improbable within the discipline of modern psychoanalysis. The individual might reinvent herself for a particular social context, either intentionally or subconsciously. Moreover, one of the foundational principles of modern psychology derives from the observation that individuals are driven by unconscious impulses that are not accessible to the rational or conscious mind; we only partially understands the forces that motivate our behaviors.

Perhaps the most unsteady element of "objective analysis" is the researcher's inevitable reliance upon language, which is forever shifting in its significations and which includes an inherent system of valuation that continues to operate even when the user specifically strives to choose non-value laden terms. For example, the researcher might choose the term "less" rather than "insufficient" because the latter more clearly suggests inadequacy. However, the term "less" itself is generally considered to be less favorable than the term "more." Saussure has taught us that language inevitably includes valuation and prioritization. Meaning within language may be generated relationally through a system of binary oppositions—such as male/female, virtue/vice, nature/culture etc. (thus undermining the assumption that a particular word retains an intrinsic and invariable meaning, a specific correspondence with reality)—but that same binary structure is neither objective nor stable (Leitch 9). The selection of one term over the other includes a value judgment even when the speaker/writer is attempting to be non-discriminating. In the above binary oppositions, the former term is generally prioritized or valued over the latter.

In addition, as Derrida has taught us, the individual speaker/writer maintains an imperfect control of the language that s/he wields (Berman 200–208). The individual consciousness is shaped by a preexisting signifying system into which the subject was born and within which s/he can only imperfectly express the multiplicity of ideas requisite to being understood. But the problem of inaccurate communication is not limited to the speaker/writer. The listener/reader generates an entirely separate potential for inaccuracy, constructing an understanding upon his or her own biases, experiences, and preconceptions and constricted by any variety of contextual influences— race, ethnicity, gender, class, sexual orientation, et. al. This inherent instability of language usage necessarily impacts the objectivity of scientific research and observation. Language will not allow the observer/researcher to create questions that are free of bias and judgment or that can communicate the intended idea with accuracy or consistency. Nor can the researcher have a reasonable expectation that the respondent will comprehend the inquiry as it was intended. The researcher's records are thus three times removed from an objective reality. The observer must mentally process the information, filtering it through her own experiences and biases; she then must capture the ideas in a shifting and evolving system of significations, one that she only imperfectly employs and understands. Once the observations have been recorded, they are further problematized by the reader who once again must filter the language through his own consciousness, leaving an unavoidable and unique contextual residue.

The problematics of objective observation are the subject of Bent Hamer's 2003 film *Kitchen Stories*, which narrates the interaction between a Swedish researcher, Folke Nilsson (played by Tomas Norstrom) and a Norwegian recluse, Isak Bjornsson (played by Joachim Calmeyer). The film allegorizes the researcher's inability to maintain objective distance and to avoid influencing the subject and environment that he observes. In addition and, perhaps, more importantly, the film illustrates Foucault's postulate that surveillance and knowledge create power and control ("The Eye of Power" 146–165). There is an inherent power dynamic in the relationship between observer and observed, an implicit judgment against the latter. The simple choice to study a particular subject assumes a problem with the same and suggests an effort at correction. Hamer's film is a veritable house of mirrors in its preoccupation with surveillance and representation, demonstrating that scientific observation is not objective and cannot necessarily produce the researcher's desired results, that the ideology of rational analysis is only one tool for the pursuit of reality and better living.

As a member of a team of Swedish researchers, sponsored by HRI (The Home Research Institute) and under the direction of Dr. Ljungberg (Leif Andree), Folke Nilsson travels to Norway for a prolonged positivistic observation of the habits of Norwegian males within their home kitchen environments. Each researcher is assigned a host household to observe for a period of weeks, and each member of the research team brings with him a small trailer, in which he will reside for the length of the study, and a tall deck or director's chair, which he places in the corner of the subject's kitchen, thus creating a vantage point from which to survey the movements of the person under observation. The researcher is permitted to come and go from the home without interference, but is not allowed to interact in any way with the resident. The observer charts the movements of the host within the kitchen. The objective of the study is to determine the typical cooking behaviors of the designated Norwegian subset in order to design an ideal kitchen environment, one that is both practical and efficient. However, the plan is flawed for a variety of reasons, not least of which is the difficulty in maintaining an objective distance from the host. As in Heisenberg's "Uncertainty Principle," the mere presence of the observer alters the subject and environment under observation. Thus Folke does not see Isak, but Isak being seen.

Isak is reluctant to be observed despite having volunteered for the project. When the question of this inconsistency is broached, he explains that he had signed up for the study because the HRI representatives had promised him a horse, a necessity in a rural home such as his where horses are still assigned practical tasks in the maintenance of the farm. Isak's current horse is dying, so the offer of the Swedish researchers is timely and advantageous. However, it is only after the Swedes arrive that he discovers the promised horse is merely a painted wooden carving. So for several days, Isak will not allow Folke into the house despite constant entreaties from a variety of people, and even after the researcher gains admission, Isak continues to interfere with Folke's efforts. Refusing to prepare his food in front of Folke, the farmer only smokes his pipe, drinks coffee, and socializes in the kitchen. Moreover, whenever he senses that Folke is recording his movements, Isak leaves the room and turns out the light and in one particular instance, turns out the light and remains in the room eating his chocolate. It is clear that Isak is offended by Folke's refusal to interact with him. Thus, paradoxically, the effort to avoid interfering with the host's culinary routine actually becomes the principal interference.

The implied smugness and superiority in Folke's objectivity disrupts the cloistered harmony and routine of Isak's life. The idea that Folke, perched on his high chair in Isak's tiny kitchen, could be ignored by the inhabitant and could avoid affecting the behavior of the same, is Kafkaesque in its absurdity and incongruity, and while Folke's elevation is only an attempt to remove him from the environment under study and perhaps also to create a vantage point from which to map the subject's movements more accurately, it is, nevertheless, interpreted as condescension and judgment. Isak is unable to ignore Folke and go about his business. Moreover, the coming and going of the researcher in so small an environment is extremely disruptive even though the Swede does not speak. In one particular scene Folke enters while Isak and his neighbor Grant are drinking coffee at the table. Folke must squeeze by the pair in order to attain his seat and once situated and prepared to record, he has so completely interrupted the easy interaction of the neighbors that they leave, turning out the light.

Folke's presence seems to demand performance, making the subject self-conscious and perhaps even embarrassed by the simplicity and poverty of his life and certainly also his apparent ineptitude in food preparation. It seems that Isak's culinary skills are limited to heating food on a hot plate, and he is unwilling to perform this task in the traditional location, avoiding the range in his kitchen except to heat water for coffee. Shortly after Folke gains admittance to the house, he starts to smell food being prepared upstairs in Isak's bedroom, outside the range of his surveillance. After the two men begin to interact, Isak still avoids kitchen food preparation, but he is more willing to talk about the same. Isak mentions that he is having "more and more trouble boiling ... potatoes properly," and he wonders what it will be like to perform the task when Norway has nuclear power. When Folke reminds him that he (Isak) does not "boil potatoes very often even though" he has "two stoves," Isak adds, "No, at least not as long as I am being observed." The admission of his reticence to prepare food in front of the researcher even after they have become friends suggests not only a fundamental objection to the surveillance, but also a fear that the study is not so much observation as scrutiny and judgment, a recognition that power is exerted through surveillance and the subsequent acquired knowledge.

What is perceived to be Isak's unwillingness to cooperate with the Home Research Institute's positivistic methodology may actually be a misunderstanding resulting from the required silence between the researcher and his subject. The fact that Isak will not prepare food in his kitchen even after he befriends his observer suggests that he was not using his kitchen for cooking even before the study. In his essay "The Eye of Power," Foucault theorizes that the architecture of the modern home constitutes the imposition of morality onto family living (148–149), functionally segregating the various bodily urges and appetites of the family, separating cooking, eating, defecating, copulating, entertaining etc. into a group of discrete spaces, and in most cases generating prohibitions against the transgression of boundaries limiting one spatial practice and another. Foucault argues that prior to the Eighteenth Century, the home was an undifferentiated space, a series of rooms that could be used to any purpose (148–49). The members of a typical family in the Sixteenth Century would sleep on the floor in the kitchen near the fireplace, the eldest son allowed to lie on the wooden slab that served as the kitchen table during the day. Only the parents had a separate room. Living alone in a large rural home, Isak is not obliged to observe the conventions of modern living. He performs many tasks in the kitchen that may be considered atavistic within the traditions of modern domestic spacing. He hangs his wet clothes, cuts hair, bathes, and frequently sleeps in his kitchen, which is also his primary site for the entertaining of guests, specifically his friend Grant, and later Folke. This multi-functional space is mirrored in Folke's living arrangements during the study. The tiny trailer that he occupies alongside Isak's house serves simultaneously as kitchen, bedroom, diningroom, and living room, perhaps pointing out the inconsistencies in our expectations of living arrangements. While in a normative living environment, sleeping or bathing in the kitchen may seem absurdly incongruous, uncomfortable, and impractical, few question the logic of combining these spaces in trailers or motor homes.

Isak's unconventional kitchen living challenges the assumptions of the HRI study, demonstrating that their positivistic approach is fundamentally flawed because it assumes a universality in the functionality of various domestic spaces. Isak sleeps in the kitchen and cooks in the bedroom. Thus the researchers are not so much objective observers as imperialistic invaders imposing materialist ideology and technology onto a culture (or at least an individual) that embraces contrary values, that is not interested in purchasing the most recent domestic technology. In effect, the arrival of the Swedish researchers constitutes a colonization as they drag their living quarters behind their cars. The colonial economy is one in which the indigenous people produce nothing that they need and use nothing that they produce, remaining economically dependent on the encroaching culture who supplies them with the materials for living. The Swedish researchers have come to observe the culinary activities of the Norwegian males, deriving information that they will then use to generate a materialist model for Norwegian cooking and sell it back to the host country at extravagant prices. In essence, the Norwegians will be purchasing their own culture from the Swedes.

The film dialogue subtly develops the invasion/colonization motif through multiple references to WWII, the Nazi occupation of Norway, and the neutral role of Sweden during the conflict, equating the latter to the presumed objectivity of the HRI study. The inability of Dr. Ljungberg of the Home Research Institute to oversee the Norwegian project as planned results from what is described as "trouble on the Eastern front," in this case problems with the Finns which preoccupy him for the length of the study. The row of cars and trailers that crosses the Norwegian border without even stopping resembles a column of tanks slated to occupy the country, and the repeated infiltrations of Malmberg into the privacy of Isak's home, visits that become increasingly menacing, suggest the Nazi administrative structure that monitored not only the docility of the subjugated masses, but also the rigor with which soldiers, spies, and collaborators enforced martial law. Isak clearly resents Swedish neutrality during World War II and repeatedly alludes to outrages of the German occupiers, citing Grant's sojourn in a concentration camp and reminding Folke that "the Swedes don't understand.... You were neutral observers during the war too." Isak's complaint captures his resentment for the HRI study. He has learned through experience that neutrality does not leave the field of conflict unaffected, but offers aid and comfort to the aggressor. The Swedes had the responsibility to stand beside their Scandinavian neighbors in resisting Nazi occupation. Isak's refusal to cooperate with the study until Folke comes down from his perch and begins to interact with him constitutes an insistence upon a qualitative rather than a quantitative study, forcing Folke to acknowledge his humanity, to study him as an individual case rather than a type or demographic based upon gender, nationality, and marital status. Isak cannot perceive the so called impartial study as benign. The objective scientific scrutiny is too impersonal, resembling the inhumanity of Nazi social and physical sciences that segregated people according to race and ethnicity. The researchers may also be reminiscent of the spies and collaborators who infiltrated and betrayed the confidences of the subjugated people during the war.

Isak's initial mistrust of Folke's presence in his home forces his personal activities "underground." His interference with Folke's observations, such as hanging laundry between himself and the researcher, leaving and turning out the lights, and removing all of the desired activities to the privacy and safety of his upstairs bedroom, outside the ken of his watchful intruder, are reminiscent of the activities of Allied resistance movements during the war. From this perspective, the cooking, particularly in its removal to the upstairs bedroom, may constitute a metaphor for scheming and intrigue, the occulted machinations of repressed but undefeated people. Isak's decision to drill a hole in the floor of his bedroom where he can spy on Folke in his chair also suggests the resistance movement's practice of watching the watchers, and Folke's periodic reports of Isak's activities to his supervisor Malmberg constitute an analogue for the clandestine reports of Nazi spies to their handlers in the German administrative structure. Clearly, Isak is still fighting the war against occupation.

However, *Kitchen Stories* is not a narrative of undiminished hostility between the Norwegians and the neutral Swedes but a narrative of healing and understanding. When Folke begins to communicate with his host, Isak is immediately responsive. He teaches Folke that more can be gained by interacting with the subject than by remaining aloof. One of Folke's fellow researchers, Green, a cousin of Dr. Ljungberg and the first Swede to breach the discipline of the positivistic study, tries to convince Folke of the futility and arrogance of maintaining scientific objectivity by refusing to speak to the subject: "What are we doing, Folke? We sit up there on our pedestals and think that we can understand everything. How can we think we can understand anything about people simply by observing them.... We have to talk to each other. People have to communicate."

The next day, Isak confirms the assessment of the project by Green: "Green is right. How can we understand each other without communicating." It is certainly true that Folke never makes any headway in understanding Isak's lifestyle until he begins to interact with him. Indeed the only times that the researcher or the audience sees Isak consuming a meal in the kitchen is when Folke provides the food. He gives to Isak the sausages and pickled herring that made him (Folke) ill, and Isak consumes them at the kitchen table, and the birthday party for Isak that begins in Folke's trailer eventually spills into Isak's kitchen where the two proceed to get very drunk, Isak passing out in Folke's chair and Folke in Isak's bed, a fitting representation of empathy. The commiseration between these two men from differing backgrounds, who have been thrust together by circumstances and who have overcome mutual suspicions to become friends, creates a visual metaphor for the reunion of the Scandinavian neighbors drawn apart by the divisiveness of war and national loyalties. Folke's capitulation to the Norwegian point of view is total. In the conclusion of the film, he has taken up residence in Isak's house, living in a fashion reminiscent of his newly deceased companion, a lifestyle that his early assessments found inferior and even atavistic.

The visual imagery of the film persistently emphasizes the greater sophistication and technological superiority of the Swedes, implying a traditional contrast between the urban and the rural. The opening sequence of the film includes a documentary commentary on the projects and goals of the Home Research Institute, revealing a woman vacuuming in an ultramodern kitchen (for the 1950's), while her activities are being monitored by a row of attentive scientists. The emphasis on objectivity, modernity, and prosperity in the imagery of the Swedish Institute will later serve as a counterpoint to Isak's impoverished and poorly arranged kitchen. When the film suddenly burns up on a projector bulb, the imagery of the Institute's kitchen is revealed to be footage viewed in a rustic Norwegian community center by a projectionist and his audience of one. When Swedes arrive, they offer a live presentation of their research objectives. The contrast between the sophistication of the presentation replete with stage lighting and audiovisual technology and the rusticity of the audience is glaring. The presentation itself implies order and regimentation. The observers are lined up on the stage, sitting in their director chairs, dressed identically in business suits, and smugly condescending to their audience. The dazzling display of institutional uniformity, formality, wealth, and power emphasizes the comparative unpretentiousness as well as the material and intellectual dearth of the Norwegians in the film. Indeed, the presentation resembles pedagogy with a collection of professorial researchers armed with knowledge and power come to teach the country folk about modern living. Moreover, the modern conveniences, evidently standard among the Swedish visitors, particularly in terms of conveyances, are ostentatious in a region where makeshift vehicles provide the necessary transportation for the residents. Grant drives his tractor everywhere he goes, and Isak's only vehicle is a horse and buggy. The visual degradation of the Norwegians in comparison to the Swedes turns out to signify only a superficial assessment of the host nation, which proves itself to have more resilience and strength of character than anticipated, actually succeeding in educating and converting the researchers.

As indicated above, the eye of the observer is not at all objective. The mere presence of the surveilling subject constitutes a judgment against the host, implying a need for development. The watchful eye embodies power, and the subject of that gaze is altered and controlled by its presence. Foucault's theoretical resurrection of Jeremy Bentham's prison architecture — the Panopticon — serves as an analogue for the transmogrification of power since the Enlightenment. In the early modern age, power was an exhibition, focusing on the person of the monarch whose physical presence embodied both the mercy and the justice of the law, his extravagant punishments serving as deterrence against the breach of peace and order (*Discipline* 47–54). After the eighteenth century, power became disembodied, shifting its focus from the person of the monarch to the careful scrutiny of the mundane and formerly private details of the average citizen's activities, and by recording, codifying, and systematizing the private lives of the social subject, the examining institutions were able to bring the average citizen within the scope of power and economy exercised through the process of normalization that forces compliance with commonplace behavioral patterns. Thus the obedient social subject becomes self-monitoring, believing that he may at any time be the subject of the evaluative gaze (*Power* 155). Social conformity results from the fear of exposure, the fear that one's unconventionality may be obviated.

In *Discipline and Punish*, Foucault invokes Bentham's panopticon prison architecture to facilitate a discussion of the relationship between surveillance and correction. The panopticon includes a central guard tower surrounded by multiple levels of prison cells, each rendered visible to the watchers in the tower. The inmates believe that they are being observed twenty-four hours a day and that there is no place from which they can escape the surveillance. Thus, they are compelled to adopt a self-correcting demeanor, rendered docile by the belief that they are the subject of the punitive gaze. However, the guard tower need not be occupied at all times. Because the inmates are in effect rendered blind by the architectural structure, the activities in the tower remain mysterious. The prisoners cannot know whether they are being watched at any given moment, so they must assume they are and avoid those behaviors that may bring punitive action. Interestingly, the physical structure of the institution fosters self-reflection, meditation, and, presumably, criminal rehabilitation, thus the name "penitentiary." The activities within the panopticon are a metaphor for the conscience, the gaze turned inward to produce normative, docile, and predictable bodies. However, the ordering gaze can also be turned against the staff within the prison schemata or within an industrial facility. Thus some watchers are compelled to watch other watchers. The guards in the tower monitor not only the inmates but also the other guards with the result that the staff are more prone to discharge their duties with the requisite efficiency and diligence (*Discipline* 195–228). The panopticism of Hamer's film *Kitchen Stories* lies in the effort of Ljungberg's study to render visible the minutiae of daily routine within the households of Norwegian men. While the information gathered by the Swedish researchers may seem unbiased and innocuous, it will also be employed in the creation of a normalizing standard of kitchen behavior that eschews eccentricity and idiosyncrasy, producing social pressure that, in turn, generates conformity.

The film is crowded with observers who, in many cases, wish to avoid detection and whose subjects are equally eager to circumvent surveillance, and in each instance, the gaze involves an implied power over its subjects. The thematic embodiment of this element of the narrative is Dr. Jack Benjaminsen (Sverre Anker Ousdal), a physician repeatedly depicted examining Grant in his office. Each time they meet, the doctor reminds Grant that he would like to have Isak submit to a checkup; however, the recalcitrant farmer will not submit to the power of the medical institutions, implicitly refusing to be subjected to the objectifying scientific gaze even when it is a matter of his health, perhaps because he knows that any concession will involve an assessment and subsequent restructuring of his life. Dr. Benjaminsen may even constitute a recuperation of the positivistic methodology of the HRI staff, demonstrating that scientific analysis is advantageous even when the scientist and his subject have a social relationship. Isak's reticence in the HRI study can be attributed to his fear that the evaluative gaze will find him wanting and that, through the acquisition of knowledge about him, will attempt to alter or control his behavior.

The film dialogue reveals that very few Norwegian subjects were willing to submit to the study, implying either that they did not relish the inconvenience or that they felt the project might involve a negative assessment of their mundane kitchen routines. Grant refuses to allow an observer into his home although he does help to place one in Isak's, an action that he later comes to regret as Folke usurps the role he (Grant) formerly occupied in Isak's life. As the friendship deepens between Isak and Folke, Grant is, on several occasions, depicted clandestinely observing their interaction through a window, usually with an expression of longing, bewilderment, or jealousy. Grant's reticence is implicitly linked to the time that he spent in a concentration camp during the Nazi occupation of Norway, an experience that may have made him suspicious of institutional scrutiny or may have simply made him resentful toward the Swedes who refused to take a side in the conflict. His surveillance of Isak and Folke carries the implied threat that he might report their growing intimacy to Folke's supervisor, Malmberg, whose role is to deter any such breaches of scientific detachment. Grant is shown in the company of Malmberg on several occasions, but his jealousy finds an outlet in a more personal act of revenge. He leaves Folke's occupied trailer on the railroad tracks in the middle of the night.

Malmberg's periodic inspections of the project constitute another form of clandestine surveillance. He arrives unannounced at the residence on multiple occasions, and while at first his visits are coded as an alliance with Folke's frustrated research efforts, they become progressively more ominous as the supervisor becomes suspicious that Isak and Folke have breached the discipline of the study. On two occasions, he arrives to find Isak sleeping in Folke's chair, and upon inquiring into the whereabouts of his researcher, he finds that Isak is willing to vouch for the truant Swede, a confirmation of the improper friendship between the observer and his subject. However, it is the discovery of Isak's additions to Folke's notes that results in the guest researcher's termination. Malmberg's final visit becomes necessary when Folke refuses to contact him as instructed; thus the supervisor intrudes upon the friends' private conversation as they make Christmas plans. When Folke announces that he is not leaving, Malmberg reminds his colleague of the terms of his employment, ostensibly coercing the fellow Swede into abandoning his budding friendship by reminding him of his contractual obligation to return his trailer to Sweden. Within the structure of the panopticon, the power of the observer is exercised against prison staff as well as inmates, forcing a compliance with the rigorous demands of the workplace, compelling self-discipline. Malmberg's unanticipated visitations initially seem to facilitate the efforts of the researchers; however, increasingly, his institutional leverage is exercised against those who were formerly his allies. His appearance and demeanor are reminiscent of the intelligence apparatus of Nazi occupations, his dark coat and hat indicative of German spies and functionaries who monitored the subjugated populations as well as the occupiers.

Isak's initial efforts to avoid observation and analysis are catalogued above, but he also becomes an observer in his own right. Drilling a hole in the floor of his bedroom just above Folke's chair, he is able to turn the tables on his guest by watching him eat his lunch, an accomplishment which, up to that point, was more than Folke had achieved. His efforts to usurp Folke's role as examiner reveals not only a fundamental mistrust of scrutiny and perhaps a lingering hostility toward Swedes, but also a belief in the power implicit in inspection and information. The effort to observe while remaining unobservable implies a more effective (if perhaps slightly unethical) means of collecting objective data. HRI's study necessitates full visibility of the researcher, which allows the subject (if I may borrow a phrase from Eliot) "to create a face to meet the faces that ... [he] meet[s]," to perform his supposed authentic routines in the kitchen. The surreptitious observation affords the subject no such opportunity. Folke's visibility constitutes too ostentatious a display of mastery, one which empowers its own opposition through its accessibility. Isak can circumvent Folke's observations by refusing to cook in the kitchen and Folke's positivistic methodology (and perhaps good manners) precludes him from forcing Isak's compliance; nor would coerced data be an accurate display of Isak's authentic behaviors. In contrast, Folke cannot or will not avoid that scrutiny to which he does not know he is subject; instead, he will display his unaffected behaviors. As demonstrated by any resistance movement during a time of war, the clandestine observer can co-opt the strength of the visible power structure by remaining unavailable to surveillance and knowledge while the controlling institutions are vulnerable to constant attack because they must remain visible in order to demonstrate their dominance and to deter the same violence that their ostentatious exhibition incites. However, if the occupying powers were invisible, then the host country would not know it had been overrun and would in effect remain sovereign.

As the two men become progressively more intimate, Isak tries to turn his observations to the advantage of his Swedish guest. It is clear that Isak has been watching Folke's trailer, at first in retaliation for the unwanted surveillance by the Swede, but later out of concern. When Grant deposits the trailer on the railroad tracks in the middle of the night, Isak harnesses his horse to pull the apparatus back to the side of his house. After Folke becomes ill, Isak offers him a Norwegian folk remedy and records his own kitchen movements in Folke's official notes, attempting to fill in for the ailing researcher, but apparently leaves evidence that he was the observer on the particular occasions, evidence that Malmberg believes has jeopardized the scientific integrity of their work.

Malmberg himself is hyper-conscious of being monitored. The Norwegian study has been placed into his care by the otherwise occupied Dr. Ljungberg, and Malmberg's diligence in this delegated office reflects his own concerns that his performance will be assessed. When they are still confidantes, Malmberg complains to Folke that Green's fraternizing with his host has placed the entire study in jeopardy, and when Malmberg finds out that Folke has also transgressed restrictions of the study, he remarks, "Does he know what he is doing to me?," implying that he expects his own efforts to be scrutinized and condemned by his supervisor.

However, when the evidence of Folke's indiscretion reaches Dr. Ljungberg, it becomes all too obvious that — figuratively speaking — there is no one in the guard tower; the inmates and staff are entirely self-regulating. Folke's notes, the same that include Isak's observations of his guest, inspire mirth rather than indignation in the scientist. The messenger does not find the doctor, his lady, and his cousin, Green, hard at work evaluating the contents of the HRI study or combating ineptitude in Finland as speculated, but, instead, he finds them drunk, urinating outside of their private plane. In his cursory assessment of the data from Malmberg, the doctor reveals a greater willingness to examine the methodology of the study, offering the incriminating evidence to Green for the cousin's amusement and remarking, "These are Folke's notes. He's hit on something essential here. Folke has been observed." Ljungberg's comments are more than drunken indifference; they constitute a reassessment of the positivistic methodology at a fundamental level, of the ingredients in their recipe for the production of reliable data. If, as Heisenberg's theory predicts, the process of observing alters the behavior of the observed, then one ought to be able to determine what the original subject was doing prior to the advent of the speculative instrument by measuring the subject's reaction to the intrusion, and this second principle is Niels Bohr's Complementarity Theory, an answer to the problems Heisenberg exposed. Dr. Ljungberg, even while drunk, recognizes that the relationship between observer and observed is binary, the two roles affecting each other. Isak's reaction to the presence of Folke in his kitchen says much about his (Isak's) need for privacy in his personal life, simplicity in his kitchen appliances, and multifunctionality in his kitchen space. But most importantly, Isak does not need a new kitchen; he needs a new horse; his kitchen is sufficient for his lifestyle. Isak's reaction to the presence of the researcher in his home, more than anything, reveals his need for companionship, a finding that lies outside the scope of the Swedish study. Dr. Ljungberg's work is flawed because it assumes a transnational standard for the ideal kitchen even at the same time that it seems to acknowledge difference. He could not predict that the subjects would use their kitchens exclusively for baths, clothes lines, haircuts, and socializing. Folke's notes are valuable not insofar as they promote the objectives of the particular Norwegian study, but insofar as they test the value and reliability of the study itself.

Bent Hamer's *Kitchen Stories* constitutes a powerful and complex meta-cinematic metaphor, raising the issue of spectatorship and creating a trope for the problems inherent in the creation of a film. The placement of the HRI observers in director chairs may be the initial clue in deciphering the meta-cinematic motif. The problems that researchers face are similar to those faced by the film director. How does one capture an authentic moment on film when the player knows that s/he is being watched and evaluated? The director cannot remain aloof from the actors but must interact, offering advice and direction, not to mention a detailed script. But even in his greatest successes, the director has only managed to record acting, an inherently inauthentic product. The constant intrusions of Malmberg and by extension Ljungberg may signify the oft lamented intrusion of producers and studio executives into the creative process of the director and actors, and the priorities of HRI supervisors and film executives are similar, a desire to produce a marketable product that will appeal to as much of the populace as possible. Even the temporary residences of the researchers during the study are reminiscent of the movie set where many of the players reside in trailers while off-screen. The setting of the kitchen has a particular relevance to the metadramatic thematic. The kitchen is usually the part of the house where the residents conduct their most complicated rituals, and thus the documenting of kitchen activities may be taken as a metaphor for the need to record the details of daily life in order to create a seemingly authentic depiction of human activities. Moreover, outside of the bedroom, the kitchen is that part of the house in which the appetites of the residents are most apparent; thus the kitchen activities create a window on human desires.

The greatest collection of watchers associated with the film are of course the theater audience, whose presence is anticipated and accounted for long before they have access to the product. The anticipated theater audience embodies the financial considerations of the film. The writers, directors, producers, and actors must anticipate the reaction of audience to the final product and make their creative decisions accordingly. The HRI is attempting to record authentic human activities, to generate a product, to package it appropriately, and to sell it back to those people from whom it was derived. The same might be true of the film industry, which, theoretically, may be said to capture the lives of its potential audience in its cinematic depictions which it then strives to sell back to those who live them. The recalcitrance of the observers/directors in *Kitchen Stories*, their refusal to abide by the stipulations of their institutional supervisors, may offer an argument for the more limited appeal as well as the aesthetic virtues of the art film, a category of cinema into which Hamer's film would certainly fall. The decision to alter the conditions under which the study of Isak's kitchen habits are conducted, to create a study that reflects upon its own methodology and acknowledges that an observer impacts the observed, runs parallel to the filmmaker's decision to create a self-reflective or thought-provoking movie in spite of the fact that, in the entertainment industry, self-reflective art is generally coded as too sophisticated for a mass audience. The discovery that Isak does not conform to the standard habits in the kitchen is a testimony to the prevalence of unique or even eccentric tastes and appetites, the same that deserve consideration in an authentic study of human activities. The art film is more preoccupied with character development than action and that character development is frequently focused on eccentricities that make the individual interesting. *Kitchen Stories* is an argument for its own necessity, for the need to offer art whose worth is not calculated exclusively in monetary terms. Thus the film records the process of its own legitimation. The Isaks in the audience deserve to have their uniqueness celebrated. After all, the meaningful data may actually lie in the exception, rather than the rule.

10

Filming and Eating Italian: *Big Night* and *Dinner Rush*

Few, if any, American ethnic groups are as consistently identified with the food they consume as are Italians (Coyle 43). Witness the predominant place that Italian food plays in each episode of HBO's *The Sopranos*, the mob boss returning home each evening to engage in a gustatory (re)affirmation of an ethnic identity that is all day under scrutiny and assault by the forces of conformity and integration — the federal authorities. Moreover, Tony Soprano's portly stature, probably resulting from an intemperate indulgence in notoriously fattening Italian cuisine, literalizes the voracious longing that drives his pursuit of power and wealth. Indeed his greedy consumption of Italian food at the conclusion of many episodes becomes a multifaceted signifier for the ethno-political content of the show. Carmella Soprano's persistent production of Italian food suggests her subordination within traditional, old world, gender hierarchies. Even when she refuses to cook for her husband, she offers him Italian food from the freezer or refrigerator. When the family eats out, their destination is invariably Vesuvio's, a location where they will find an authentic Italian cuisine as well as a management sympathetic toward their lifestyles, where the chef not only serves the food that confirms ancestry, but also demonstrates appropriate deference to the powerful crime boss, acknowledging the values that, right or wrong, have been appended to Italian cuisine. Soprano's voracious consumption of Italian food may also suggest the damage that he perpetrates — both as a fictional character and as an actor in yet another Italian mafia narrative — by defaming his own ethnic heritage. He literally eats his own culture.

Peculiar culinary indulgences are often the final remains of a culture that has been thoroughly integrated into a more powerful, more diverse, or more contemporary social system. The members of a particular ethnicity retain their taste for specific foods and spices long after they have discarded other manifestations of cultural difference such as dress and language. The unique national or regional recipes and tastes of a people remain the most prominent declaration of a distinctive heritage within multi-cultural society, putting culture on display by permitting diverse populations to sample a legacy that is temporally, geographically, or genetically remote. However, it is naive to assume that the culinary productions of an integrated ethnic consciousness are unadulterated by the host nation's values and appetites. For example, when visiting Mexico, one might look in vain for food that resembles American Mexican cuisine, unless, of course, one visits border towns or tourist centers. I recall my own abortive attempts to find chips and salsa in central Mexico. Chips were easy enough to find as was salsa, but it was very difficult to find them being served together. Similarly, many authentic Italian dishes would be unrecognizable to the same Americans who claim to love Italian food or who may even be of Italian extraction. The transmogrification of ethnic foods into a commodity suitable for an American market necessitates the alteration of both the cuisine and the conditions under which it is prepared and served. The American market is driven by pragmatic considerations that influence both the quantity and the composition of the food.

Two recent films— Stanley Tucci and Campbell Scott's *Big Night* (1995) and Bob Giraldi's *Dinner Rush* (2001)—create a similar conceptual parallel between the progressive integration of ethnic Italians into the American mainstream and the evolution of their native cuisine. While each narrative addresses the adaptation of inner city restaurateurs to social change, the former documents the struggles of recent immigrants who refuse to compromise their indigenous culinary practices in order to accommodate the American appetite, a commitment that threatens to bankrupt them. The latter depicts the transition — both culinary and social —from ethnic Italian-American to the trendy and the mainstream. Each film captures conflicting cultural priorities in the relative dispositions of opposing family members. *Big Night*'s fraternal squabbling conveys incongruent views of the compromises requisite to success in the competitive American market. *Dinner Rush* focuses on an inter-generational conflict between father and son who embody alternative views on restaurant management and the progressive transformation of Italian cuisine. Taken together, the two films are virtually companion pieces documenting transformations in Italian food and culture in the second half of the twentieth century.

Big Night

Tucci and Tropiano's *Big Night* details the efforts of recent immigrants, Primo and Secondo, who struggle to make a success of their restaurant, while simultaneously maintaining the integrity of their native cuisine, and they maintain their commitment to authenticity even when it becomes evident that their dishes are not appealing to their clientele. The brothers are divided in their dispositions toward the future of their restaurant, and the clash of their personalities is central to the narrative (Iammarino 185). Primo—the gustatory artist who refuses to compromise his work in order to appeal to the philistine tastes of Americans who want quantity rather than quality in their food and who believe that restaurateurs should pander to the clientele's lowly appetites—is willing to allow his business to sink into insolvency rather than make even minor pragmatic concessions to Mammon. Primo's answer to the brother's financial problems is to return to Italy where they can serve patrons who understand and appreciate authentic Italian cuisine. Primo cannot be drawn out of his "palace of art" long enough to consider the practical concerns of running a business in an unfamiliar environment where the clientele are ignorant of or indifferent to his cultural traditions. He verbally abuses an unsatisfied customer who complains of the lengthy period of time that her order has taken and who, upon receiving her risotto, requests an order of spaghetti to supplement the small portion she has already received. The customer is further aggravated when she discovers that she cannot get meatballs with her pasta, but must order those separately as well. The inclusion of two starches in a single meal enrages the temperamental chef. When Secondo demands that Primo fill the woman's order, the latter calls her a "criminal" and a "philistine" and hurls a pot at the kitchen door.

Primo's artistic integrity includes a repudiation of American pragmatism and commercialism. He is the immigrant who refuses to melt into the pot, who refuses to conform to the business axiom that "the customer is always right." When his brother Secondo suggests that they remove risotto from the menu because it is both too expensive and too time consuming in preparation, Primo facetiously agrees and suggests that they replace it with hotdogs. Secondo reveals that the chef nightly rages against his customers' offensive gustatory instincts. So incapable of considering the financial ramifications of his intransigence, Primo is willing to feed for free those who he believes understand his artistry. His barber Alberto receives free food from the restaurant because he calls the chef "maestro" and listens to his complaints about the vulgar clientele of Primo's restaurant. Primo also feeds a local artist in exchange for the paintings which hang in The Paradise. The gesture includes a recognition of a kindred spirit who suffers poverty for the opportunity to create, for the integrity of his art. When the brothers plan a feast in a last ditch effort to gain some publicity to save their business, Primo is gracious and well behaved because the invitational gathering fills his restaurant, not with paying customers, but with people who have the erudition requisite to the appreciation of authentic Italian cuisine. Moreover, the fact that the diners are not paying for their meal eliminates any pretenses upon which the diners could demand dishes that are not on the set menu. The film suggests that the environment most conducive to the exchange and appreciation of genuine art is one in which money is not central. Money is corruptive of art.

Primo is hostile toward the Americanized Italian restaurant across the street because he reviles the compromises the proprietor, Pascal, has made in order to achieve financial or business success. Pascal gives his customers what they want — meatballs and large portions of pasta. He mass produces food. The brothers remark that every dish at Pascal's looks as if it were from a can, while all of Primo's dishes are made upon order. Pascal has learned one of the principal laws of American economics, that business must capitulate to public taste even if that taste is repugnant; that fine art must negotiate with popular culture in order to create a space and opportunity for an art form that retains at least some elevated attributes. Primo calls the fare served at Pascal's a "rape of cusine" and would consign the proprietor to "prison for the food he serves." The rape analogue seems appropriate

Secondo (Stanley Tucci) quarrels with his girlfriend Phyllis (Minnie Driver) as she helps to prepare the lavish feast calculated to save The Paradise restaurant in Tucci and Campbell Scott's *Big Night* (1996).

Bottom: Primo (Tony Shalhoub) and Secondo (Stanley Tucci), recent immigrants and proprietors of the failing Paradise restaurant, share a meal before work in Campbell Scott and Tucci's *Big Night* (1996).

because Pascal does not kill the cuisine; he merely pollutes or corrupts it. The interaction between these two proprietors demonstrates the "incompatibility between art and business" (Coyle 49).

Big Night repeatedly equates the preparation, consumption, and appreciation of Italian food to religious idealism. Primo proclaims that "to eat good food is to be close to God" and "The knowledge of God is the bread of angels." This idea is developed more thoroughly in the ecstatic responses to the feast that he prepares. "Ecstasy" is a devotional experience that involves the transportation of the faithful's soul from the limitations of the physical body to a communion with the infinite, with God. Generally the experience has a noetic quality in which a divine message is translated into human understanding. The participants in Primo and Secondo's feast are forced to wait for their ecstatic release until they can scarcely abide their hunger. When the participants finally prepare to dine they are ravenous; nevertheless, they approach the table in a reverent or even ritualistic fashion, and the feast begins slowly, each testing the first course and registering visual signs of intense pleasure. The anticipation of each new dish heightens the pitch of the feast, hilarity and delight growing upon the group almost imperceptibly at first until the gathering begins to greet each new

Bob (Campbell Scott) and Gabrielle (Isabella Rosellini) chat while they wait for jazz artist Louis Prima to arrive and for the dinner to begin in Scott and Stanley Tucci's *Big Night* (1996).

course with shouts of pleasure. The previous sobriety, awkwardness, and inhibition among the group dissolve as they dance to *Mambo Italiano* and burst into the kitchen to congratulate the chef. The final entree, Il Timpano, signals the ecstatic height of the feast because the dish embodies both heart and mind. Ostensibly, the dish named after a kettledrum refers to the shape of the pot in which it is prepared. However, the drum also suggests a crescendo or climax within the orchestrated feast. The pounding of the timpani often signals a moment of peak drama or the grand introduction of a new movement within a musical composition and so within the gustatory symphony of the film. The aptly named dish may also suggest the overwrought hearts of the participants who can scarcely believe that there is still more food, that the main course is yet to be served. The implicit pounding of the heart signifies the passions—both erotic and spiritual—that the feast has provoked. Finally, the visual image of the Timpano suggests the human brain in both shape and texture, and the idea that the dish includes many surprises in its interior, containing all the best things in the world, further reinforces its role as a representation of the mysterious and illimitable content of the human brain. When the brothers cut the

Timpano for their guests, their actions dramatize the impact their food has had on the diners, exposing emotions and desires, making Gabriella an honest woman by moving her to reveal that Louis Prima was never really invited to the party, exposing Pascal as a manipulative and heartless businessman bent on the destruction rather than the salvation of The Paradise, revealing the disappointments of a female diner who cries because her mother was such a poor cook, and forcing a confrontation between Primo and Secondo regarding their financial mistakes and their conflicting plans for the future. In this sense, the ecstatic feast is indeed revelatory, transporting the characters into a greater understanding of themselves and those around them.

The religious thematic is further allegorized in the names, actions, and locations of the narrative, invoking the mythology of the "American Adam" and "the new world garden." Like so many immigrants before them, the brothers came to America believing that they would discover a "paradise" of opportunities, where their culinary genius would be appreciated and rewarded. They named their restaurant in accordance with this expectation. However, they soon discovered that the new world was a post-lapsarian garden where vulgarity and commercialism had long ago stolen America's innocence. In this context, their restaurant was indeed a culinary paradise; they had thus far refused to compromise their values and virtues in order to create a product that appealed to a mass market. Their Paradise is a strictly regulated environment in which great pleasure is accessible but only on the proprietors' terms. The customer must submit to the will of the chef and the chef to history. Enjoyment at The Paradise requires a capitulation to influences larger than the individual will — the power of tradition. Here adherence to recipe as well as the rigid compliance with dietary traditions allows chef and diners pre-lapsarian access to the divine. However, ecstacy is incompatible with economics, and paradise cannot exist in a fallen world.

The Paradise's more successful rival restaurant is equated to hell, the calm of the former disturbed by the racket and traffic of Pascal's. The soft lighting and tasteful decor of Paradise is replaced by the deep red tones, dark interiors, live music, clamorous crowds, and heaps of pasta with meatballs at the competitor's establishment. The infernal imagery of Pascal's is visually reinforced by the brief and inexplicable scene in which the proprietor seems to deliberately set fire to one of his chefs, the same proprietor who has offered to invite jazz singer Louis Prima to support Secondo's final effort to gain publicity for his restaurant. Pascal is the devil who has stolen into The Paradise to destroy the tiny enclave yet unpolluted by American commercialism and consumerism, a sanctum of culinary virtue and artistic

Secondo (Stanely Tucci) confronts Pascal (Ian Holm) when he discovers that the rival restaurateur has willfully sought to ruin The Paradise in order to get the brothers to work for him in Scott and Tucci's *Big Night* (1996).

integrity. While the brothers have longed to emulate their rival's financial success, Pascal has coveted Primo's culinary genius, hoping to lure the uncompromising chef into his chaotic gustatory empire. Like Milton's Satan in the pre-lapsarian garden, Pascal is lured by the beauty and virtue of the denizens of Paradise, not because he wishes to celebrate or sustain their goodness, but because he wishes to destroy it out of envy and competitiveness. Perhaps he perceives the addition of Primo to his staff as an incremental step in his program for business success: "Give people what they want and then later you can give them what you want." Ostensibly, this advice encourages Secondo to make concessions to popular taste in order to achieve success as a restaurateur. However, once the Pascal's devious plan to ruin The Paradise has been successfully executed the advice to Secondo obtains a more insidious meaning. He only pretended to give the brothers what they want (support for their struggling establishment) so that he could bring them under his power. Secondo confronts Pascal about the deception, assuring him that his ruse will never bear fruit: "You will never have my brother... He is real; you are nothing."

In the confrontation between two proprietors, Pascal is interrupted while nonchalantly playing the piano like a vaudeville devil, unrepentant for his villainy and undisturbed by Secondo's rage. Pascal reveals that he destroyed The Paradise "out of respect" and that duplicity is requisite to success in business: "I am a businessman. I am anything I need at be at any time." The successful American businessman cannot afford to share Primo's integrity. Like Milton's hell, the American market is an inverted hierarchy of value, where the worst receives the greatest reward and the best is reviled (*PL*, Book I, 159–160, 254–255). This insight explains Pascal's outburst when sampling Primo's cooking: "This is so fucking good I should kill you." Pascal recognizes that goodness and integrity cannot exist within the postlapsarian world of the American consumer market, and his destruction of The Paradise is calculated to limit the suffering of the virtuous and simultaneously reinforce his own ascendancy as the premier restaurateur. Secondo's final imputation against Pascal ("He is real; you are nothing") tries to reassert a traditional standard of good and ill. Regardless of his lack of financial success, Primo has a connection to an ethnic tradition larger than himself, an identity derived from centuries of culinary and cultural evolution, while Pascal has kicked himself loose of history, a culinary apostate without connection to any respectable standard of taste or artistry, aligned only with the dollar. In short, Pascal's desertion of his cultural heritage has left him without any identity, only a series of masks to distract and beguile those who cling to his empire, and, hence, he is "nothing."

Secondo's repudiation of Pascal does not come easily because he shares the latter's desire for financial success. However, he discovers that his own apotheosis would require the sacrifice of his brother's dream, and he cannot offer so much. When the brothers discover that they have been duped by Pascal, they blame each other for the failure of their business. Secondo explains, "I needed you to sacrifice," and Primo returns "If I sacrifice my work, it dies; it is better if I die." The syntax of Secondo's revelation is equivocal. It could mean either that he needed Primo to make a sacrifice or that he needed to sacrifice Primo, and the brother's rebuttal acknowledges both meanings of the statement, equating the death of his art to his own death. Here the brothers begin to resemble the unhappy pair in the garden, who following their degradation (at least according to Milton) fall to recriminations, Adam blaming his wife for their mutual ruin and their expulsion from paradise (*PL*, Book IX, 1114–1199). Like Secondo, Eve was willing to compromise with the devil to repudiate traditional authority in order to advance her state. Yet, the unsettling gender dysphoria created by the application of the biblical myth makes another archetype a more probable analogue for the film script. Cain and Abel accurately predict the fraternal bond of Primo and Secondo and encompass the sacrificial motif in the film dialogue. If the order of birth is any indication, Primo would suggest Cain and Secondo, Abel, yet their respective virtues remain incongruous with the scriptural analogy. The discrepancy is, nevertheless, resolved by the American context of the action. Extending the correspondence further, the temperamental god of the allegory is the American consumer market which is consistently denigrated in the film. Indeed as discussed above, the market constitutes an inverted hierarchy of good and bad. Thus it is Secondo/Abel's efforts to appease a finicky god that are the most efficacious, even as they are undermined by Primo/Cain's integrity. The success of Pascal's reveals that appeasing the temperamental god of American consumerism requires an alliance with the film's devil figure. America is hungry and requires the sacrifice of one's indigenous cultural identity. Pascal has already made that sacrifice and been rewarded with power and material wealth.

The name Pascal may allude to the Paschal Lamb of the first Passover, which celebrates the Jews' liberation from bondage in Egypt. Thus in the shifting significations of the film, the sacrifice that Pascal has made of his authentic national cuisine signals the bondage of Italian culture within the boundaries of North America. Pascal's restaurant was passed over by the capricious market forces that destroy so many businesses. Primo is the first born who is destroyed by his failure to sacrifice to the vengeful and capricious god of consumer economics; thus he longs to return to his nation of origin. Secondo, more susceptible to the allure of American success, will not return to Italy despite the failure of his business efforts.

Big Night exposes the shortcomings of the American Dream. The placement of the brothers' restaurant on the Jersey shore suggests their tenuous grip on the continent. They could return to Europe or, figuratively, be swept out to sea at any time. While Secondo's behavior suggests that he shares the dream of many immigrants and that he intends to remain in America regardless of his restaurant's fate, he learned too late or was unable to convince his brother that American success comes on American terms. Here an immigrant has the opportunity to dream and to strive, but success rarely comes without soul killing capitulations to the mass tastes.

Dinner Rush

Bob Giraldi's *Dinner Rush* continues many of the ideas broached in *Big Night*, but finally suggests that artistic integrity in food preparation can be progressive and need not be fettered to historical/cultural traditions. Gigino's has undergone a transformation from a family owned business serving Italian American cuisine to a trendy Manhattan eatery producing dishes that resemble avant garde art. The owner of the establishment is not happy with the food that Chef Udo Cropa, his son, serves because it no longer resembles the Italian cuisine prepared by Udo's mother, the restaurant's original cook. However, as a businessman, Louis has to acknowledge that his son's cooking has made Gigino's extraordinarily successful of late, packing in diners every night. *Dinner Rush* eulogizes the passing of an era in the Italian American experience. The dominance of the quasi-ethnic Italian restaurant is challenged by the trend toward more multicultural tastes. The incremental integration of ethnic Italians into a pluralized culture has made some significant strides, yet the relationship between the ethnic Italian and the progressive urban cultures is mutually influential/beneficial, a process that can be observed in the film's mob narrative in which the legitimate and illegitimate businessmen become increasingly indistinguishable.

As with *Big Night*, the action of *Dinner Rush* occupies a brief span of time — in this case a single pivotal evening in the life and operations of a restaurant — and documents the terminal moment in the establishment's ownership/management when it moves from a front for an illegal bookmaking operation to a completely law-abiding business. All evening while chef Udo and his staff are attempting to solve the emergent problems of an extremely successful and over-booked restaurant, the proprietor Louis is attempting to resolve a few problems of his own. In a manner of speaking, his gambling operation is also "over-booked" in so far as it is attracting some unwanted attention from people who are making it difficult to function — Black and Blue, two violent mafia upstarts from Brooklyn who murdered the proprietor's partner and are attempting to muscle their way into both the legal and the illegal operations of the restaurant. While Udo and his personnel are cooking up special dishes for their patrons, Louis and his covert staff are preparing a dish for a different type of "patron" — "a dish best served cold." The narrative of the film, which at first seems merely documentary, hinges upon the gradual revelation of Louis' obscure designs, demonstrating that he is every bit the craftsman that his son has become, simultaneously orchestrating a variety of activities with far more composure than his genius son displays.

The center of the film is the godfather's table where Louis greets, counsels, and bestows favors upon customers and staff alike. He shares the table with a colleague who turns out to be the lawyer and confidant who has drawn up the papers to transfer ownership of Luigi's from father to son, a fact that the father keeps concealed from his demanding progeny who is forced to beg for more control of the restaurant. In a manner of speaking, the godfather has two sons — one biological, Udo, and the other spiritual, Duncan. These two young men suggest the polarities between which Louis is pulled, the two potential futures for the restaurant. Udo, who attended an expensive culinary arts school in order to become one of the hottest chefs in Manhattan, has refused to emulate his father's professional choices by following him into the illegal bookmaking business. His professional efforts suggest a new start for the restaurant and the family, a future unfettered by mob affiliations. Duncan, on the other hand, is "a pathological gambler" who inadvertently drew the attention of the more hardened gangsters, Black and Blue—first to Louis' bookmaking operation and, subsequently, to his restaurant, an interest that resulted in the murder of Louis' partner, Enrico. Duncan works to ingratiate himself with Louis by cooking Italian dishes for the owner, dishes that Udo refuses to prepare in his gourmet establishment. While Louis cannot approve of Duncan's compulsive behavior, he understands the youth more than he does his own son. Duncan has chosen a path in life similar to his own, and Louis' efforts to divest himself from his illegal business include a simultaneous effort to liberate Duncan from both his debt to Black and Blue and his obsession with gambling. While there is never any indication that Louis considers leaving the restaurant to Duncan, there is a possibility that if he can resolve the evening's professional dilemma, he will be able to maintain the status quo for the present. It is only after he realizes the demanding mobsters are not going to accept his reasonable offer of the gambling operations, an agreement that would respect the independence of the legitimate business, that Louis elects to divest himself of any significant participation in the daily operations of his business.

Udo and Duncan work well together in the kitchen when they are cooking side by side, but Duncan also embodies that part of the restaurant over which Udo does not yet exercise control, the same part that the son pleads with the father to relinquish. Udo and Duncan have opposing work ethics. While the attentions of the former are unremittingly fixed on the efficient operations and quality productions of the restaurant, Duncan's concentration is divided between cooking, wagering, smoking, and making love to his girlfriend. While both Louis and Duncan seem relatively comfortable, juggling both legal and illicit activities during the dinner rush, Udo longs to chase away all residual manifestations of the restaurant's mafia connections, indeed all activities that do not positively contribute to the increased efficiency of the legitimate operations. Udo fires a novice chef for cutting with a dull knife, complains of Duncan's divided attentions, and demands that his father tell the gangsters on the balcony to "get lost." While Udo's professional efforts are calculated to emphasize the legitimate side of the business, he has more in common with gangsters than he may be willing to admit. Udo rules the restaurant with rigor and remorselessness, a behavior that Duncan describes as Udo's "little power trip." Indeed, his demeanor in his business dealings is more harsh than that of dangerous mobsters, at least until the guns start flaring. The mobsters are polite, but firm with each other. Udo shouts at and reprimands his employees in front of their co-workers and complains constantly of their performance. However, Udo does drop his severe tone when he greets the customers, with whom he is both gracious and solicitous. He greets tables of artists and critics, the former perhaps because he relates his own work to their creative endeavors and the latter because the success of his establishment hinges upon positive publicity. Udo has literally slept with the critic Jennifer Freely (Sandra Bernhard) in order to promote his professional activities.

There is even a spatial allegory of the parallels between the father and son's respective business practices, a spatializing that puns upon the word "underground." Moreover, there seems to be a class structure that is spatially constituted within the establishment. Udo keeps all of his worst behavior "underground," treating harshly the cooks in his basement kitchen where he verbally reprimands and dismisses employees at will. He reserves his respectful and respectable facade for the dining rooms where he treats his labor more graciously, working with them as peers, perhaps even respecting their judgment. Similarly, his father maintains a demeanor of respectability when he is seated at his table or interacting with the customers in his dining room. He is ostensibly polite with Black and Blue while they dine in his restaurant. When they demand that he relinquish a percentage of his restaurant profits, he generously offers them his bookmaking operation. However, when he finds them intransigent in their demands, he has them executed in his basement toilet, thus continuing the spatial imperative that all of the dirty work, all of the activities unsuitable for public scrutiny, be executed "underground." The film thus suggests that both the gambling and restaurant operations have their occulted activities.

There is also a spatial hierarchy in the dining room, one that suggests the ascendancy of particular influences over others. Both father and son entertain demanding guests who require special handling. When Black and Blue arrive without a reservation, their ominous demeanor and their solicitation of the owner are sufficient to place them immediately at one of the enviable balcony tables. From their lofty perch, they are able to scrutinize the operation that they hope to wrench from the control of the rightful owner. They dine for free and are treated with deference by both the servers and the owner. When Udo's unexpected guest, the food critic Jennifer Freely, arrives, she is unable to get a table on the balcony in spite of her complaint to Udo, who promises to get her one of the better tables as soon as something opens up. Despite her important role in the restaurant's recent success, she has to wait a long time for her food, but she is, nevertheless, able to order dishes that are not on the menu and to have her food prepared by the master chef himself. Just as the arrival of the mobsters sets the hidden machinations of Louis' illicit organization in motion, the surprise entry of the food critic inspires Udo to tighten his grip on his own hidden empire; the cook staff are instructed not to allow any imperfect dish to leave the kitchen. Udo's promise to move Jenn to the balcony as soon as something opens up turns out to be a figurative rather than a literal pledge. Her ascension will take place as soon as the restaurant's mob connections can be broken in order to allow for the inclusion of contributory or beneficial influences. At the conclusion of the film when the bodies of mobsters have been removed from the basement and the customers have all vacated, it is Jenn who remains alone with Udo in the dining room.

For a time, the mobsters in the balcony create a rival to the owner's table. Just as Udo complains that he has to visit the "godfather's table" to beg for the materials he needs to operate the restaurant, Louis is required to ascend to the balcony to answer the demands of his unwelcome guests, and the mobsters are every bit as intransigent as is the father solicited by the son. The owner is pulled between contrary influences, a structure reminiscent of the medieval *psychomachia*, an internal struggle between the vice and virtue. Even as the son insists that the father assign him full control and ownership of the restaurant, Black and Blue demand that they be given a substantial interest in its profits. Louis must decide which of the antithetical influences — licit or illicit — that he is going to honor. The dilemma also suggests the duality of Louis' identity, one embodied in the discrepancy between his Italian and American names, between his name as represented in its diminutive form in the title of the restaurant — Gigino's for Luigi — and the Americanized version that he responds to when invoked — Louis. By the end of the film, Louis has literally divested himself of his specific Italian identity. He has handed over his namesake, the restaurant, to his son, he has broken his connection to the syndicate. He reminds his dinner companion Gary, "We're out of the bookmaking business; for now on, I am just a legitimate restaurateur."

Louis' progeny, Udo, is a completely integrated personality who has no interest in exploiting his Italian heritage for business success, although he does demonstrate his cognizance of it when he explains the restaurant's name to Jennifer Freely's companion. His menu and his staff are a picture of Manhattan's diversity. He refuses to prepare traditional Italian dishes; he neglects to pay tribute to the mob hierarchy represented in his father's initial solicitation of Black and Blue; he retains few or no Italians in his kitchen or his wait staff; and he caters to a diverse crowd of upwardly mobile urbanites rather than ethnic Italians looking for a taste of home. When

Louis informs Udo that he is signing the restaurant over to him, he also expresses his pride in the young man's decision not to follow his father into the illegal bookmaking business. However, the father does not accept the passing of his lifestyle with as much relish as his protestations suggests. In conversation with his son earlier in the film, he becomes nostalgic:

> Louis: You know sometimes I would like to take this place back to the way it was when your mother ran it, but we can't; can we?
> Udo: Why do you always have to live in the past?
> Louis: No past, no money for school, no famous chef.
> Udo: No gangsters on the balcony.
> Louis: ... Those guys think they are entrepreneurs.
> Udo: Tell 'em to get lost.

Udo's imperative to his father reveals his repudiation of traditional ethnic connections, and the father's actions during the evening assist his son in his campaign to rid the establishment of any residual illicit influences. Louis' transition to legitimate businessman is signified by several deaths, the first being his partner who is murdered by Black and Blue in the opening minutes of the film. The other deaths are those of the same mobsters who killed his friend and tried to muscle a piece of his restaurant. The murder of Black and Blue coincides with Louis' well-timed and very public withdrawal from the restaurant. He signs the restaurant over to his son, reforms the wayward Duncan, pays tribute to the police officer seated in the main dining room, and makes a very public departure from the premises just before the shots are fired in the basement lavatory. Louis has been cooking up a special of his own while seemingly sitting idle at the owner's table — his well crafted exit has ensured that the restaurant is free of any mob liabilities and has made a New York City Police detective witness to his early departure and consequent innocence.

When Louis reveals that he will retain a small percentage of the restaurant after he transfers ownership, he highlights one of the recurring thematics in the film — the progressive similarity between legitimate and illicit business practices. The father's decision to retain a portion of Luigi's profit is certainly reasonable, but it is thematically similar to Black and Blue's effort to squeeze a share of the restaurant out of the owner. The film offers the cynical or even comic observation that Manhattan is so rough the traditional gangsters lack the subtlety, sophistication, and savvy to compete. The dissimulation of Manhattanites is too much for the heavy-handed extortions of traditional mobsters. The hitman Ken Roloff (John Corbett) observes, "When did eating dinner become a Broadway show?" Ostensibly, his comment refers to the pretensions of the diners as well as the difficulty and expense of getting a table, but it may also allude to the idea that patrons and staff alike are playing roles. Many of the people in the restaurant have adopted alternative identities: the mobsters are becoming entrepreneurs; the bookie is becoming a legitimate restaurateur; the waitress is an artist; and the Wall Street broker is a hitman. The destruction of Black and Blue results because they are the worst actors; they cannot play the role of entrepreneurs convincingly. While they believed that they were determining the action within the restaurant, in reality Louis was directing his subterfuge to its bloody conclusion, and the mobsters never recognize the hitman because he only plays a murderer in his night job. His demeanor as a nice guy is in many ways authentic; thus Black and Blue do not know to guard against him.

Perhaps the most interesting manifestation of the discrepancy between appearances and reality and the union of licit and illicit business activities is realized in the description of Udo's restaurant subsequent to the double murder. Jenn reminds him that in New York the publicity from a mob hit will guarantee that his establishment is booked solid for a year. Ironically, even as Luigi's divests itself of mob related activities, it gains a lucrative reputation for gangster violence. When the restaurant actually was a front for an illegal bookmaking operation, the mob associations were unwelcome, something to be hidden from public view, but the appearance of mob affiliations appeals to the pretensions of the jaded, thrill-seeking, and voyeuristic Manhattan patrons. In brief, Manhattanites no longer fear the mob culture that has shaped the public image of Italians, particularly Sicilians, throughout the twentieth century. It has become an entertainment as witnessed in the many mob narrative in popular culture. Enrico's grief-stricken daughter offers a eulogy on the passage of an era: "The problem with your world, no one gives a shit about it anymore. Welcome to the new world." Her insight is paradoxical, however, because it seems to suggest that no one is interested in the mob anymore, but this is not the case as Jennifer points out at the conclusion of the film when she lauds the murders as great publicity. "No one gives a shit" about that world in the sense that they are no longer intimidated by it; they are no longer willing to capitulate to its extortions. The mobsters lament the decline of their influence and appeal to Louis' shared values: "I don't go in so much for the *nouveau cuisine*. Rumor has it you don't either."

Both *Big Night* and *Dinner Rush* narrate pivotal trends in the Italian-American culture. Both equate the preparation of food to art and business, the consumption of food to sex, and the appreciation of food and its dining rituals to cultural heritage. While *Big Night* illustrates an abortive genesis of authentic Italian cuisine in America, resulting from the businessman's reticence to compromise with local tastes, *Dinner Rush* is elegiac in its lament for the passing of the ghettoized Italian American identity and its attendant flavors. However, unlike Primo, Louis and Udo are businessmen willing to keep pace with culinary trends in order to maintain a successful enterprise. While Louis' son, like Primo, is the uncompromising genius, fortunately Udo's work has found an appreciative audience in the cosmopolitan environment of Manhattan, riding a trend toward a more international cuisine.

11

A Chef in Love:
The Fable of a Communist
and Culinary Re-Evolution

Long before the breakup of the Soviet Union in the last decade of the twentieth century, the failure of the great social experiment had become glaringly apparent. The great Mammon of western culture had bankrupted the communist bloc by forcing it to compete with unprecedented military spending, and the Delilah of bounteous food and cheap consumer goods proved too much for the Soviet people after decades of privation. The mythology of the Soviet revolution promised a utopian transformation in the structure of society, a paradise for the worker in which the rewards of labor would be distributed with equity among the populace, an entire nation laboring for the advancement of a common wealth, the mass of riches and influence no longer situated among a small group of cultured elite. The socialist revolution was to be a re-evolution for humanity, a new beginning in which the paradigms of social interaction could be re-invented. However, in order to create a rupture in the social organization that had prevailed throughout the industrial revolution, the Soviet Union needed to withdraw from the family of European nations, to break the influence of western traditions that emphasize self-reliance, materialism, and sumptuousness. Yet in the chaotic formative years of the re-evolution, the designers must have faced a daunting task, attempting to wipe away centuries of western tastes and traditions. What was to be done with the remnants—physical, intellectual, and spiritual—of the residual culture? How could the revolution sweep away the collective memory of sumptuous living, and how could the monolithic Soviet influence erase the cultural traditions of subjugated ethnicities?

Many of the above questions are addressed in Nana Djordjadze's *A Chef in Love* (1996), a film that allegorizes the clash of cultures that attended the Soviet revolution in the province of Georgia. The narrative details the escapades of a French chef, Pascal Ichac, who, searching for new tastes and new dishes, comes to the Russian province of Georgia and falls in love not only with Princess Cecilia Abachidze, but also with the land, its people, and its cultural traditions. The French chef suggests the cultural influences of high western traditions on the Eastern province, the same that the Soviet system will attempt to sweep away in favor of authentically and exclusively nationalistic tastes. The pre–Soviet Georgians' love for the chef and his food is indicative of their affection for Western Europe. However, this fascination with French high culture is localized within the privileged classes of Georgian society, allegorized most plainly in Princess Cecilia's affair with Pascal and her refusal to abandon him even after her forced marriage to a communist revolutionary. The film documents the central role that Pascal played within Georgian society in the brief period before the revolution and his progressive marginalization afterward. The film constitutes a eulogy for the Soviet system, so Pascal's continued residence on the roof of his former restaurant at the conclusion of the film suggests the inability to wipe away the cultural influences of the Western bourgeoisie as well as its availability to resume its place at the center of cultural taste once the nationalistic Soviet system collapses.

The first half of the film narrates the mutually beneficial and mutually influential relationship between French and Georgian cultures, figured in the love affair between Chef Pascal and the Princess Cecilia. Abounding with imagery of sensual pleasure and social harmony, these portions of the film emphasize the pastoral innocence of the pre–Soviet province. The audience's first introduction to Pascal and Cecilia is the sound of their love making as they inadvertently awaken their hosts with their midnight romps. The succeeding imagery of the grape harvest continues the motif of sensory and sensual pleasure. The scene depicts a harvest picnic underneath grape vines and trellises. The Georgians sing of their prosperity while they pick and consume the grapes directly off the vines. Pascal resembles the shaggy bearded Dionysus of ancient Mediterranean culture, hanging grape clippings on each side of Cecilia's head as he kisses her, while another celebrant conveys the lamb to be "sacrificed" for afternoon kebabs. Later, Cecilia washes Pascal's feet so that he can crush grapes in a vat, a clear metaphor for squeezing each drop of pleasure from life.

The riotous "love affair" between Princess Cecilia and Pascal suggests the influence of refined French tastes on the Georgian elite. The lovers' activities outside of the bedroom include the enjoyment of culinary delectables, fine wines, and opera. Here, the role of western European influences on the political apparatus of pre–Soviet Georgia is also emphasized,

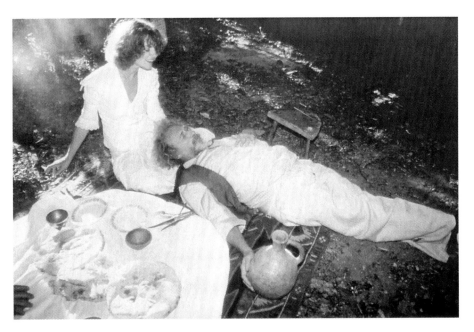

French chef Pascal Ichac (Pierre Richard) and Princess Cecilia Abachidze (Nino Kirtadze) enjoy a traditional Georgian grape harvest and picnic in Nana Dzhordzhadze's *A Chef in Love* (1997).

suggesting that the western powers help to sustain the social structure that has become odious to the dictators of the proletariat. While attending the opera, Pascal's heightened senses save the Georgian president's life (and perhaps his own) by detecting the smell of powdered magnesium from a bomb under the President's chair. The chef's heroic actions result in his lionization, and he is invited to feast with the President and his staff, while the leader reveals his familiarity with Pascal's culinary writings, quoting the accomplished gourmand. In order to show his gratitude as well as his love of French cuisine and culture, the President helps Pascal and Cecilia open Tblissi's first authentic French restaurant, The Eldorado—a name which means "the gilded," perhaps an allusion to "the gilded age" in which Georgia experienced a brief and prosperous period of independence between the respective Turkish and Soviet dominations, or perhaps a symbol of the enshrinement of French civilization in the culture of the pre–Soviet republic. Subsequent changes in the restaurant signify the subsequent transformations in Georgian society culminating in the appropriation of both by the red army.

The film offers two visual and narrative analogues to Pascal's restaurant — the roadside inn where the audience is first introduced to Cecilia's future husband and Soviet revolutionary Zigmund Gogoladze and the modest traditional restaurant where Pascal guesses the ingredients in his Koupatis. These alternative images of the Georgian culinary experience frame Pascal's restaurant, revealing either the antithetical culinary traditions or the past and future of indigenous cuisine. Pascal and Cecilia are waylaid by the overly zealous proprietors of a country inn who accost the couple at the roadside and virtually force them into their decaying establishment. When the couple finds their food unpalatable, they effect their escape, but not without first rescuing a doomed pig from the slaughter. The incident at the country inn allegorizes the politics of the Soviet revolution in Georgia and particularly the distaste that the former cultured elite will harbor for the vulgar communist palate. The scene literalizes the disparaging semantic equation between the wealthy privileged classes and pigs. After Pascal abducts the doomed pig at gunpoint, Zigmund locates his gun, races down the hill to intercept the car, and intentionally shoots the pig rather than the human occupants of the vehicle. The action reveals his socialist sentiments, or perhaps it is supposed to be this incident which first arouses his proletarian indignation. The initial encounter between Pascal, Cecilia, and the roadside proprietors also creates a heavy-handed metaphor for the Soviet revolution in Georgia. The happy prosperous couple are accosted at knife point from the roadside and dragged into an establishment where

Chef Pascal (Pierre Richard) conveys his lover, Princess Cecilia Abachidze (Nino Kirtadze), to the site of his new restaurant, The Eldorado, the first French restaurant, in the Pre-Soviet Georgia in Nana Dzhordzhadze's *A Chef in Love* (1997).

bungling chefs are ill-equipped to offer any of the culinary services that they have touted, the customers held prisoner by an ineffective system characterized by incompetence and dearth.

The hungry couple seek sustenance subsequently in a traditional Georgian restaurant where they are entertained by dancers and musicians indicative of the Greek and Mediterranean influences on Georgian ethnic identity. Pascal and Cecilia are able to enjoy traditional Georgian fare and to interact with the talented proprietor, who quizzes Pascal on the composition of his dinner. This latter establishment suggests the rich cultural past of the region and creates a foil to the incivility, sparsity, and vulgarity of the impending Soviet regime. The symbolic placement of The Eldorado between the country inn and the traditional restaurant emphasizes its role in Georgia's political transition in that brief period between Turkish domination and the Soviet revolution.

The director films three picnic scenes which suggest the progressive ascendancy of separate cultural influences in the region. The first of these is the grape harvest, characterized by a quiet gathering of friends and family who mix work and merrymaking in celebration of the abundant crop. The imagery suggests social harmony and Edenic leisure while the peasants lounge under the vine trellises eating, drinking, and singing. While the

Chef Pascal (Pierre Richard) guesses the hidden ingredients in a traditional Georgian dinner in Nana Dzhordzhadze's *A Chef in Love* (1997).

grape harvest reveals the life and traditions of the common people, Pascal's picnic with the Georgian President is a formal affair with all of the ritual of a state dinner. While the peasants rest on the ground enjoying their repast in the initial picnic, the guests of the President sit at a formally set table replete with cloth, fine china, and centerpieces. The host offers formal toasts that acknowledge the President's appreciation for both France and its accomplished citizen Chef Pascal, who is invited to undertake a traditional challenge of drinking an ox horn full of wine. Here, as in the grape harvest, the proceedings retain a quiet dignity despite the progressive inebriation of the guests. Moreover, the participants are dressed formally for the occasion and are representative of the various ministers of state both military and civilian. The final picnic scene depicts the vulgarities of the Red Army. As in the previous scenes, the celebrants eat, drink, sing, and dance, but the military affair breaches the bonds of decorum; the participants become slovenly drunks gorging themselves and growing progressively more riotous. The affair concludes with a collective bout of diarrhea when all of the diners are forced to evacuate the toxic lunch that Pascal had prepared for them, a dish which, he explains, contained "crow."

It is difficult to determine whether Pascal's "crow" is literal or figurative, suggesting the humiliation of the diners or for that matter his own humiliation as he is progressively reduced to a mere cook, but throughout the final gathering, Pascal has made his discontentment obvious. In the previous bucolic celebrations, he was allowed to participate and was considered a guest of distinction; however, in the final picnic, he delivers the food unceremoniously and retreats from the festivities to mope. His dissatisfaction has less to do with his inability to participate than with the usurpation of his lover by Zigmund, who has forced Cecilia to marry him. Within the political allegory of the film, Cecilia's coerced marriage to Zigmund suggests the constrained union of the old and the new. Princess Cecilia, who represents the aristocratic order of the past, is compelled to embrace the revolutionary present as embodied in Zigmund. Pascal's progressive marginalization within the film suggests the diminished role of western European influences on the new Soviet society. Similarly, Pascal's gourmet cuisine and refined dining practices no longer appeal to a culture that repudiates those manners, customs, and tastes reminiscent of the residual social hierarchy. The Soviets take great pride in their low and vulgar tastes, and they revile any residual customs that would tend to derogate the practices of the proletariat.

The film creates a similar dichotomy between the genteel and the uncouth in its depictions of the Soviet appropriation of The Eldorado. Prior to the revolution, the French restaurant was a gathering place for the

Chef Pascal (Pierre Richard), an unidentified character and Princess Cecilia (Nino Kirtadze) celebrate the opening of their elegant French restaurant in Nana Dzhordzhadze's *A Chef in Love* (1997).

country's most prosperous and refined citizens. The Georgian President toasted the establishment at its grand opening, and subsequently, the restaurant was patronized by those with an appreciation for gourmet French cuisine and elegant dining. The restaurant is elegant and dignified, the patrons appreciative and cultivated. However, following the revolution, The Eldorado is commandeered by the Red Army, whose esteem for Pascal's talent is scant. Upon arrival, the Soviet general insists that Pascal fry the goldfish from the aquarium in his foyer. Pascal's pleas that the fish are old and inedible are ignored. Even when Pascal delivers the required dish and demonstrates that a dog will not eat it, the general persists, explaining that he has already eaten "that which a dog wouldn't touch," and demands that Pascal serve the food. The commander's very public display of indifference to fine food is intended to emphasize the Soviet contempt for the trappings of bourgeois taste and western influence. His appetite is disciplined by the propaganda of revolution and the dearth of war. The dictatorship of the proletariat seeks to elevate the vulgarities of common laborer not by replacing them with more refined tastes but by affecting the exaltation of the low. In the inverted hierarchy of the Soviet revolution, that which was low is raised up; that which was last is first.

Following the Soviet occupation, the atmosphere of The Eldorado radically and permanently alters. Gone are the elegantly dressed and dignified diners of the Republic, and they are replaced by uniformed personnel who treat the dining room as both a mess hall and a barracks. The quiet dignity of The Eldorado is replaced by riotous celebrations and their aftermath, including the refuse of drunken binging both human and otherwise. While there is no evidence that the Red Army continues to insist on inedible food, their behavior certainly emphasizes contempt for the manners of polite society. Beyond the disarray of the dining room where the evidence of riot and revelry is permanent, the most ostentatious display of the appropriation of the formerly elegant restaurant by the forces of vulgarity is the hanging of a garish Soviet flag from the balcony of the main dining hall. With the raising of the Soviet flag, Pascal's establishment is no longer his own, and he is merely an interloper increasingly forced to the margin. Indeed the film creates a geography of marginality involving the interior terrain of The Eldorado and its accompanying apartments. Angered by Pascal's decision to feed the Red Army "crow" during their rural junket, Zigmund vindicates his humiliation by seizing Pascal's elegant flat above the restaurant where he will reside with Pascal's former girlfriend, Princess Cecilia. He sends the chef to live in the attic, a symbolic gesture that for the remainder of the film signifies the sublimation of the French and by extension refined western influences within the Georgian psyche during the Soviet domination of the region. Pascal's displacement, however, does not end his meddling. He continues to hold sway over the affections of the former Georgian elite, embodied in Cecilia, who visits him in the attic periodically, bringing him the laughingly inadequate comestibles concocted in the new Soviet kitchen.

As with the restaurant of Greenaway's *The Cook, the Thief, His Wife and Her Lover,* The Eldorado constitutes an interior geography of the human body and in this case the Soviet Georgian body politic. The stomach, represented by the restaurant itself, has become vulgarized by the Soviet occupation of the building. Since the hammer and sickle banner was raised in the dining room, the occupants have become increasingly disordered eaters. Indeed, Cecilia carries a letter from confined Pascal to the cook offering his polite suggestions for improving the cuisine, and Cecilia finds that the new Soviet cook, a degraded elderly woman peeling potatoes, is illiterate and cannot appreciate the culinary master's insights. Thus Cecilia begins a false correspondence with Pascal in which she impersonates the new Red Army cook, offering a polite, encouraging, and learned reception to the Pascal's overtures. Of course, the new cook is privy to none of the subsequent interaction. If the kitchen is the new unrefined Georgian stomach, then the building's living quarters constitute the heart where Zigmund tries to maintain his unfaithful wife's affections, but the heart is full of betrayals. Zigmund never really possesses his wife because she cannot abandon her first love for Pascal, and she repeatedly steals into the attic where she enjoys and nurtures the declining Pascal. The former princess and her French lover even steal into the main bedroom of the residence where Zigmund is forced to listen to their love making from the next room. Cecilia considers a scandalous betrayal of her husband through a double suicide of Pascal and herself in Zigmund's own bed. Cecilia's refusal to abandon her fascination with Pascal and by extension western culture eventually leads to her murder by her husband, an action that frames the film narrative, as her child remembers the day of his mother's death at the hands of the man he falsely assumes was his father. The betrayals of the Georgian heart — or its continued love affair with western culture — extend into the attic or the mind where Pascal is forced into solitude and almost forgotten, following the red army's occupation of the building and the simultaneous triumph of vulgarity. Zigmund seeks revenge against the man whom he perceives as an obstacle to his wife's devotion. However, despite repeated efforts, Zigmund cannot bring himself to murder Pascal; instead he redirects his rage toward Cecilia. The repeated failure to kill the French chef suggests the inability of the Soviet system to root out the collective memory of a bygone era when the Georgian appetite tended toward the more refined tastes of western Europe. The Soviets can dominate the physical bodies of the subjugated masses, but they cannot possess the hearts and minds of the same. They cannot make their political thralls content with vulgarity and dearth.

Zigmund's efforts to murder Pascal while the latter is sleeping in his impoverished rooftop garden allude to Shakespeare's *Hamlet*; Zigmund has recently attended a production, and it occurs to him that he might pour mercury into the ear of the sleeping gourmand. The contemplated action would seem to equate him to Shakespeare's Claudius, who murders his brother, King Hamlet, in order to possess his throne and his wife, Gertrude. However, the dramatic roles from the play are not so easily applicable to the film. Ironically, in a physical sense, Zigmund already possesses Princess Cecilia although her heart does not belong to him. Zigmund's abortive efforts to murder his rival are more indicative of Prince Hamlet, since both characters are unable to follow through in an unenviable task that will bring order to the state. In addition, the Marxist revolutionary's inability to maintain his murderous resolve is obviously driving him mad. In his final effort to kill Pascal, Zigmund is distracted by a bee that emerges from Pascal's mouth, and the soldier runs off across the rooftop firing blindly into the air attempting to kill an insect. The image simultaneously signifies that the man is driven mad by frustration and that his antagonist is inconsequential; the threat that Pascal poses is illusory or is at best symbolic. Perhaps Zigmund cannot bring himself to murder Pascal because he harbors his own sublimated affections for that which the Chef represents.

If nothing else, he loves the woman who loves his enemy, perhaps thus invoking the oedipal triangle that is so common in the interpretation of *Hamlet*. Zigmund fears symbolic emasculation by his fatherly rival, and there is no doubt that the revolutionary is undermined by the continued influence that the French chef exercises over Cecilia. The familial triangle also extends into the political allegory of the film since the aristocratic Cecilia can easily be conceived as a maternal or parental influence, her class having preceded the Marxists in power over the Georgian state. Zigmund's inability to win her allegiance suggests the Communists' inability to win the hearts and minds of the Georgian populace. The incestuous implication of a union between Zigmund and Cecilia is also reconcilable to both the Freudian family drama and the socio-political commentary of the film. Zigmund, a native Georgian turned Soviet sympathizer, may be understood as the disaffected child of the previous social order, represented by Cecilia. Zigmund perceives Pascal as an interloper who usurped the affections of the mother — the state. However, as in the Oedipal triangle, the child can never really possess the mother because he fears the father's influence/violence. While Pascal cannot be understood as physically threatening, his continued presence does seem to threaten the national unity under the Soviet occupation. He embodies the potential restoration or the memory of a desirable past, and thus he impedes the revolution that requires a complete overturning of the past.

The failure of the Soviet system to purge its sphere of what it perceives as decadent western European influences is also represented in the visit of Lenin's emissary, comrade Kollontay, who harbors an affection for Pascal, with whom she had once had a romantic affair. Upon her arrival in Tbilissi, she seeks out her former lover and intrudes upon him in bed, reminding him how they first met on a train when she was impersonating the German Princess Ann. Her narrative reveals a half hearted commitment to the goals of the revolution even from a person who is a close associate of the architect of that social transfiguration. Her impersonation of royalty seems to be a particular betrayal of the revolutionary objectives, and her continued appetite for the refined tastes of French cuisine reveals her inability to reconcile revolutionary objectives with culinary dearth. Unlike the Red Army General, she is not willing to eat that which a dog would not touch.

The frame of the film is a contemporary narrative of discovery in which a Georgian gallery director in the 1990's is opening an exhibit of ethnic Georgian art, some of which includes culinary motifs. Anton Gogoladze believes that he is the child of communist revolutionary Zigmund Gogoladze and Cecilia Abachidze; however, he discovers that he is actually the child of Cecilia and Pascal Ichac, conceived on the night when Cecilia and Pascal contemplated suicide in Zigmund's bed. This revelation is facilitated by Marcelle Ichac, the niece of Pascal, who seeks out Anton to provide him with information about his family. That information turns out to be a new understanding of his lineage and the discovery of a new relative: Marcelle is actually his cousin. This family reunion is consistent with the political and historical parable of the film. The frame of the historical narrative takes place after the collapse of the Soviet bloc and the subsequent cultural liberation of the Georgian republic. The reunification of family members and particularly the discovery of his half French ancestry becomes the fulfillment of Pascal's prediction that "Communism will disappear one day, fine cooking won't." Anton's discovery of his origins parallels the cultural awakening of the Georgian populace following the collapse of Soviet influence. He is forced to revise his understanding of his ethnic heritage to admit that Western Europeans are his cousins. The fact that Marcelle Ichac is a "gastronomic photographer" reinforces the cultural connection between east and west. Food is one of the principal markers of cultural difference and affinity; the discovery of the mutual love of gourmet cuisine unites cousins and cultures.

The emergence of Georgia from its long Soviet isolation roughly coincides with the creation and release Djordjadze's *Chef in Love* in 1996. Georgia's independence was officially recognized by Russia in 1992 and the first President was Edvard Shevardnadze, the former Soviet official and ally to Mikhail Gorbachev, the Soviet premier who sought closer connections with the West and presided over the collapse of European communism. The allegorical tale of the pre–Soviet Georgia's love affair with refined western European tastes simultaneously eulogizes the past affection and signals the regeneration of those valuable cultural affiliations. In the predictable gesture of contemporary identity politics, Anton, and by extension Georgia, reclaims its cultural identity by rediscovering its cultural past, by embracing all of the influences on its genesis rather than those that exclusively reinforce the Soviet ideology.

12

The Artist in Exile:
Babette and "Alexander's Feast"

In the late 17th Century, poet and playwright John Dryden composed two works contributing to the celebration of St. Cecilia's Day—*A Song for St. Ceilia's Day* (1687) and *Alexander's Feast* (1697). Each extolled the power of music over the human passions—both carnal and divine. The former attributes the creation and harmony of the universe to music, concluding with an encomium on St. Cecilia's miraculous voice which, according to the poem, made an angel mistake earth for heaven. The latter poem depicts the musician Timotheus entertaining Alexander the Great at a feast following the conquest of Persia. The poem celebrates the mastery of the musician/artist who is able to subdue the world's conqueror with sound. This chapter will address the parallels between Dryden's Cecilia poems and Gabriel Axel's film *Babette's Feast* (1987), based on Isak Dinesen's short story of the same name. Previous scholarship on *Babette's Feast* has concentrated primarily on the narrative of forgiveness and mourning as well as the revelatory powers of the culinary artist (Rashkin 357, 367; Michelson 37; Podles 67; and Petersson 284). This discussion will invoke some of the same ideas, but will examine them through the Neo-classical lense of Dryden's aesthetics.

Babette's Feast depicts the sojourn of an exiled French chef, Babette, among an isolated sect of Lutherans living on the coast of Denmark, a change of location from Dinesen's short story which takes place in Norway. Babette joins the household of Martine and Philippa, the daughters of the deceased charismatic preacher who founded and led the small group of ascetics living in the Scandinavian village, Norre Vossborg; her desperate plea for charitable employment as chef and maid wins the sisters' sympathy, and while they are initially reluctant to take on the financial burden of a servant, they become progressively dependent upon the contribution of the French woman. Babette lives among the Lutherans without incident for over fourteen years, committed to the austere lifestyle of the village, preparing dishes no more complicated than split cod and ale-bread soup and revealing nothing of her more sumptuous and indulgent past.

The sisters, Martine and Philippa, have devoted their lives to simple living. Both chose to remain at home caring for their father rather than follow their respective suitors, and in their more advanced age, they remain committed to the maintenance of their father's religious work, attempting to hold together the sect that has become fractious following their father's death. In youth, Martine had been courted by an ambitious young soldier, Lorenz Lowenhielm, who eventually rejected the life of modest self-denial that would have been his legacy had he chosen to marry into the sect. Philippa had likewise been courted by a famous French singer, Achille Papin, who, convalescing on the Danish coast and drawn by the sound of Philippa's voice, ventured into a church service. Following the ceremony, Papin offered to give Philippa voice lessons, but when he became overly passionate following a practice duet from *Don Giovanni*, Philippa sent him a letter requesting to withdraw from the lessons. In both cases the daughters reject

In procession to church, the young Martina (Vibeke Hastrup) and Phillippa (Hanne Stensgaard) are accompanied by their father (Pouel Kern), the minister and founder of Norre Vossborg's austere religious sect, in Gabriel Axel's *Babette's Feast* (1988).

worldly love, ambition, adulation, and wealth, remaining exclusively devoted to spiritual goals that they believe can only be achieved through denial of sensory and sensual appetites: "In the Dean's flock, earthly love and marriage were considered to be of scant worth and merely empty illusions." Following their mutual disappointments, Lowenhielm goes on to become a general in the army and an advisor to Queen Sophia, and Papin returns to the privileged and celebrated life of a Parisian opera star.

Babette's arrival at the home of Martine and Philippa is precipitated by the slaughter of her husband and son at the hands of General Galliffet, who was attempting to pacify a populist uprising in Paris. Achille Papin, who appreciates the artistry of Babette's cooking, sends her to the remote Danish coast where she will be safe from the general's sword. Babette remains silent about her past for fourteen years. When she wins 10,000 francs in the lottery, the sisters fear that she will use the money to return to Paris, and her offer to cook an authentic French feast in celebration of the hundredth anniversary of their father's birth does not ease their apprehension as it suggests that Babette is preparing for her departure with a gesture of gratitude. Instead, Babette spends her entire fortune on a rich and elaborate meal that awakens the repressed passions and sleeping sensibilities of the abstemious Puritans, demonstrating that spiritual ecstasy can be achieved more readily through the indulgence of the appetites than through self-denial (Rashkin 357). The purpose of the meal may be to celebrate the chef's ability to move her audience through her art and perhaps to assert the virtues of French culture over those of the austere Danes.

Babette's elaborate and mysterious preparations for the feast are alarming to Martine and Philippa, who fear that she may be engaged in a witch's sabbath in their kitchen. Martine warns her dinner guests that they may find the food offensive and laments that she has, in her concession to Babette's wishes, introduced "dangerous or maybe even evil powers" into the celebration of her father's memory. The Danes agree that they will not comment on the food no matter how bad it tastes, remarking that "It will be as if we never had the sense of taste." The diners approach the table with great trepidation on the evening of the feast, fearful of what they might be served. However, the solemnity of the period is not entirely the result of their concerns. Although the gathering is a celebration, the light hearted enjoyment that should attend such an event is antithetical to the disposition of the participants, who could be expected to behave with gravity and sobriety in their most whimsical moments. Their vow to behave as though they "never had the sense of taste" is second nature to them as their spartan living, and their insistence on consuming only the most bland cuisine suggests that their taste is, indeed, undeveloped.

The diners' vow of silence creates a unique tension that illustrates the power of Babette's cuisine more convincingly than if they had raved over it. The greedy consumption and the expressions of delight on the faces of the diners are sufficient to convey the triumph of the exotic dishes over their subdued emotions. Their vow not to comment on the food, however, does not leave them silent; they channel their delight into encomia on the life of their deceased leader. When Babette serves her signature dish, Cailles en Sarcophage, General Lowenhielm, a visitor to the celebration, recalls the first time that he consumed the dish in a Parisian restaurant, Café Anglais, and recalls the accomplished female chef who was renowned for her "ability to transform a dinner into a kind of love affair, a love affair that made no distinction between bodily appetite and spiritual appetite." While the Lutherans were able to hold their tongues during the appetizers, the quail in its pastry coffin provokes the expressions of love for the dead Dean, a spiritual ecstasy instigated by sensory pleasures, a love fest, not for the food itself but, more appropriate to the dish and the occasion, for the dead. In a manner of speaking, the food and drink loosen their tongues and allow them to commune with the dead (Rashkin 2), a result that would indeed suggest a culinary seance orchestrated by the kitchen sorcerer's concoctions.

It is via Babette's quasi-magical artistry in the kitchen that Axel's film intersects with Dryden's encomia on music, Timotheus, and St. Cecilia. The legend of Cecilia dates to the 5th century: Cecilia told her recently wed husband, Valerian, that an angel attended her, defending her virginity from any who might touch her. When the husband insisted that she reveal her angel, she explained that he could only see it if he were baptized. Submitting to the sacrament, Valerian returned to his lodging and found an angel hovering over his wife while she prayed. The conversion and, subsequent, good works of Valerian and his brother Tibertius resulted in their martyrdom. Cecilia went on preaching until she too was condemned. Following the abortive attempt to cut off her head, the future saint continued to preach and pray to the faithful while she lingered near death for three days. Cecilia is venerated as the patron saint of music because she is credited with having invented the organ and because she is said to have heard heavenly melodies during her marriage ceremony. Dryden embellishes upon the legend of St. Cecilia, creating a myth of origin for the inclusion of organs in church services. In "A Song for St. Cecilia's Day," her organ sounded so much like the imagined heavenly choir that it inspired divine love and compelled an angel to mistake "earth for Heaven." Similarly, in "Alexander's Feast," the poet concedes that even Timotheus' art must "yield" to Cecilia's greater power. While the former's music inspired a mortal to heavenly ambitions, the latter's "drew and angel down."

One of the primary parallels between *Babette's Feast* and Dryden's Cecilia poems involves music's ability to invoke the heavens. Achille Papin discovers Philippa's extraordinary vocal talents when he hears her voice issuing from the Norre Vossborg chapel. In the subsequent singing lessons, he raves that she will have all of "Paris at her feet": "You will be a like a star in the heavens.... The Emperor will come to hear you and so will the modest seamstress.... You have the talent to distract the rich and to comfort the poor."

In the letter of introduction carried by Babette, Papin consoles himself that he could not enjoy Philippa's singing in this life, but that he hopes to hear her again in Paradise, adding that her voice will "charm the angels." The revelatory quality of Philippa's melodies is more explicit in Dinesen's story than in the film: "For here were the snowy summits, the wild flowers and the white Nordic nights, translated into his own language of music, and brought him in a young woman's voice. Like Lorenz Lowenhielm he had a vision" (26).

Papin's vision regards the glory, for both himself and Philippa, that would follow his introduction of the young diva to the Parisian stage: "Achille's expectation grew into certainty and his certainty into ecstasy. He thought, 'I have been wrong in believing that I was growing old. My greatest triumphs are before me! The world will once more believe in miracles when she and I sing together'" (27).

While Achille Papin himself is certainly not the angel that Philippa's voice called down, he is just as certainly responsible for the "ministering angel"—Babette—whose presence and talents improve the lives of the melancholy sisters. He recognizes an artistic kinship between Babette and Philippa, and when the former is forced into exile, he sends her to the Lutherans on the coast of Jutland where her presence is not unlike a celestial visitation. Her willingness to work for free and to conform to the lifestyle of her employers and her ability to improve the simple dishes consumed by the Danes bring an unexpected boon to both the sisters and their community. Babette's labors in the household free the sisters to perform charity work among the elderly and infirm, and her improvement of the charitable meals that the sisters distribute is evidenced by the distaste of the beneficiaries when Babette takes a few days off. Despite expectations of hardship when they agree to take in Babette, the sisters find that their finances actually improve once the French lady comes to dwell with them. Moreover, it is clear that the sisters themselves regard Babette as heaven sent. When she announces that she has won the lottery, the sisters expect her swift departure and console themselves that God's earthly bounty is only temporary: "The Lord gave and the Lord took away." However, the true nature of Babette's talent and contribution is not known until after her feast.

In the concluding scene of the film, Philippa recognizes that Babette is a kindred artist and that Achille Papin's praise of her singing was equally true of Babette's kitchen artistry. Philippa quotes Papin's letter of introduction in her praise of Babette's skills: "But this is not the end, in Paradise you will be the great artist that God meant you to be — Ah, how you will delight the angels." One way of understanding the revelatory impact of Babette's feast on her diners is to suggest that she did indeed call an angel down into their dining room, an angel of communion and forgiveness. Indeed her feast is routinely equated to the transubstantiation of the host at the Last Supper (Raskin 369; Beck 213; Mickelsen 37; Podles 566), a physical act of consumption that creates a spiritual unity and transcendence, making the deceased Dean present either within the food that she serves or within the dining room. During the dinner, the quarrelsome congregation are transfigured into the loving and forgiving group that was the Dean's legacy.

Another way of understanding the effect of Babette's feast is to consider the tradition of spiritual ecstasy, the same that is invoked in Dryden's poetry when Cecilia's music solicits the heavens. The ecstasy is a tradition in devotional writing in which the faithful are temporarily transported out of their bodies in order to commune with the divine. The experience is pleasurable, revelatory, and transformative, the subject returning to consciousness with a renewed faith and understanding of God's design either for the individual or the world (Eliade 4–5), but Babette's invocation of the deceased leader seems more pagan than Christian insofar as it reveals that divine revelation can be achieved through the indulgence as well as the deprivation of the senses. The extreme pleasure that defines the spiritual ecstasy is rarely the inducement to the same, but rather a result of the transcendental experience. In this sense, Martine was not entirely inaccurate in her equation of Babette's cooking to sorcery. Babette is the kitchen shaman, her goal to open the portal between the earthly and the divine so that the members of the tribe can commune with or seek guidance from their dead ancestor. Within the shamanic ritual, the group regains its sense of tribal unity. The feast may even be equivalent to the ingestion of psychoactive substances by tribal members in order to facilitate the visionary state. The dinner includes a variety of wines and champagnes that weaken the diners' inhibitions and loosen their tongues. The recitation of events from their communal past, those specifically related to the wisdom and miracles of their dead leader, also conforms to the paradigm of the tribal ritual where the group might hear a recounting of their common mythology or the heroics of a memorable hunt or battle. The dancing and singing of the Lutheran brethren around the village well following the feast seems to be more of a spontaneous residual memory of their pagan past than a celebration of their communal Christian virtues since dancing is undoubtedly forbidden among this austere puritanical sect. If Cecilia's great virtue was to convert the pagans of ancient Rome to Christianity, Babette's work may be intended to reacquaint the Christians with the more fleshly religions of their distant past, rehabilitating the uses of earthly pleasure and demonstrating that the spiritual can just as easily be attained through indulgence as through self-denial, through the complex as through the simplistic. Thus body and soul are reconciled (Rashkin 357).

Dryden's poem "Alexander's Feast" constitutes an more complex analogue to Axel's film than is "A Song for St. Cecilia's Day." The parallels include but are not limited to the similarity of titles. The relationship between the film and the poem hinges largely upon the presence of General Lorens Lowenhielm at the feast. When, thirty years earlier, Lorenz forsook his pursuit of Martine, his rationale included a desire to win earthly fame, to sample the pleasures and glories that would be denied him if he settled among the isolated Lutheran sect who see no virtue in worldly pursuits, and it is clear upon his return to Jutland for the Dean's anniversary feast that he has sampled Europe's luxuries and won renown both at home and abroad. Indeed, he married a handmaid of Queen Sophia and became a member of the royal court. However, he does not return to Jutland with complete confidence in the decision he made so long ago to abandon his pursuit of Martine. Just as Achille Papin regrets the decision to leave Jutland and return to the Parisian stage, concluding that fame is "the grave that awaits us all," General Lowenhielm questions the wisdom of his ambitions. Staring at himself in the mirror, he challenges his youthful self to prove that his desire for glory was worthy of the sacrifice of so great a beauty as Martine, his first love. He sums up his life in the simple sentence, "Vanity, all is vanity." When he arrives at the celebration dinner, he is very gracious, yet he is literally wearing his accomplishments on his sleeve and his breast, his elaborate dress uniform perhaps a defense against regret and self-doubt.

Lowenhielm is the embodiment of martial triumph that parallels the image of Alexander in Dryden's poem. The Greek conqueror, fresh from his conquest of Persia, is reveling in his victory when Timotheus labors to entertain him with his subtle music. Dryden's poem celebrates the power of the artist to manipulate and enslave the world's conqueror, altering the soldier's passions with each subtle shift in rhythm and melody, shuttling him from pride and vanity to melancholy and love and finally to hatred, valor, and revenge, which results in the burning of Persepolis. Timotheus alters his music when he perceives that Alexander has become overwrought with a single passion. Just as in Axel's film, the conqueror is made more pliable by intoxicating drink. The third segment of Dryden's poem celebrates the virtues of Bacchus, specifically defining wine as the "soldier's pleasure" bringing "pleasure after pain." Thus the artist's audience is made more susceptible to the aesthetic craft through the intervention of intoxicants. Interestingly, Alexander never realizes that he is being swayed by the machinations of a great artist. He celebrates only his own vulgar power and success.

The influence that Babette's culinary art exercises over her diners can be seen most readily in the behavior and commentary of the General, not because his transformation is the greatest, although it may be, but because he is the only one who has not vowed to remain silent about the repast. In addition, the general is the only member of the celebration with sufficiently refined taste and worldly experience to know the rarity and virtue of the dishes and beverages he consumes. And each new course of the meal inspires a verbal tribute to the merits of the particular dish. The meals also cause him to reminisce about his past, inviting a variety of emotions. He recalls with pride the triumphant dinner in Paris with Colonel Galliffet when he was first introduced to *Cailles en Sarcophage,* and he speaks of the popularity of the Dean's collected sermons in Queen Sophia's court. Later he becomes melancholy, waxing nostalgic about that which he has lost and offering an inspired speech on the union of the seemingly antithetical virtues—righteousness and bliss. Finally, he is moved to proclaim his undying love for Martine, confessing that she has retained a special place in his heart all the years of his absence and that she will continue to occupy that place until his death. All of the General's sentiments are orchestrated by chef Babette, who moves him from surprise, delight, and pride to erudition, golden melancholy, and finally spiritual love, this from a man who upon his arrival at the Dean's house might be described as stiff, sober, and perhaps a bit imperious.

The artist's manipulations of the heroic figure in both Axel's film and Dryden's poem includes an element of deception, one that capitalizes on the respective figures' vanity. Alexander is never aware that the passions he experiences, including that which moves him to burn Persepolis, are not his own, but are created by a skilled musician plucking the strings of both his lute and his emperor. In a matter of speaking, it is the artist, following in the wake of Alexander's triumph, who defines the extent and nature of his conquest, and the conqueror himself behaves in conformity to the mythology that has been constructed to celebrate him. In Dryden's poem, Alexander destroys the Persian capital because the recounting of his own heroic deeds requires such action, the desire for revenge inspired by Timotheus' tribute to his fallen Greek comrades. Thus the hero is driven by the desire to construct his image and legacy in compliance with the artist/historian's adulation, by the desire to confirm his own mythology. Timotheus' recounting of Alexander's divine origins magnifies the emperor's power, increasing his hauteur and lordliness, and the musician's praise of Bacchus' treasure and its particular appeal to soldiers spurs the conqueror to drink and makes him still more vulnerable to artistic sleights.

Similarly, Lowenhielm is deceived by the luxurious feast and inadvertently by his fellow diners. Because the Lutherans have taken a vow of silence, the General assumes that such delicacies are commonplace among the Danes. He mistakes silence for knowledge and worldliness. Moreover, the triumphant toast that he makes celebrating the union of mercy and truth and righteousness and bliss can be read as a complete misunderstanding of the meaning of the feast, leaving him, in spite of his egalitarian gestures, just as expectant and vain as he was during his youthful visitation. The Lutherans have not become more open to worldly bliss, and there has been no permanent union of his alternative life choices—righteousness or pleasure/glory—save in the brief period that the celebrants have been under the spell of Babette's divine cooking. He leaves with an affirmation of his life choices, but the circumstances of his revelation do not support his conclusion. He is still trapped in the paradox of his own vanity, believing that he can have both that which he embraced and that which he rejected thirty years before. However, once he has distanced himself, both spatially and temporally, from the ecstasy of Babette's feast, it is doubtful that the transcendence of that brief period will continue to comfort him, that he will persist in his belief that a melancholic nostalgia and a faith in spiritual union after death is sufficient to compensate for the loss of his true love. Babette's art creates the illusion that the corporeal and the divine can be reconciled in this life, but once the dinner party has concluded, the separate spheres are once again irreconcilable. Babette has only made the General and his companions comfortable in the life choices that they have made, reaffirming the values, both physical and spiritual, to which they were already committed. Thus the feast may be defined as a euphoria, affirming a false sense of well-being, not actually altering the diner's reality save insofar as it has made the worldling and the ascetics better able to understand that which motivates their philosophical antithesis. Thus the feast offered insight, demonstrating that there are alternative routes to the divine, but it does not rattle anyone's commitment to their formerly chosen path. It does, however, make them love and understand each other despite their differences, which may indeed be a pseudo-miracle.

At an allegorical level, Axel's film narrates the clash between conflicting religious, political, and national ideologies: the French Catholic and the Danish (formerly Norwegian) Protestants (Branson 2). The Lutherans regard the luxurious lives and sensory indulgences of the French as sinful, a fact made more explicit in Dinesen's short story than in Axel's film, but nevertheless cinematically clear when Martine registers her scandal over the wine that Babette has brought into the Dean's house. Conversely, Babette is bewildered by the spartan lifestyle and particularly the bland and unappealing diet of the Danes. When Martine teaches her how to boil split cod and make ale bread soup, Babette is scarcely able to conceal her disgust and disbelief, yet she dutifully makes the same every day of her sojourn among the Danes. While Babette certainly represents the refined and sensually indulgent culinary practices of the French Catholics, her political position is not antithetical to that of the Lutherans, as her motivation for fleeing to Jutland is to escape the repercussions of her family's involvement in the communards' revolt against the ruling French elite, an uprising brutally suppressed by General Gailliffet. Although the citizens of Norre Vossborg are not politically involved, forsaking worldly concerns, they are

Babette Harsant (Stéphane Audran) haggles with a fisherman (Lars Lohmann), selecting fish for the simple diets of her employers in Gabriel Axel's *Babette's Feast* (1988).

committed to the simple philanthropic life. The lesson of Babette's dinner is intended more for the sisters than for the general. Babette strives to demonstrate that they do not have to deny themselves pleasure and joy in order to live righteously, in order to honor their father's work, that it is possible to feel closer to the Dean by indulging the senses than by starving them, and, perhaps, even that spiritual love is a nearer kin to pleasure than to privation. If this is the text of Babette's gustatory sermon, there is no evidence that the homily has a lasting effect on her congregation, perhaps only because the narrative closes immediately after dinner. Philippa's final reassuring remarks to Babette following the revelation of the French woman's history and talent is not an invitation to practice her art at Norre Vossborg, but the same reassurance she received from Achille Papin, that she will be able to practice her art in the hereafter, is offered to Babette, a statement that does not constitute a repudiation of the Dane's commitment to forsake worldly pleasure in preparation for the divine, but offers Babette the opportunity to participate in the same ideology of self-denial. In a sense, both artists are in exile, unable to practice their skills in this corporeal frame, but reserving their "best" for the heavenly choir and the nuptial feast of the Lamb.

The artistic manipulations of both Dryden's Timotheus and Axel's Babette are powerful analogues to the role of the poet (Dryden) and the cinematic artist (Axel). In his *Essay on Criticism*, Alexander Pope recognizes the parallel between Timotheus and Dryden: "The power of music all our hearts allow/And what Timotheus was, is Dryden now" (382–383). The poet literally alters Alexander's moods in his poem with each stroke of his pen. Similarly, the only true revelation achieved by Babette's food is actually Axel's or Dinesen's victory. A textual or cinematic feast can only be metaphorical, never substantive or nourishing, except in an entirely intellectual or spiritual sense. The diners at Babette's table are an analogue for the cinematic audience; the equation between gourmet food and spiritual enlightenment are parallels not merely to the impact of a film on its audience, but more specifically to the intellectually nourishing effect of quality or art cinema, of which Axel's film is a glowing example. Just as Babette's exotic foods refine the taste of her diners, Axel's film instructs its audience on the finer points of the cinematic art. The art film unifies the body and the spirit by translating the corporeal object into idea and emotion. Thus Axel remains the true Timotheus and her audience the vulgar and willful Alexander, who are never fully conscious of their subordination to a great artist even as she drives them through a variety of emotions—admiration, hope, disappointment, desire, hunger, love, and an illusory transcendence.

13

Family Suppers and the Social Syntax of Dissimilation

The structure of the gustatory ritual within a collective environment has long been understood to symbolize social coherence for those who partake in this repetitive process of consumption. Indeed, the activities at the table not only affirm religious, ethnic, national, class, and racial identities of the participants within their broader cultural environment, but also expose variation within the dining party itself, such as gender, generation, and power, and the disruption of this culinary observance often suggests the dissolution of the group consciousness or unity. The banquet scene of Shakespeare's *Macbeth* reveals the progressive impact of the titular character's precipitous breach of social etiquette. As a host to King Duncan, Macbeth had been obliged to offer sustenance and safe lodging, but his "most sacrilegious murder" of his guest disturbs the good order of the realm, a condition manifest in Macbeth's inability to preside over a feast for his own court. The intrusion of Banquo's ghost into the proceeding transforms what had been an orderly and amiable gathering into a riot. The guests who had arrived and seated themselves according to rank and class are asked to leave without consideration of the same, with Lady Macbeth demanding, "Stand not upon the order of your going,/But go at once" (III.iv.120–21). The disruption of the banquet is preceded by Macbeth's duplicitous invocation of his as yet unrevealed murder victim, Banquo, for whom he feigns concern. Thus he undermines his own authority through the solicitation of an outsider who has been radically excluded from the proceedings by the paranoia and violence of the host. The meal intended to symbolize the order and sanctity of his reign descends into chaos, permanently redirecting the suspicion of murder and apostasy onto himself and undermining the same power his social efforts had sought to consolidate.

The representational burden of the disrupted banquet in Shakespeare's play is the same frequently conferred upon the family dining scene within contemporary film. As an example, consider the deterioration of the conventional orderly family as depicted in the progressively more tense dining scenes of *American Beauty*. When the family patriarch hurls a plate of vegetables at the wall and rearranges the conditions of their dining ritual, he effectively stages his domestic revolution, claiming the power previously enjoyed by his wife. Similarly, the struggle of Jessica Lange to hold her family together in *Men Don't Leave* reveals itself in her effort to compel her children to participate in a weekly observance, which includes sharing a meal, an inconvenience against which the youngsters chafe. The Swedish film *A Song for Martin* illustrates the advancing dementia of a composer battling Alzheimer's through the steady decline of his table manners at a series of family gatherings. His decline culminates with his urinating in a planter at a local restaurant during his own birthday celebration.

This chapter will explore the dialectics of the family feast. While much can be, has been, and will be said about the ways in which a family dinner confers identity through inclusion, this discussion will also focus on the necessity of exclusion in the maintenance of domestic harmony. Who is not invited to the table? Who are the interlopers, and what is the effect of their intrusion on the social coherence of the family unit? The films to be explored are *Soul Food* (1997), *Eat Drink Man Woman* (1994), and *Tortilla Soup* (2001). In each narrative, the unity of the group is threatened by exterior influences, and in each, the bond is restored by the sharing of food. In addition, all three films depict a family alienated and isolated, facing assimilation by a quasi-hostile culture that threatens to swallow up their unique ancestral heritage, thus necessitating the maintenance of rigid familial boundaries.

Soul Food

George Tillman's *Soul Food* depicts an African American family thrown into turmoil by the illness and subsequent death of the matriarch, Big Mama, whose wisdom, traditions, and cooking skills served to stabilize the potentially fractious group. The Sunday dining ritual that the family has maintained for over forty years was and is a restorative, a folk remedy, reminding the members of their origins and alliances. Thus the dinners are a retreat from the world that threatens to draw the disparate elements of the group in new directions, toward new values and new loyalties. The tradition is a bulwark against assimilation and the subsequent obliteration of all that is unique within the nuclear and racial families. The dinners offer coherence in a postmodern world where meaning and direction are lost.

Tillman's film is a continuation of two longstanding, perhaps now cliché, thematics within African American literature: heritage and duality. The black writers of the late nineteenth and early twentieth century recognized that the African American community needed to rediscover its origins, to embrace its indigenous cultural traditions in order to reclaim pre-bondage identities and self-respect. The institution of slavery sought to wipe away the cultural memory and consequently the sense of racial unity among its thralls—the languages, the myths, the religions, and the traditions. Conversely, African American art strove to retain or reclaim the unique ethnic and racial heritage of the recently liberated population. However, little could be done to obliterate three hundred years of indoctrination by western institutions, particularly while the suppressed population remained within the confines of the dominating culture's sphere of influence—spoke its language, worshiped its God, obeyed its laws, observed its holidays, attended its schools, accepted its prohibitions, ate its food, and embraced its material priorities. Thus W.E.B. Dubois, in *The Souls of Black Folk*, postulated that African Americans have two souls, one white, one black (5). Inside each African American a struggle is waged between conflicting loyalties and desires—the impulse to conform to dominant cultural institutions and the desire to embrace a primal African essence that has remained dormant within the subjugated populace, passed on through art and biology over the many centuries of repression.

Big Mama's dinners are not merely an opportunity to enjoy home cooking and the good company of family. They are lessons in cultural legacy, efforts to retain a connection to the past that shaped not only the family's current prosperity, but also their all too recent tribulations at the hands of a hostile white culture. When conflict arises at dinner between her two eldest daughters—Teri (Vanessa Williams) and Maxine (Vivica Fox)—Big Mama reminds them of the struggles that she and her late husband endured in order to purchase the house she occupies, and she emphasizes the necessity of consolidating family loyalties to militate against exterior threats. Big Mama's Sunday dinners constitute a charmed circle against the total assimilation and subsequent dispersal of her family. The recounting of oft repeated narratives illustrating the past ordeals of the family, the consumption of consecrated foods, the sense of love and belonging, all conspire to repulse external destabilizing pressures and influences.

The family traditions were formed through exclusions and ones not always based upon biology. In the broadest sense, the intruder at Big Mama's feast is white culture, the absent presence that must be consistently repulsed in order for the Joseph family to retain its collective identity. The heritage of the family is particularly meaningful in contrast to the western cultural institutions that sought to dissolve it. Within the film, there is a dearth of

The Joseph sisters — Teri (Vanessa Williams), Bird (Nia Long), and Maxine (Vivica Fox) — are annoyed when they see Bird's husband dancing with an old girlfriend at his wedding (George Tillman's *Soul Food*, 1997).

explicit criticism of the white establishment for the suffering of the African American family. The single example of the same, voiced by Lem (Mekhi Phifer) because his prison record excluded him from reasonable expectations of employment, is rebuked with prejudice by his wife. However, the historical subtext of the narrative includes a prolonged indictment of the deplorable conditions that inspired the family traditions. The young narrator Ahmad (Brandon Hammond) reminds the audience that "soul food" grew out the miseries of slavery. The black populace, having little to celebrate, turned to food preparation as a means of showing love: "So that's what those Sunday dinners were all about. It was more than just eating; it was a time to share our joys and sorrows." Of course, the unenviable conditions of the slaves' lives were the direct result of the greed and inhumanity of the white establishment. Thus the gustatory traditions of the family were formed to consolidate spiritual and material resources against those institutions that sought to exploit or annihilate them.

The racial legacies are stronger within the elder generation — Big Mama and Uncle Pete. The adult siblings of the subsequent generation are more fully assimilated to contemporary American culture, which concerns itself primarily with the acquisition of wealth and individual ambitions. When

Big Mama falls into a coma, the warring siblings begin to drift apart because the embodiment of their familial and spiritual bonds has been removed, and no one has yet assumed the responsibility. The family must learn that the social cohesion sustained by Big Mama's Sunday ritual can indeed survive her death. However, it falls to the youngest member of the family to remind his parents of the importance of heritage. Young Ahmad manufactures a pretense to get the family together for Sunday dinner, telling each member that he has discovered the mythic cache of money that was reputed to be hidden in Big Mama's house, a tale which the matriarch had always denied. Ahmad's appeal to the several family members invokes the self-serving appetite for wealth that most have fallen into following Big Mama's death. He leads each member to believe that she would be the only one to share in the newly uncovered wealth. Once they arrive to discover all the other family members in attendance, they automatically fall into their traditional roles in the kitchen and dining room, and, subsequently, they are forced to address their differences over their restorative soul food.

The revelation of Ahmad's deception precipitates the crisis that eventually leads the family to reconciliation. Being summoned from the kitchen to the dining room to explain his deception, the lad absentmindedly leaves a towel on the burner, which results in a fire. The collective effort to smother the flames and save their ancestral home reminds the adults of the dangers of leaving the maintenance of their legacy to a child. The adult siblings had been feuding over whether to sell the house. Teri, the most successful and self-absorbed and the most fully assimilated into the mainstream values of self-interest, wanted to dispose of the house to pay Mama's hospital bill while the other siblings, Maxine and Bird, wanted to retain the symbol of their cultural and familial legacy. The fire reminds everyone that they do not want to lose the house, and once they have arrived at this collective understanding, reclusive Uncle Pete precipitately enters the kitchen with his television, no doubt intending to evacuate the premises with his prize possession. Dropping it, he inadvertently reveals a cache of money hidden in its casing. The symbolism here is quite heavy-handed but, nevertheless, effective. The money facilitates the family's recognition of the value of their collective bonds, and it is no accident that the money is revealed in the kitchen, signifying the great value of the activities taking place in that environment — the value of soul food.

The food that the Joseph family consumes — Southern fried chicken, deep fried catfish, chitlins, pig's feet, black-eyed peas, sweet potato pie, egg pie, sweet corn bread, greens, macaroni and cheese etc. — suggests the cultural duality that Dubois identified within the African American soul. There is nothing particularly African about the comestibles that the family savors;

however, many of the dishes are racially distinctive within American cuisine (pig's feet, chitlins, greens, black-eyed peas) and still others possess a regional significance (deep fried catfish, corn bread, Southern fried chicken, sweet potato pie, etc.). Soul food embodies the historical impoverishment of and constraint upon African Americans by the culture that enslaved them. Many of the items cited above became a part of the black population's diet because the ingredients were the most readily obtainable by those unable to purchase finer cuts of meat and more desirable vegetables. Indeed, one might postulate that soul food represents the leavings of the great American banquet at which African Americans were not allowed to dine. It is a tribute to the culinary art of the black community that it was able to create these delicious dishes from the foods scorned by whites. The Joseph family continues to dine on the same dishes they have always consumed despite their newly attained affluence. Consuming soul food is consuming hard won history and cultural identity; it is a communion of the oppressed for whom digesting their own lamentable histories is an act of exclusion and defense, consolidating family loyalties against lingering racial hostility as well as total assimilation by the dominant culture.

The Joseph family attempts to repair internal conflicts by resuming their observance of the Sunday dinner ritual in George Tillman's *Soul Food* (1997).

Eat Drink Man Woman

Director Ang Lee's film *Eat Drink Man Woman* depicts the struggles of a Taiwanese master chef and widower, Chu, to keep his family together by insisting that the four members meet each Sunday to consume a multicourse dinner. Chu's three adult daughters—Jen, Chien, Ning—long to leave their father's house, which has become oppressive, as has his weekly observance, which Chien refers to as the "Sunday dinner torture ritual." During the opening credits of the film, Chu prepares the elaborate feast that no one will enjoy while the intermittent scenes reveal his daughters' individual struggles to attend. As the narrative progresses, the Sunday ritual is exposed as an empty gesture, bringing neither gustatory nor social enjoyment; the participants are merely going through the motions. Despite Chu's fascinating proficiency in exotic and ancient Chinese culinary techniques, his artful meal remains unpalatable for the diners, the empty gestures of a chef who can no longer taste and who creates elaborate meals to hide the fact that he no longer knows how to please and support his daughters, and within the family conversation, the audience can detect thinly veiled hostility.

Chu can no longer assess the appropriate ingredients and seasonings requisite to the completion of an enjoyable dish. At work, he can exploit the palate of Old Wen, his colleague and friend, who testifies to the success of Chu's culinary efforts: "I have only your face to judge my recipes by." However, at home, the generational tension between the father and his daughters, particularly the second, Chien, who is the most successful cook, has left him no one whose judgment he considers trustworthy. When Chien criticizes his soup, the father is resistant, assuming that she is merely being difficult, but when she announces that she has bought a condo without consulting him in advance and is planning to move out, he is stunned and demoralized. This scene helps the audience to decipher the metaphor of Chu's inability to taste, which parallels his incapacity to control and direct his daughters' lives. He no longer knows what ingredients are necessary for their happiness, and, ultimately, the daughters must be allowed to contribute their own unique ingredients (in the form of husbands and career choices) to the family repast before the enjoyment of the tradition can be restored.

The dissolution of Chu's family ritual is clearly inevitable from the beginning of the film, each daughter leaving either to pursue a husband or a career, yet the significance of the "Sunday torture ritual" is not lost. The artful dishes that the master chef prepares embody Chinese tradition, and the weekly observance constitutes Chu's efforts to compel his daughters to acknowledge their heritage both as a family and as an ethnicity. The daughters' inability to appreciate fully either the food or the companionship of the weekly dinner illustrates their growing alienation from Chinese culture. Taiwan is a country that is torn between powerful conflicting influences. While the inhabitants remain heavily bound to mainland China, when it comes to traditions, the antithetical leverage of Western culture is everywhere apparent in the film, particularly in the daughters' lives. Indeed, the generational dispute between Chu and his daughters can be coded as a clash of these two cultural giants, the older generation embodying the original legacy of China, and the younger, the more recent influence of America. The father's decision to sell his house and take the unconventional step of moving in with a young wife illustrates his final capitulation to the emerging culture, and while there is no evidence that the food he prepares has changed, his new ability to enjoy alternative recipes (for food and living) has been initiated.

The Chu household may be lagging behind the vanguard of Taiwanese society at the beginning of the film. The house itself is the only traditional Asian structure on a block filled with modern apartment buildings, and it is repeatedly constructed as an oasis from the bustle and uniformity of the overcrowded city outside. The house is spacious, private, exotic, and peaceful. Despite the daughters' obvious assimilation to Western values and lifestyles, they are all shocked by Chu's announcement of his marriage to Rong, the eldest daughter's closest friend, and by his decision to sell the ancestral home, thereby letting go of the past and embracing change and modernity. Before his conversion, the father had, by virtue of his extensive knowledge of the mysterious and exotic culinary practices of Chinese culture, been the embodiment of cultural wisdom who conferred identity on his daughters by connecting them with a tradition larger than themselves. His meals are a bulwark against assimilation. Each of the daughters is threatened by absorption into the emergent set of values that offer to change the world into a single cultural entity and, subsequently, wipe away the unique heritage of the Chinese/Taiwanese. Again Chu renders his assessment of the dwindling influence of Eastern virtues using food metaphors: "There's no sense in cooking exquisite food anymore. After forty years of Chinese food in Taiwan, everything is mixed up just like rivers running into the sea. It's all one flavor! Even a mess of slop can pass for Joy Luck Dragon Phoenix." Chu's resignation as a chef signals his willingness to abandon tradition and accept the progressive assimilation into the Western melting pot; his second marriage is his first act of revolt against cultural orthodoxy.

Chu's daughters are already heavily influenced by Western values at the beginning of the film. Jen is a Christian; Chien is a highly competent Western style businesswoman who seeks advancement in the airline company that employs her and is reassigned to the company office in Amsterdam; and Ning, who works at an American style fast food restaurant, meets a man, gets pregnant, and starts a family with him before finishing school. Yet despite their several rebellions against parental authority and, by extension, Eastern values, the daughters expect their father to remain conventional and are stunned by his decision to sell their ancestral home and remarry. When he announces at dinner that he will marry Rong rather than her mother Mrs. Liang, his daughters think he has become confused with drink. The daughters' rebellion against parental guidance necessitates that the parent retain a commitment to the values that they defy, but when Chu refuses to maintain his place within the semiotics of the social unit, he destabilizes the daughters' identities, revealing the retention of their Chinese socialization. Chien assumes the father's place in the kitchen of the ancestral home, becoming the repository of cultural wisdom represented in Chinese culinary arts. She, like all the family members, has become a hybrid of Eastern and Western culture. While she will move to Amsterdam, she promises to return in a few months to visit, and her cooking skills will be an emissary of Asian culture to Europe.

Chu is not the only parent in the film who is concerned about the creeping westernization of his family. Li-Kai, Chien's professional colleague, is a Taiwanese national who lives in America and who complains that his son is growing up to be an American. In returning to Taiwan, he imagines that he is returning to the cradle of his ancestral culture, but he finds the environment altered. He cannot find a single Chinese gift for his son. As he and Chien browse for souvenirs, she finds an item that appears Chinese, but Li recognizes that it is based upon a western cartoon. Thus even a man reared in Taiwan can no longer distinguish between the merging cultures. Similarly, Mrs. Liang returns to Taiwan from America, no doubt searching for a new husband, one who will restore her link with her origins, only to find that the fountainhead of her native civilization has changed in her absence. She laments the vulgarization of her children in America, partially fashioning her complaint in culinary terms: "And my youngest hitched up with a white guy who plays an electric guitar in his garage all weekend — a disaster! He eats hamburgers with onions every day. And when I tried to cook fried rice, the smoke alarm would go off. I'd rather die than live there."

Of course, Mrs. Liang's relief at returning to Taiwan is short lived. When Chu announces his intentions to marry her daughter rather than her, she raves against the cultural degradation of her homeland, condemns the match, and begs to return to America.

The restoration of Chu's taste at the end of the film is facilitated by his willingness to allow his daughter Chien to cook his dinner, and while her recipes do not taste quite right to him, he realizes with great surprise that he can, once again, taste. With the decision to let his daughters ply their own music, he understands that child rearing is not like cooking; the parent cannot know what to expect from the ingredients with which s/he works. Even the most methodical process can produce varying results in the respective adult subjects: "Life isn't like cooking after all. I can't wait until all the ingredients are properly laid out before starting to cook. Anyway after the first bite, the only thing that counts is the taste."

The chef's reference to taste in the final line suggests that appearance is less important than pleasure in eating and happiness in life. He did not produce the conventional family that he may have wanted, each member following a traditional path through education, profession, courtship, and marriage, but the happiness of family members is the most desirable outcome. Just as Chu salvaged the disastrous Shark Fin soup for the banquet at the beginning of the film, transforming it into "Joy Luck Dragon Phoenix" and winning the admiration of caterers and diners alike, he must allow his daughters to stir and season the soup that is their lives, particularly if he hopes the final result to be their fulfillment, but he can salvage his own life by reclaiming a family in ruin, by choosing a young divorcee, Rong, who already has a daughter, Shan-Shan, rather than the elder Mrs. Liang. The resulting social unit is no paradigm for the conventional family, but it, nevertheless, brings happiness to its members.

Tortilla Soup

Maria's Rapoll's *Tortilla Soup* (2001) is the American/English language adaptation of Ang Lee's *Eat Drink Man Woman*. The father and daughters have been transported to L.A. with their ethnicity altered to Latino. While they remain, as in Lee's film, displaced or, perhaps more appropriately, replaced people, the cultural influences or value systems that draw the family in opposing directions do not appear as disjunctive as the similar conflict in Taiwan. The discrepancy between China and the USA constitutes more of a gulf than that between Mexico and Southern California. Nevertheless, the Naranjo family, particularly the father, Martin (Hector Elizondo), remains vexed by a cultural paralysis, unable to return to their unadulterated Mexican heritage or to their place of origins, but equally ineffectual in moving forward and becoming fully assimilated into American culture. Obviously, as in the original film, the daughters are much more successful than their father in their absorption into urban American life, yet they too remain cultural hybrids, synthesizing the values of their geographic origin and those of contemporary California.

In Lee's film, the geographic proximity of Taiwan to mainland China is an important thematic feature, mirroring the shared social and cultural heritage of the two nations. However, the two countries, having moved in radically different directions in the second half of the twentieth century, are left bitterly opposed to one another, and arguably the satellite nation, Taiwan, has become a sanctuary for the Chinese culture that has been repressed under communist mainland rule, yet that same culture is threatened by western economic influences made necessary by international alliances in the maintenance of its national boundaries. On the island, the ancient Chinese culture is safe from the authoritarian directives of the mainland, but faces a progressive modernization and a perhaps a more appealing form of economic assimilation. *Tortilla Soup* creates a similar geographic and demographic scenario. The connection between California and Mexico is not merely proximity nor is it political. The Southwestern United States was appropriated from Mexico in the nineteenth century. Thus the Naranjo family may not be more recent immigrants from Mexico, but leftovers from a time before the land's (re)acquisition, original Californians. Both locations, Southern California and Taiwan, may be adjacent to the civilization that engendered them, but there are radical incongruities. Indeed, in both films, the subject families could be construed as economic refugees from their respective homelands. Certainly, Taiwan (like Hong Kong until recently) constitutes a haven for Chinese communism's discontents; likewise, Americans automatically assume (often wrongly) that Mexicans entering the United States, either legally or illegally, are attempting to escape the widespread poverty of their homeland.

Martin is a purist attempting to keep the merging cultures separate, irritably refusing to allow his family to speak Spanglish because it debases both languages. He demands English or Spanish, and when the daughters begin to quarrel at the table, he reminds them that they are to venerate the ritual of dinner: "We honor dinner. We have good manners, and we have pleasant conversation." Shortly thereafter, he is called away from the formal repast to manage a culinary crisis at work. Martin is equally troubled by the violation of tradition in his daughters' respective lifestyles. When Carmen announces her intention to move out of his house, she justifies her actions to her sister Leticia (Elizabeth Peña) by invoking the differences between Mexican and American culture. Martin's desire to have his daughters remain at home until married may be a cultural practice common to their homeland, but not necessarily to Southern California. Chef Naranjo constitutes a significant departure in characterization from the Ang Lee's stoic Chef Chu. Consistent with the ethnic stereotype of Latinos, Martin is a man prone to passion, anger, and irritability although he may be losing some of his heat. While the introduction of Ning's boyfriend and her intention to move out of her father's house provokes little emotion in Chu, Martin rages in the analogous scene, accusing Andy of trying to steal away his daughter. Predictably, Martin is most adamant about the integrity of the food he prepares. When his second daughter, Carmen (Jacqueline Obradors), criticizes his soup explaining that he should not have removed the seeds from the seranos, Martin asserts that he "respects tradition." His coworker, Gomez, remembers how uncompromising his partner was when they owned their own restaurant. He resisted any criticism of his work even from his customers. Maribel's boyfriend Andy is the first to identify Martin as an artist, and Martin has some very old-fashioned notions of the qualities requisite to culinary art, and the first of these is related to gender. Carmen, the daughter who developed a powerful interest in and talent for cooking, complains that her father kicked her out of the kitchen. And while Martin explains that he wanted her to go to school, to do "something significant with [her] life," Carmen offers an alternative interpretation: he "didn't think a woman would make a good chef." Elsewhere, Carmen complains that her father thinks all of her dishes are "mutts," a term appropriate to his culinary philosophy. Since a "mutt" is a mixed breed of dog, Carmen's dishes must similarly blend traditions. Perhaps her recipes capture the tastes of America as well as those of old Mexico; doubtless, they are more spicy than her father's. Martin also displays contempt for American foods. Orlando (Paul Rodriguez), Leticia's husband, offers to take Martin to a ball game and to buy him hot dogs and sodas, but the latter quips, "I'll tell you what; you take care of the tickets, and I'll take care of the food."

The uniquely Mexican cuisine that Martin prepares emphasizes peppers, a vegetable traditionally associated with the heat of passion. The original culinary dispute between Carmen and her father at the beginning of the film is waged over her father's too timid use of serano peppers. By removing the seeds, the chef radically reduces the heat of the vegetable, and this difference in father and daughter reveals their respective approaches to life. Much of the passion went out of Martin's life when his wife died, and he blames his restaurant and his cooking. His wife's death may also be the incident that initiated the decline in his ability to taste. Carmen, whose cooking will eventually reawaken her father's taste for food and life, wants Martin to meet someone who will rekindle his desires. The conclusion of the narrative emphasizes the necessity of change in the efforts to keep life interesting. Martin's selection of a young wife rather than the elder Hortensis (Raquel Welch) signifies his desire to experience the passions of youth, and it is when his daughter prepares the same soup as that over which they disagreed at the first dinner that he regains his taste. The first sensation is the taste of seranos, which he describes as "too sharp." Carmen's rebuttal that they make the dish "a little more interesting" says as much about life as about cooking. The introduction of sharp tastes parallels the embrace of desire and change.

Speaking of Dinner

Meaning and identity within the dinner party is constructed dialectically, structured like language; food is a "system of signs" (Douglas and Gross 1–4). The image of family matriarch/patriarch is the signifier that temporarily fixes meaning within the system. The divergent members of the group draw the meaning in their lives from their relationship to the parental figure at the head of the table. The syntax of this visual construction suggests that each child is an elaboration on the subject who is the matriarch/patriarch, but as with all language, the efforts at explanation fall short of capturing the meaning that was first spoken and intended or, in this case, embodied in the chef. Each articulation includes a variation on the subject. Similarly, the food passed around the table, the same that reminds the diners of their shared cultural and biological heritage, varies with each articulation/preparation only approximating the original taste, and as the dishes round the table, the palate of each diner remixes the ingredients and produces a unique reaction and meaning. The ordering of the dishes is syntactical as well. Just as a given language has a finite number of grammatical paradigms through which to express an idea, the ordering and ingredients of a dinner are rigidly dictated by the rules of propriety (Douglas 44). The traditional dinner needs only one meat dish, one starch, one sweet, and perhaps several vegetables. The placement of the dishes along the signifying chain or within the process of the dinner reveals the participants' cultural and class standing. The family that consumes dessert first are vulgar and contemptuous of decorum. If an American dinner leaves the salad for the final course, the diners are conscious of a breach of ritual; however, many European ethnicities routinely consume the salad at the conclusion of the meal. Moreover, one does not generally serve sandwiches, a lunch food, at dinner, and the presence of the same at the evening meal undermines the social meaning, the seriousness of the repast. One would not consume sandwiches or fast foods at a holiday dinner; such a practice would identify the participants as irreligious or unpatriotic. Even the importance of each meal varies according to geography. In American culture, the evening meal is usually the largest except on Sundays when an afternoon feast is prepared. In contrast, Mexican culture places the main meal at about one or two in the afternoon reserving leftovers for the supper.

In each of the above films, the Sunday dinner is offered as a stabilizing ritual that confers identity, purpose, and unity onto the participants. The person who prepares the food in each case signifies family and ethnic tradition. The dinner itself involves a display of respect with the participants revealing reverence for religion and deference to the past struggles of the biological and racial, ethnic, or national families. The display of obedience constructs the microcosm of the nuclear family as a metaphor for the macrocosm of society, and the conformity of the participants signifies the creation of obedient familial as well as obedient social subjects. The ironic outcome of the several characters' efforts to preserve the Sunday ritual is the revelation of dissolution rather than the maintenance of the families. One does not need to make a Herculean effort to restore cohesion to a healthy institution.

That the maintenance of the ritual is required at all suggests that the members of the group are being drawn apart and that the practice is in danger of disappearing. It is not only the disagreements between family members at the various dinner parties that reveal the instability of the system, but also the social pressures that require both observance of tradition and the devotion to an economic imperative that draws them apart the rest of the week. The fact that the families do not meet for dinner the other six days in the week is an indictment of the same system that feigns an interest in the cohesion of the household. The modern subject in a capitalistic society must first be a producer or laborer and a consumer and then a member of a family. The material demands of modern urban cultures (in all three films, embodied in the monolithic American consumer culture) are the forces that undermine the family's effort to celebrate their unity.

14

Food Fights: The Martial Chefs and Magical Arts of Asian Cinema

In the final scene of Yimou Zhang's visually spectacular *The House of Flying Daggers* (2004), the titanic struggle between two Tang Dynasty warriors—Jin (Takeshi Kaneshiro) and Leo (Andy Lau)—attains mythic status, the warriors translated into virtual forces of nature. As snow unexpectedly falls upon the previous midsummer setting of the narrative, the director creates a visual parallel between the bitter and prolonged combat of the warriors and the contentious change of season, as nature gods vie for dominion over the earth embodied in the female protagonist, Mei (Ziyi Zhang). Perhaps the director only conveys the intransigence of the dueling swordsmen whose strength, determination, and skill defy temporal limitations or perhaps the director jettisons the rational development of character and narrative in favor of art and cinematic magic, literalizing the metaphorical equivalent between winter and death.

The transcendence of rational and physical limitations within Asian cinema shares much with the magical realist movement in literature and film, the same that emerged from central and south America in the first half of the twentieth century. In "Magical Strategies: The Supplement of Realism," Scott Simpkins, paraphrasing Angel Flores, argues that the aesthetic "does not depend either on natural or physical laws or on the usual conception of the real in Western Culture.... [It is] a narrative in which the relation between incidents, characters, and setting could not be based upon or justified by their status within the physical world..." (142).

The events and characters in Zhang's films frequently defy gravity as well as the limitations of human dexterity and sensitivity. Characters fly through the air in the fight scenes, inflict destruction that would seem optimistic for a tank, and suffer physical torment that defies human endurance while all this time remaining graceful, unruffled, and unfatigued.

The magical martial arts of the Asian cinematic aesthetic are not limited to fight films but play a recurring role in Hong Kong cinema about the competitive vocation of food preparation. Several recent films fit an unusual classification that I will call the "Asian food fight film": Stephen Chow and Lik-Chi Lee's *The God of Cookery* (1996), Tsui Hark's *The Chinese Feast* (1995), and Chi-Ngai Lee's *The Magic Kitchen* (2004). Each portrays the Hong Kong restaurant industry as a combat between gangs with rival cooking styles, and each of the narratives concludes with a cooking contest in which the underdog protagonist bests the expected winner. In *The God of Cookery* and *The Chinese Feast*, the antagonist is arrogant, vaunting, and dishonest, while in *The Magic Kitchen*, the final contest becomes an act of self-overcoming on the part of the protagonist rather than a triumph over a prideful opponent. In all three narratives, the principal chef experiences a fall prior to the final conflict and must regain sufficient fortitude to face apotheosis, and in each, the triumph over the rival combatants is accompanied by edification, a new understanding of the meaning of cooking and its representative role in human relations.

The God of Cookery

Stephen Chow and Lik-Chi Lee's film begins with a meta-cinematic commentary. The arrogant, vaunting, and merciless master chef, Stephen Chow, the God of Cookery, appears to be adjudicating a culinary competition in which each of the contestants fails to live up to the judge's standards and is cruelly rebuffed. When the final contestant reveals the steaming hidden contents of his "Secret Roast Goose," having tricked the judge into a hasty and inaccurate preliminary assessment of his dish, the God refuses to retract his score, shifting his criticism to the contestant himself, who, in Chow's estimation, is too "ugly" to cook, his appearance spoiling the diners' appetites. Chow's judgment, swift and uncompromising, humiliates and destroys the contestant. Having given each of the participants a score of zero for minor faults, Chow makes his own dish, a candied dessert which he magically constructs in mid-air, the ingredients solidifying in defiance of gravity and forming the Chinese character for "heart." The master chef simultaneously tosses flower petals into the air that land on the hardening dish, adding, "We must rely on our heart to make the perfect dish." Of course, his platitude remains ironic until end of the film since no one has shown less heart than the merciless God of Cookery.

The expectations of the cinematic audience are undermined in the next scene when Chow meets with his former contestants on the roof of his corporate headquarters to assesses their performances. The contest was staged, designed to create stimulating television programming. However, his heartless assessment of the ugly chef's acting reveals that the master is every bit as proud and demanding as his television persona. These opening scenes act as a meta-narrative for the remainder of the film. The magic and hyperbole of Chow-the-character's cooking program, *The God of Cookery*, parallel the same in Chow-the-director's identically titled film. Chow plays himself, writing, producing, and directing the film in reality just as he does the cooking show in fiction. The odyssey of self-discovery that the fictionalized Chow experiences in the film mirrors the movie mogul's efforts to create a movie with heart in which the protagonist discovers that humility is the most important skill a chef can wield. The fictionalized story of the chef who falls from grace through pride and proceeds to lift himself up, becoming a more virtuous and compassionate person as well as a better cook, allegorizes the process of filmmaking, the culinary artist's tribulations embodying those of the cinematic hunger artist as he prepares the various ingredients of his film narrative.

The God of Cookery is exposed as a fraud early in the narrative by a seemingly unassuming and solicitous assistant who turns out to be a trained chef determined to humiliate, destroy, and ultimately replace Chow. Bull Tong (Vincent Kok) reveals his skills unexpectedly while Chow is being filmed at a ribbon cutting ceremony for his new restaurant. He taunts and reviles his employer before offering an on-camera cooking demonstration intended to expose Chow as a fraud. Tong's exterior clothing bursts off of his body revealing an underlying suit, and when he slams his fist on the demonstration table, the fish and vegetables fly upward and are sliced and carved in midair before they land in a serving bowl, meticulously arranged and sculpted in the shape of hearts. Mocking Chow's own earlier moralizing, Tong adds that one must "have the heart to cook." Ironically, Tong does not have the "heart" for cooking either. Although he has exceptional skills in food preparation, Tong becomes as imperious, abusive, and demanding as his predecessor, the competitive Hong Kong food business having exchanged one tyrant for another, the oppressed having become oppressor in his turn.

Chow's fall from power and affluence deposits him in an even more brutal and competitive food market. Wretched and homeless, he prowls among the sidewalk vendors of Temple Street where gang warfare determines which business is permitted to sell particular dishes. The street conflict is an analogue for similar battles within the corporate world, and the progressive restoration of Chow's confidence and marketing expertise requires that he keep low company, that he combat his opponents openly until he is once again prepared for the subterfuge of the boardroom. In his spiritual/professional odyssey, he is reduced to the preparation of the simplest dishes to achieve an enlightenment based upon humility and simplicity. Eventually he unites the rival gangs in a business venture selling their newly created dish "Explosive Pissing Beef Balls" which propels them to the top of the culinary industry where Chow is once again able to compete for his former title, God of Cookery.

Chow's [re]education includes spiritual, culinary, and martial arts preparation at the Shaolin Monastery where he is inadvertently deposited following an assassination attempt. He employs this improbable combination of skills in his successful bout with Bull Tong, a match that resembles a martial arts combat or the rivalry between wizards as much as it does a cooking contest. As is common in the magical realist aesthetic, the mundane is transformed through hyperbole or sometimes through the literalization of figures of speech until it resembles the mythic and the heroic (Faris 171). Chow arrives at the contest at the last moment skimming and floating across the surface of the bay and leaping through a second story window. The subsequent food preparation involves the display of supernatural skills such as shortening the cooking time of complicated dishes through the application of body heat. Chow even fries an egg in his hand, resurrecting the ancient skill of "Fire Fist." The men demonstrate a superhuman skill with knives in the preparation of the dish "Buddha Jumping Wall," and their aggression toward the ingredients spills over into their interpersonal relations as they fling food and hot oil at each other. Tong kicks a table, causing a collection of knives to fly at Chow, who successfully catches all of them simultaneously. Next, Tong hurls a meat cleaver, which Chow kicks back in Tong's direction. The judge of the contest compliments Tong on his flying skills when he glides through the air hurling himself at his opponent, and when Chow beats back his assailant with a folding chair, she praises his skill in using a chair as a bludgeon as though it were a traditional culinary art. The judge's untroubled acceptance of the extraordinary events in the demonstration room is consistent with the nonchalant acquiescence to the supernatural in the magical realist narrative, where characters regard metaphysical phenomena as common occurrences unworthy of note (Zamora and Faris 3).

While Chow's training at the Shaolin Monastery included the mastery of Kung Fu, his apotheosis at the conclusion of the film necessitates humility and lowliness rather than vaunting pride; indeed his refusal to provoke divinity with the presumptuous title the God of Cookery actually saves him from their avenging wrath. When his version of the complicated "Buddha Jumping Wall" explodes, Chow has three minutes to create another dish. Invoking his newly attained religious virtues, he prepares the simple dish, BBQ Pork Rice. The judge experiences a spiritual ecstasy when she tastes the simple dish, which expresses Chow's grief over the loss and mistreatment of his homely business partner Turkey. He has finally learned to cook with heart, to convey his love and emotions to his diners. However, his lesson in humility is not yet complete. The divinity who subsequently descends to punish Tong for his tragic pride and ambition spares Chow because he has learned that everyone and no one can be a God of Cookery. He has ceased to strive beyond the place of common humanity, and he is rewarded with love and success.

The conclusion of *The God of Cookery* reveals the dual heritage of Hong Kong. While traditionally a Chinese province, Hong Kong was maintained as a British territory since the 1840s until its return to Chinese control in 1997. The social politics of the film reveal the tension between western capitalism and eastern communism among the denizens of Hong Kong. While the film condemns the shady business tactics of massive food corporations, it also offers material success in the industry as the primary goal of the characters, a value that is not explicitly interrogated within the film although it may be undermined implicitly in Chow's stoic indifference to the outcome of the cookery contest. The villainy and greed of the food moguls is contrasted with the ingenuity, skill, and enthusiasm of the masses who stage their own challenge to the rule of large corporations. Chow's revolution begins in the streets where he exploits the values of the large firms to their destruction. The opulent, arrogant, and insensitive lifestyle of the food mogul is rejected at the conclusion when Chow embraces Buddhist virtues of simplicity, humility, poverty, and serenity. While the religious or philosophical dimensions of the film's conclusion may be antithetical to the atheistic position of China's communist government, both philosophical systems promote the simple life, one not driven by the mania of owning things.

The Chinese Feast

Tsui Hark, director of *The Chinese Feast*, organizes his film around a series of cooking contests of progressively less formality, culminating in the final scene which restores the high ritual of the first. Thus the film continues the heroic structure also present in Chow and Lee's *The God of Cookery*. Master chef Lui Kit (played by Kenny Bee) undergoes a dramatic decline in stature resulting from his failure to value the interpersonal over the professional. Thus he falls at the height of pride and experiences prolonged suffering and degradation until he is rehabilitated by a collection of misfit cooks who require his long dormant skills in defense of one of the oldest restaurants in Hong Kong. Consistent with the other two films in this discussion, *The Chinese Feast* equates masterful skills in the kitchen with the dexterity and discipline of the martial arts, and the blinding speed with which the chefs execute their tasks once again invokes the narrative strategies of magical realism. Considerably less magical than *The God of Cookery* (which even includes divine intervention), *The Chinese Feast* nevertheless necessitates the audience's suspension of disbelief, the acceptance of culinary miracles.

The film opens with a formalized contest between Lui Kit and Lung Kwun-Bo (Man Cheuk Chiu), both participants calm and respectful of each other's talent. However, the concentration of Kit is interrupted by a plea from his lover in the hospital. At first refusing to concede, he eventually abandons the contest to join her at the hospital only to find that he is too late. She is out of surgery and has left him a note upbraiding him for his insensitivity, for placing his professional pride over his lover's personal welfare. Kit abandons his cooking utensils in the hallway of the hospital and disappears, suffering a complete mental and emotional breakdown. He is later discovered stocking shelves in a small grocery store, all of the refined sensibilities that made him a master chef having abandoned him, dulled by alcohol, poverty, and clinical depression.

The second cooking contest constitutes a parody of the first. Scores of aspiring chefs, positioned along lengthy rows of cooking stations, prepare to compete for an employment opportunity in a Toronto hotel restaurant. The only participant unable to take the proceedings seriously is Sun (Leslie Cheung). Positioned half way back in the middle row, he is conspicuous as the only chef who is not wearing the traditional white coat and hat, his black leather jacket and ostentatious demeanor disrupting the otherwise orderly proceedings. While Kit had ignored his lover's pleas by participating in the master chef challenge, Sun, who does not even know how to cook, entered the recruitment contest in hope of being sent to Toronto where he can join the woman he loves. Kit's mastery and integrity contrasts sharply with Sun's ineptitude and dishonesty. The desperate lover has stuffed his jacket with restaurant bought dishes that he can pass off as his own work. However, despite his deviousness and vulgarity in professional pursuits, he does, unlike Kit, place personal relations before pride and professional ambition. Thus in at least one way, he retains more integrity than Kit.

When he is disqualified for cheating in the contest, he obtains employment in the local Qing Han Restaurant where he hopes to learn to cook. However, he rapidly discovers that his presence in the restaurant is a practical joke played on himself and the owner, Au Siu-Fung (Kar-Ying Law). He has become a pawn in the ongoing rivalry between Fung and Lung

Kwun-Bo. Sun, having been sent to the restaurant to disrupt its efficiency through his ineptitude, once there, finds himself the subject of Fung's hijinks for having been recommended by Lung. He does fall for Wai (Anita Yuen), the owner's daughter, who is every bit as much of a disruption as Sun and who enjoys baiting her conservative father. In spite of superficial animosities, the unlikely collection of individuals band together to save the Qing Han from Wong Wing (Xin Xin Xiong), director of the Supergroup, who is determined to take over the Hong Kong food industry, one restaurant at a time, beginning with the oldest establishment in the district — Fung's Qing Han.

Wong Wing initiates the third and most informal contest, which arises spontaneously from the antagonist's inspection of Fung's kitchen. Without invitation, Wing commandeers a wok and begins preparing his "Crispy Noodle with Beef," all the time explaining his masterful techniques, which involve a dazzling dexterity with pans, knives, and ladles. He produces an artful dish in an impossibly brief period of time, his sleight of hand responsible for the careful wrapping of noodles around portions of beef. The crispy aspect of the noodles constitutes his own innovation as he lights the dish on fire, defying the onlookers' expectations. Not to be outdone, Au prepares his own version of "Sweet and Sour Pork," spinning ladles and knives with extraordinary speed and concluding with nuggets of crispy pork on a bed of vegetables that fan out beneath in colorful rows. The rivalry that has grown between the two men cannot be satisfied by the spontaneous cooking demonstrations. Wing challenges Fung to a formal contest in which the participants will prepare the 108 dishes in the "Qing and Han Imperial Feast." Wing wagers 5 million gang bi (Hong Kong dollars) and Fung control of his restaurant. The challenge seems more appropriate to a martial arts film than to a narrative about the food industry. Wing insists that Fung acknowledge him as his master, and Fung feels honor bound to accept the challenge or lose face among his kitchen staff. However, when his entire staff resigns having been bribed by Wing, Fung suffers a heart attack and is unable to compete. Thus his daughter and her haphazard collection of confederates must defend the restaurant on his behalf, and this includes his former rival Lung.

With Au Siu-Fung out of commission, the group must rehabilitate Kit, the only chef who knows the 108 dishes of the "Qing and Han Imperial Feast." However, lifting Kit out of his degradation involves more than just cleaning him up. His first cooking display for many applauding chefs is a complete failure. While he retains his practical skills — preparing a visually stunning dish in a matter of moments — he has, nevertheless, lost the acute sensory perceptions that made him a master chef. The subsequent scenes in which the team [re]train Kit's senses constitute a rubric for the composition of an excellent cook. The team explains the role each of the five senses plays in the chef's work, and when they have completed their instruction, Kit is once again ready for competition.

The rehabilitation of the master chef is parallel to the restoration of ritual and order in the fourth and final cooking challenge. The moral structure of the final combat echoes the same in *The God of Cookery*. The protagonists, who display humility and integrity, face an opponent who is imperious, vaunting, devious, and immensely talented. However, in tragic fashion, Wing's own pride and arrogance lead to his downfall. When the two teams have identical scores at the end of the third and last day, the judges give the award to Kit and the Qing Han crew because Wing's personality constitutes a blemish on his work. The dishes prepared on each of the three days of the feast are obviously intended to showcase the exoticism, creativity, and extravagance of Chinese cuisine. The three meats featured in the main courses are each products derived from endangered species and seem particularly challenging because the very idea of consuming them is offensive from both ecological and purely gustatory perspectives. The preparation of bear palm, elephant trunk, and monkey brain is a shining example of the cinematic practice Frank Chin designated "food pornography" (qtd. in Ma 62), not in the offensiveness of the ingredients, but in the ostentatious exploitation of exoticism in the promotion of one's cultural/culinary distinctiveness.

The martial qualities of the narrative remain on display in the final competition. The chefs wield their utensils with blinding speed while all the time maintaining form, discipline, confidence, and resolution. The contest itself is coded as a boxing bout, at least in the visual representations of Wong Wing and the Supergroup. Wing wears traditional Chinese clothing that resembles the silk warmup coat worn by boxers before and after a match. Moreover, like a fighter between rounds, Wing is massaged and doctored by his team of assistants. Such imagery codes him as an ambitious scrapper and street fighter who will not compete fairly or lose with dignity and humility, but will do everything necessary to win. The Qing Han team are disadvantaged because they have integrity and honesty. The street fighter/gangster on the Qing Han team — Sun — has been tamed and civilized, revealing none of the desperate trickery that he demonstrated in the chef recruitment competition at the beginning of the film. However, after Wing puts phosphorous on Kit's towel so that it catches on fire and Kit is burned and no longer able to chop, the Qing Han team learns to use subterfuge, not by disrupting Wing's efforts but by anticipating and circumventing any further trickery from the opposition.

The magical elements of the narrative are much more subtle than in the climax of *The God of Cookery* where a deus ex machina resolves the conflict, an angel literally intervening and destroying the villainous chefs. The wizardry of the characters of *Chinese Feast* lies partially in the rapidity and skill with which the artful dishes are prepared and partially in the ancient esoteric knowledge requisite to the production of such dishes. The magic lies less in the preparations of the chefs than in the exoticism and creativity of the Chinese culinary tradition, the chefs coded as shamans who are not only conversant with the deep tracts of occulted human knowledge but capable of leading their diners on a spiritual and emotional journey. The original Qing Han Imperial Feast was held to unify the Qing and Han ethnicities following the discrimination against the Han Chinese by the Manchurians. The feast was intended to reconcile the separate groups by synthesizing their traditional foods. Appropriately, the Qing Han restaurant team have learned the lesson of the ancient feast when the film is concluded. The former rivalries of Fung/Lung and Lung/Kit are resolved and the people work together for a common cause in defense of their region. In contrast, the antagonist, Wing, knows how to prepare the Qing Han feast but does not understand its social significance. It is his own selfish ambition that destroys his efforts to subdue and rule the food industry of Hong Kong.

The Magic Kitchen

Paradoxically, *The Magic Kitchen* (2004), written and directed by Lee Chi-Ngai, is less magical than *Chinese Feast* and *The God of Cookery*, but more magical realist. Abandoning the hyperbole of the earlier films, the events of *The Magic Kitchen* remain, for the most part, grounded in reality save for the family curse that Yau (Sammi Cheng), the female protagonist, believes has been placed upon herself and four generations of her female ancestors. The martial attributes of the narrative are equally muted, relegated to the distant past. Any food preparation is completed without the superhuman speed and miraculous dexterity of Chow, Tong, Kit, and Wing, nor does Yau retain the culinary and cultural erudition or the confidence of the foregoing master chefs. She is reticent in her pursuit of the culinary arts. Her exceptional skills do not derive from careful study and a desire to master the art of Chinese cooking, but from her mother's magical cookbooks which convey both recipes and family history.

Yau narrates the story of her family curse, which began with her grandmother's grandmother, Ju, who was a master of both martial and literary arts. A great chef, Auyoung, loved her, but she refused him until he agreed to transfer his culinary skills to her. "Using the galactic rotation stance, Ju sucked away Auyoung's culinary talents." When Ju's father discovered that Auyoung could no longer cook, he banished his daughter and hired a shaman to place a curse on her and on all those who succeeded her in the female line: they will be excellent chefs, but the men that they love will abandon them. Ju's ambition constitutes the original sin for which the family's women are punished without offending. The protagonist of *The Magic Kitchen* must lift the hex placed upon her female progeny and progenitors by succeeding at both the culinary and the romantic arts.

The Magic Kitchen is an unusual love story in which Yau must abandon her residual affection for Yao (Andy Lau), a man with whom she had a relationship several years before and with whom she was never able to consummate her love, the family curse intervening every time they sought to become intimate. Yau and Yao are inadvertently reacquainted at the beginning of the film, and Yau is forced to wrestle with her residual emotions which are particularly troubling when Yao begins to date a close female friend of Yau, one on whom Yau herself has a crush. By the time Yao is available again at the end of the film, Yau has discovered that love was always accessible to her through her friend Ho (Jerry Yan), an assistant in her private restaurant, "The Magic Kitchen." Ho quietly harbored an affection for Yau for many years while she was preoccupied with others, but she must recognize and appreciate affection where it already exists rather than reignite a passion that has been extinguished for years.

As with Tita in Arau's *Like Water for Chocolate* (1992), who can convey her erotic passions to her brother-in-law through her "Quail in Rose Petal Sauce," Yau has the capacity to transmit emotions through her cooking. Her friend May (Maggie Q) describes Yau as a culinary shaman, a technician of ecstasy: "They all say Yau has magic fingers. Even the most ordinary dishes turn sublime in her hands. Some even find her cooking blissful." Yau describes the first time she recognized the sensuality of food: when she served her friends crab, the consumption of the dish became orgiastic. On that night, she fell in love with May. However, Yau's supernatural culinary skills are her maternal legacy, not her own creation. She relies exclusively upon her mother's magical cookbooks, the same that contain the family recipes of five generations. Indeed Yau has no confidence in her gustatory skills without her mother's recipes. She initially refuses to participate in the King Chef cooking contest, fearing that she would not have time to consult her mother's books since the ingredients are announced on live television. Even after Ho convinces her to compete, she freezes when they announce the secret ingredient since she has never before cooked with "the world famous Hokkaido fresh milk" or any milk for that matter, but through Ho's ministrations, she is able to create new recipes spontaneously and not only demonstrate her proficiency in the contest but also break free of her mother's models for dinner and for life. She is able to lift the curse.

Yau's extrication from the bondage of her mother's legacy always remained within her power. In her narrative of the family curse, Yau's mother indicated that the grandmother's grandmother, Ju, was not only a martial, but also a literary artist. Thus she offered the key to understanding the curse to which she and her progeny would succumb; it was never magic, but metaphor. Yau realizes that the curse was symbol for her mother's marriage. She could not lure her wandering husband home no matter how much food she cooked. She used to prepare huge feasts for just herself and Yau, expecting her husband to return at any time. The mother's recipes were an expression of longing and grief, and so long as Yau continues to prepare the same dishes, she will continue to experience unrequited or unfulfilled love. She will continue to pursue unavailable men, refusing to recognize love where it lies — with Ho, the only person in her life "completely devoted to love." Mother's recipes are paradigms for living an unfulfilled life. Yau must create her own recipes for happiness rather than pining after a lost love and expressing her regret through food. When the contestants in the King Chef rivalry are tied after the first session, Yau refuses to compete any further, arguing that cooking is love and bliss and neither of these should be subject to contest.

Yau arrives at an understanding similar to that which edifies Chow in *The God of Cookery* and Kit in the *Chinese Feast*. All three chefs conclude that they must emphasize interpersonal relations over culinary competitiveness and pride. Cooking is labor on behalf of others, a facilitation of the enjoyment and sustenance of others, and those others must be the primary focus of the endeavor. Chow earns the restoration of his divinity through the expression of humility following the God of Cookery contest. In addition, he earns the love of his newly beautified partner Turkey. Kit regains the love of his former lady, Ms. Cheuk, by accepting her assistance in his culinary enterprises, and thus his failure to attend her agony at the hospital is redeemed. Kit is also elevated by the companionship of his professional rivals who help him to regain his former stature and who share equally in his triumph. Yau realizes that she need not look beyond the devotion of Ho for a fulfillment of her romantic longings, and she does not need to win the King Chef contest because she has already learned the meaning of cooking and has no desire to triumph over her opponent. In contrast to the other two narratives, *The Magic Kitchen*'s rival contestant is not an arrogant, vain, and ambitious villain, but another humble chef who is either moved by Yau's concession or already familiar with the lessons that Yau has only recently learned. He agrees to leave the contest a draw.

The Magic Kitchen shares with The God of Cookery a meta-cinematic motif, a thematic dimension in which the narrative seems to be commenting on itself, showcasing its textuality or its status as a fiction. Yau meets an aspiring film director, Tony, who lives in her building and who appreciates the multi-dimensional smells of her cooking. He enlists Yau's assistance in the creation of a film script that essentially captures the circumstances of their living arrangements, a tenant in an apartment building falls in love with a female chef, whom he has never met, but who lives in the same structure. His only contact with the other tenant is the smell of her culinary creations. Yau insists on making the script autobiographical. When Tony argues that their protagonist should own a private restaurant and maintain a female assistant, Yau alters the gender of her cinematic coworker to conform with the factual details of her life. The film script that Tony composes is The Magic Kitchen, which contains a narrative of its own creation and solicits the co-authorship of its principal protagonist. This type of self-reflexive gesture is generally intended to foreground the fictionality of the story, eliding the so-called transparency of realist fiction or the effort to create the illusion of reality. Magical realist and postmodern narratives frequently contain textual representations of their own composition (D'haen 192). In the concluding pages of Garcia Marquez's One Hundred Years of Solitude, a manuscript is discovered that narrates the events of the novel including that very moment in which the manuscript is uncovered.

Perhaps the meta-cinematic or meta-fictional dimension of The Magic Kitchen comments on the dramatic arch in the development of the protagonist. The insistence that the film narrative reflect the real circumstances of Yau's personal and professional life constitutes an acceptance of those aspects of her life that she previously resisted. She never liked being a chef and only pursued the profession in order to maintain her mother's legacy and her mother's private restaurant, and she has formerly resisted the obviously lovestruck assistant Ho, who has pined after her for years, slavishly devoted without any requital of his faithfulness. The insistence that her life be portrayed accurately suggests a new acquiescence. The circular aspect of the meta-cinematic motif — the fact that the composition of the narrative overlaps with the events it portrays — may be mirrored in the structure of the mythic family curse, which can only be lifted when the karma has come full circle, and the progeny of Ju have redeemed their injury of Auyoung.

The parallel between the culinary and the cinematic artists is particularly strong in the above films. Repeatedly, the magic of filmmaking is mirrored in the magical chefs of Asian cinema. Their sleights of hand and magical techniques elide the real time requisite to the production of an elaborate recipe and their attention to sensory detail parallels the director/screen writer's effort to evoke sensual/sensory pleasures in a medium that can stimulate the auditory and visual only. The film director must rely upon parataxis in the creation of his narrative. He cannot create a compelling narrative in real time. Few events of any complexity take place in an hour and fifty minutes, nor can a story that is told in real time account for simultaneous and interrelated narratives of other characters, short of creating multiple frames within the full cinema screen, as in the film *Time Code* (2000) or the television series *24*. A cinematic chef spontaneously composing a complex recipe that may take hours or even days to prepare — as in a televised cooking combat where the contestants are not given advanced notice of the dishes to be composed — must be given magical powers, as is Chow, to speed of the process of cooking, or else the chef's activities must be edited to abbreviate the time necessary for the completion of an elaborate dish. Thus the cinematic chef constitutes a rich analogue for the predicament of the screen writer and director, who must account for elapsed time, who must create visual and auditory transitions between images in order to enable the audience to follow the story line. Moreover, the culinary magic displayed by the onscreen chefs is simultaneously cinematic magic. The same techniques the cinematic chef uses to speed up the cooking process are those used by the director to tell the chef's story. Finally, just as cooking requires the collection of a variety of ingredients that are shaped and processed into a culinary masterpiece that is pleasing to the eye, tongue, and nose, filmmaking requires the collection and arrangement of diverse sounds and images into an aesthetically pleasing narrative, prepared for the consumption of an audience hungry for entertainment.

Conclusion

The chapters in this volume cannot do justice to the wide variety of culinary images in contemporary film, nor can they fully sample the broad selection of movies that can be categorized in the food film sub-genre. However, the chapters represented here generate an overview of the multiplicity of roles that culinary narratives and images can play in cinema. This final commentary will labor to reveal some of the broader uses of food imagery in cinema, categorizing various fusions of the culinary and cinematic art forms. My purpose is to reveal that this monograph as well as those works that have come before, such as Anne L. Bower's edited collection *Reel Food: Essays on Food in Film* and Gaye Poole's *Reel Meals, Set Meals: Food in Film and Theatre*, are hardly exhaustive of the genre, particularly insofar as the momentum in the production of food films seems to be increasing.

A surprising number of films adopt a single or a limited number of food items as controlling or defining metaphor[s] within the composition. Rafael Montero's *Cilantro and Parsley* (1996) limits the food commentary to a single analogue between the titular herbs and an incompatible couple. Cilantro and parsley appear to be the same plant, but their respective tastes and smells reveal the substantial differences. Juan Carlos Tabio's *Strawberry and Chocolate* (1993) utilizes a similar central metaphor that defines the contrast between characters. The two ice cream flavors capture the distinction between an overly serious Cuban revolutionary and his flamboyant gay neighbor. While their appreciation of flavors may differ, they both enjoy ice cream, a traditional symbol of life's intense pleasures. *Bread and Tulips* (2002), by Silvio Soldini, depicts the liberation of an unappreciated and emotionally abused wife; the food metaphor in the title reveals the simplicity of her new existence in which she needs no more than beauty and basic sustenance. *Catfish and Black Bean Sauce* (directed by Chi Moui Lo, 1999) addresses the dual heritage of two Vietnamese youths who have been adopted and raised by an African American family, but who are reunited with their biological mother. The catfish and bean sauce signify the collision of cultural polarities in the characters of the youthful adoptees who are forced to choose between the people who raised them and the woman who birthed them.

In some cases, the food metaphor may be character defining. Rachel Flax (played by Cher) in Richard Benjamin's *Mermaids* (1990) feeds her daughters nothing but party hors d'oeuvres, a food which embodies her tendency to runaway from her difficulties with men. Much to her daughters' dismay, Rachel relocates whenever her relationships become overly complicated or messy. The hors d'oeuvres embody her inability to commit to life's main course. An effort to work out her problems rather than relocate would bring her greater fulfillment in life, the implication being that difficulties always lie in the path to happiness. Moreover, Rachel's gustatory choices mirror her gaudy and coquettish sartorial preferences, both she and her dinner are appetizing, but not sustaining. Allison Burnett's 1997 film *Red Meat* also adopts a single culinary metaphor to illuminate character. Three men meet once a week to eat red meat and talk about their respective conquests of women. Of course, just like *Mermaid*'s Rachel Flax, the men are sensualists, not interested in relationships, but only in sex and personal gratification. Red meat is then a metaphor for men's primal drive to hunt and glut themselves intemperately on their captive quarry.

Food may also act as a structuring device in the cinematic narrative. The Swedish film *A Song for Martin*, directed by Bille August (2001), depicts the deterioration of a Swedish composer/conductor who develops Alzheimer's. Martin's progressive decline is revealed through his increasingly irrational behavior at the dinner table. His decision to take his wife to the same restaurant twice in one evening because he cannot remember the earlier dinner is one of the first disturbing signs of his creeping dementia. The act that lands him in an institution occurs during a birthday celebration at a local restaurant where he publicly urinates in a potted plant.

American Adobo, directed by Laurice Guillen (2001), follows five Filipino/Americans through a series of parties where they reaffirm their cultural identity by sharing a dish native to their country of origin. Greenaway's *The Cook, the Thief, His Wife, and Her Lover* (1989) maintains a culinary organization, each chapter of the narrative represented by a tableau of the restaurant's daily specials. Moreover, each menu presages the environment in which the wife and lover will meet for their tryst.

In addition to its more utilitarian function in narrative structure and character development, food in cinema can be classified according to thematics. For example, a significant number of films focus on holiday food rituals (Jodie Foster's *Home for the Holidays* [1995], Gurinder Chadha's

What's Cooking [2000], and Peter Hedges' *Pieces of April* [2003]), —family dining (Sam Mendes' *American Beauty* [1999], Billy Bob Thornton's *Sling Blade* [1996], Stanley Kramer's *Guess Who's Coming to Dinner* [1967], and Norman Jewison's *Moonstruck* [1987]), weddings and courtship (Joel Zwick's *My Big Fat Greek Wedding* [2002], Melissa Martin's *A Wedding for Bella* [2001], Ang Lee's *The Wedding Banquet* [1993]), and birthdays (Henry Jaglom's *Eating* [1990]).

Many food films employ restaurant settings for much or sometimes all of the narrative. In addition to the long list of such movies already discussed in this volume (*Big Night, Dinner Rush, Scotland, PA, Tampopo, The Chef in Love, The Chinese Feast, The Magic Kitchen, Mostly Martha,* and *The Cook, the Thief*), one could include Michael Curtiz's *Mildred Pierce* (1945), Jon Avnet's *Fried Green Tomatoes* (1991), Jan Egleson's *The Blue Diner* (2001), Garry Marshall's *Frankie and Johnny* (1991), James Mangold's *Heavy* (1995), Reuben Gonzalez's *Mambo Café* (2000), Harvey Frost's *Recipe for Disaster* (2003), Cedric Klapisch's *Un Air de Famille* (1996), and Rob McKittrick's *Waiting* (2005), to name only a few more. A subcategory within this same grouping would be dinner conversation films, many of which take place in restaurants. The most well known, of course, would be Louis Malle's *My Dinner with Andre* (1981), but more recently Bob Odenkirk's *Melvin Goes to Dinner* (2003).

The close parallel between the gustatory appetite and eroticism is a commonplace thematic in such films, many of which focus on a female chef who uses her culinary skills to manipulate men's romantic desires. Alfonso Arau's *Like Water for Chocolate* (1992), not only the most well known film addressing the relationship between the sexual and culinary appetites but also the most well known food film in general, tells the story of lovelorn Tita, forbidden to marry by her mother, who, because of a family tradition, expects Tita to remain single so she can nurse the elder woman in old age. Tita's culinary creations have the ability to express her grief nonverbally. When her sister marries the man she loves, she cries into the wedding cake batter; the tainted mixture causes the wedding guests to weep and vomit uncontrollably. Through her recipes, she communicates her passions for her lost love. When she prepares quail with rose petal sauce, the concoction causes all of the diners at the table to become sexually aroused, one sister growing so overheated that she tries to cool herself in a shower, but her body heat ignites the outlying building. Similarly, Fina Torres' *Woman on Top* (2000) features the culinary talents of chef Isabella Oliveira (Penelope Cruz) who has the ability to manipulate men's sexual desires through her spicy Latin recipes.

Other recurring topics in cinematic food narratives include the following: food, politics, and social class (Luis Buñuel's *The Discreet Charm of the Bourgeoisie* [1972], Francis Veber's *The Dinner Game* [1998], and Stacy Title's *The Last Supper* [1995]); food and weight management (Jonnhy To and Ka-Fai Wai's *Love on a Diet* [2001], Mike Leigh's *Life Is Sweet* [1990], James Mangold's *Heavy* [1995], Mike Meiners' *Diet* [2002], and Henry Jaglom's *Eating* [1990]); food and magic (once again Arau's *Like Water for Chocolate* [1992] and Torres' *Woman on Top* [2000], but also Gabriel Axel's *Babette's Feast* [1987], Laurice Guillen's *American Adobo* [2001], and Lee Chi-Ngai's *Magic Kitchen* [2004]); fast food and lifestyle (Danny Leiner's *Harold and Kumar Go to White Castle* [2004], Stephen Frears' *The Van* [1996], Nisha Ganatra's *Fast Food High* [2003], Brian Robbins' *Good Burger* [1997], Jonathan Fahn's *Fast Food* [2000], and Billy Morrissette's *Scotland, PA* [2001] to select only a few names from a very long list); and cannibalism (Marc Caro and Jean-Pierre Jeunet's *Delicatessen* [1991], Anders Thomas Jensen's *The Green Butchers* [2003], Paul Bartel's *Eating Raoul* [1982], Antonia Bird's *Ravenous* [1999], Jon Avnet's *Fried Green Tomatoes* (1991), and Richard Fleischer's *Soylent Green* [1973]).

The above classification is not meant to be exhaustive or rigid. Many of the categories overlap, and none of the films deal exclusively with food related issues. However, the list offers some insight into the varied uses of food in cinema where it must always function as either metaphor or metonymy. The meals and snacks depicted onscreen are never meant to be consumed for pleasure or sustenance, but instead to signify or to stand in for human experience. The subjects who eat onscreen are rarely silent, and when they speak, their food is not often the subject of conversation, the consumers more occupied with the vicissitudes of their daily lives than with their sustenance. They discuss their romantic, familial, professional, ethnic, racial, gender, national, aesthetic, or political preoccupations, rarely the quality or virtues of their comestibles, and, paradoxically, even when the subject of the dialogue is food, the food is not the subject, the meaning of food is. Real food feeds the body, reel food the mind. The consumption of nourishment is a biological drive, the importance of which remains to sustain life. Other aspects of food and particularly film food are cultural, related to the meaning of consumption, preparation, service, and production of the same. Rarely does the dialogue of the narratives discussed in the foregoing pages touch upon the biological necessity of food. Martha offers her recipes as patterns for living; for Ginny Cook, food is the burden of wealth and empire; for the Joseph family, tradition and identity; for Louis Cropa, a racket; for Georgina, sex; for Joe McBeth, ambition; for Primo and Secundo, their ethnic past and material future; for Vianne Rocher, magic; for Babette, redemption; for Mr. Hilditch, predation; and for Antonia, a celebration of life, family, and regeneration.

Appendix: Food Films

American Beauty. Dir. Sam Mendes. United International Pictures, 1999.
American Adobo. Dir. Laurice Guillen. Outrider Pictures, 2001.
Antonia's Line. Dir. Marleen Gorris. First Look Pictures Releasing ,1995
Babette's Feast. Dir Gabriel Axel. Orion Classics, 1987.
Big Night. Dir. Campbell Scott and Stanley Tucci. Samuel Goldwyn Company, 1996.
Blue Diner, The. Dir. Jan Egleson. First Look Home Entertainment, 2001.
Bread and Tulips. Dir. Silvio Soldini. First Look Pictures Releasing, 2000.
Cat Fish in Black Bean Sauce. Dir. Chi Moui Lo. First Look Home Entertainment, 1999.
Chef in Love. Dir. Nana Dzhordzhadze. Sony Pictures Classica, 1997.
Chinese Feast. Dir. Hark Tsui. Mandarin Film Distribution, 1995.
Chocolat. Dir. Lasse Hallstrom. Miramax Films, 2000.
Cilantro and Perejil. Dir. Rafael Montero. Instituto Mexicano de Cinematografia and Telinor, 1995.
Cook, The Thief, His Wife, and Her Lover, The. Dir. Peter Greenaway. Miramax Films, 1989.
Diet. Dir. Mike Meiners. Cinemetro Films, 2002.
Dinner Game, The. Dir. Francis Veber. Lions Gate Films,1998.
Dinner Rush. Dir. Bob Girladi. Access Motion Picture Group, 2000.
Discreet Charm of the Bourgeoisie, The. Dir. Luis Bunuel. 20th Century Fox Film Corp., 1972.
Eat Drink Man Woman. Dir Ang Lee. Samuel Goldwyn Company, 1994.
Eating: A Very Serious Comedy about Women & Food. Dir. Henry Jaglom. International Rainbow, 1990.
Eating Raoul. Dir. Paul Bartel. 20th Century Fox International Classics, 1982.
Family Resemblances. Dir Cedric Klapisch. Leisure Time Films, 1996.
Fast Food. Dir. Jonathan Fahn. Atom Films, 2000.
Fast Food High. Dir. Nisha Ganatra. CCI Entertainment, 2003.
Felicia's Journey. Dir. Atom Egoyan. Artisan Entertainment, 1999.
Frankie and Johnny. Dir. Garry Marshall. Paramount Pictures, 1991.
Fried Green Tomatoes. Dir. Jon Avnet. Universal Pictures, 1991.
God of Cookery, The. Dir. Stephen Chow and Lik-Chi Lee. Universe Films, 1996.
Good Burger. Dir. Brian Robbins. Paramount Pictures,1997.
Grande Bouffe, La. Dir. Marco Ferreri. ABKCO Films Inc., 1973.
Green Butchers, The. Dir. Anders Thomas Jensen. New Market Films, 2003.
Guess Who's Coming to Dinner. Dir. Stanley Kramer. Columbia Pictures, 1967.
Harold and Kumar go to White Castle. Dir. Danny Leiner. New Line Cinema, 2004.

Home for the Holidays. Dir. Jodie Foster. Paramount Pictures, 1995.
House of Flying Daggers. Dir Yimou Zhang. Sony Pictures Classics, 2004.
Kitchen Stories. Dir. Bent Hamer. IFC Films, 2003.
Last Supper, The. Dir. Stacy Title. Columbia Pictures. 1995
Life Is Sweet. Dir. Mike Leigh. October Films, 1990.
Like Water for Chocolate. Dir. Alfonso Arau. Miramax Films, 1992.
Love on a Diet. Dir. Johnny To and Ka-Fai Wai. Twin Star Entertainment, 2001.
Magic Kitchen. Dir. Li Chi Ngai and Chi-Ngai Lee. Twin Co. LTD, 2004.
Mambo Café. Dir. Reuben Gonzalez. Unapix Entertainment, 2000.
Martha Inc. Dir. Jason Ensler. Lions Gate Films, 2003.
Melvin Goes to Dinner. Dir. Bob Odenkirk. Arrival Pictures, 2003.
Men Don't Leave. Dir. Paul Brickman. Geffen Film Co., 1990.
Mermaids. Dir. Richard Benjamin. Orion Pictures Corp., 1990.
Mildred Pierce. Dir. Michael Curtiz. Warner Bros., 1945.
Moonstruck. Dir. Norman Jewison. Metro-Goldwyn-Mayer, 1987.
Mostly Martha. Dir. Sandra Nettelbeck. Paramount Classics, 2001.
My Big Fat Greek Wedding. Dir. Joel Zwick. IFC Films, 2002.
My Dinner with Andre. Dir. Louis Malle. Cinegate LTD.,1981.
Pieces of April. Dir. Peter Hedges. United Artists, 2003.
Prospero's Books. Dir. Peter Greenaway. Miramax Films, 1991.
Ran. Dir. Akira Kurasawa. Orion Classics, 1985.
Ravenous. Dir. Antonia Bird. 20th Century Fox Film Corp., 1999.
Recipe for Disaster. Dir. Harvey Frost. Metro-Goldwyn Mayer, 2003.
Red Meat. Dir. Allison Burnett. Peninsula Films. Inc. 1997
Scotland, PA. Dir. Billy Morrissette. Lot 47 Films, 2001.
Sling Blade. Dir. Billy Bob Thornton. Miramax Films, 1996.
Song for Martin, A. Dir. Bille August. First Look Pictures Releasing, 2001.
Soul Food. Dir. George Tillman Jr. 20th Century Fox Film Corp.,1997.
Soylent Green. Dir. Richard Fleischer. Metro-Goldwyn-Mayer, 1973.
Strawberry and Chocolate. Dir. Tomas Gutierrez Alea and Juan Carlos Tabio. Miramax Films, 1994.
Tampopo. Dir. Juzo Itami. New Yorker Films, 1985.
Tortilla Soup. Dir. Maria Ripoll. Samuel Goldwyn Company, 2001.
Thousand Acres, A. Dir. Jocelyn Moorhouse. Buena Vista Pictures, 1997.
Time Code. Dir. Mike Figgis. Columbia TriStar Domestic, 2000.
Van, The. Dir. Stephen Frears. Fox Searchlight Pictures, 1996.
Waiting. Dir. Rob Mc Kittrick. . Lions Gate Films, 2005.
Wedding Banquet, The. Dir. Ang Lee. Samuel Goldwyn Company, 1993.
Wedding for Bella, A. Dir. Melissa Martin. Panorama Entertainment, 2001.
What's Cooking. Dir. Gurinder Chadha. Lions Gate Films, 2000.
Woman on Top. Dir. Fina Torres. Fox Searchlight Pictures, 2000.

Bibliography

Abbott, Elizabeth. *The History of Celibacy.* Cambridge, MA: Da Capo, 2001.

Aguiar, Sarah Appleton. "(Dis)Obedient Daughters: (Dis)Inheriting the Kingdom of Lear." *He Said, She Said: An RSVP to the Male Text.* Eds. Mica Howe and Sarah Appleton Aguiar. Madison: Fairleigh Dickinson UP, 2001. 194–210.

Allen, Stewart Lee. *In the Devil's Garden: A Sinful History of Forbidden Food.* New York: Ballantine, 2002.

Amerine, Maynard A. "Flavor as a Value." *Food and Civilization.* Eds. Seymour M. Farber, Nancy L. Wilson, and Roger H.L. Wilson. Springfield, IL: Charles C. Thomas, 1966. 104–120.

Ansen, David. "Twice as Sweet as Sugar." *Newsweek* 18 Dec. 2000: 77.

Ashkenazi, Michael. "Food, Play, Business, and the Image of Japan in Itami Juzo's *Tampopo.*" *Reel Food: Essays on Food and Film.* Ed. Anne L. Bower. New York: Routledge, 2004. 17–26.

Bakerman, Jane S. "'The Gleaming Obsidian Shard': Jane Smiley's *A Thousand Acres.*" *MidAmerica* 19 (1992): 127–137.

Beck, Ervin. "Dinesen's *Babette's Feast.*" *Explicator* 56 (1998): 210–203.

Beneke, Timothy. *Proving Manhood: Reflections on Men and Sexism.* Berkeley: U of California P, 1997.

Berman, Art. *From the New Criticism to Deconstruction: The Reception of Structuralism and Poststructuralism.* Urbana, IL: U of Illinois P, 1988.

Bernier, Chris. "Chocolat." *Creative Screenwriting* 8 (2001): 12–13.

Boose, Lynda E. and Richard Burt. "Introduction." *Shakespeare the Movie: Popularizing the Plays on Film, TV, and Video.* Ed. Lynda E. Boose and Richard Burt. London: Routledge, 1997. 1–7.

Boswell, Parley Ann. "Hungry in the Land of Plenty: Food in Hollywood Films." *Beyond the Stars III: The Material in American Popular Film.* Eds. Paul Loukides and Linda K. Fuller. Bowling Green, OH: Bowling Green State University Popular Press, 1993.

Branson, Stephnie. "Dinesen in Three Dimension: A Comparison of Irony in Two Films of Dinesen's Stories." *Literature Film Quarterly* 28 (2000): 49–54.

Braziller, George. *The Blood of Kings: Dynasty and Ritual in Maya Art.* New York: George Braziller Inc. and the Kimball Art Museum, 1986.

Brennan, Martin. *The Hidden Maya.* Santa Fe, NM: Bear & Co., 1998.

Carr, Glynis. "Persephone's Daughters: Janes Smiley's *A Thousand Acres* and Classical Myth." *The Bucknell Review* 44 (2000): 120–136.

Chakravarti, Debnita. "Feel Good Reel Food: A Taste of the Cultural Kedgeree in

Gurinder Chadha's What's Cooking." *Reel Food: Essays on Food and Film.* Ed. Anne L. Bower. New York: Routledge, 2004. 17–26.

Coe, Michael D. *Breaking the Maya Code.* New York: Thames and Hudson, 1992.

Coe, Sophie D., and Michael D. Coe. *The True History of Chocolate.* London: Thames and Hudson, 1996.

Cooper, Rand Richards. "Hallucinogens for All." *Commonweal* 128 (2001): 19–20.

Counihan, Carole, and Penny Van Esterick, eds. *Food and Culture: A Reader.* New York: Routledge, 1997.

Coyle, Margaret. *"Il Timpano*—'To Eat Good Food Is to Be Close to God': The Italian-American Reconciliation of Stanley Tucci and Cambell Scott's *Big Night." Reel Food: Essays on Food and Film.* Ed. Anne L. Bower. New York: Routledge, 2004. 17–26.

Culler, Jonathan. *Ferdinand de Saussure.* Ithaca: Cornell UP, 1986.

_____. *On Deconstruction: Theory and Criticism After Structuralism.* Ithaca: Cornell UP, 1982.

D'Arcy, Chantal Cornut-Gentille. "Peter Greenaway's *The Cook, the Thief, His Wife, and Her Lover." Literature Film Quarterly* 27 (1999): 116–124.

Delphy, Christine. "Sharing the Same Table: Consumption and the Family." Trans. Dianna Leonard. *Sociological Review Monograph* 28 (1979): 214–231.

D'haen, Theo L. "Magic Realism and Postmodernism: Decentering Privileged Centers." *Magical Realism: Theory, History, Community.* Eds. Lois Parkinson Zamora and Wendy B. Faris. Durham, NC: Duke UP, 1995. 191–208.

Dinesen, Isak. "Babette's Feast." *Anecdotes of Destiny and Ehrengard.* New York: Vintage, 1993. 21–59.

Douglas, Mary. "Deciphering a Meal." *Food and Culture: A Reader.* Eds. Carole Counihan and Penny Van Esterick. New York: Routledge, 1997. 36–54.

_____. *Purity and Danger: An Analysis of the Concepts of Pollution and Taboo.* London: Routledge, 1966.

_____ and Jonathan Gross. *"Food and Culture: Measuring the Intricacy of Rule Systems." Social Science Information* 20 (1981): 1–35.

Drury, Nevill. *The Elements of Shamanism.* Rockport, MA, 1991.

Dryden, John. "St. Cecilia's Day" and "Alexander's Feast." *Selected Works of John Dryden.* Ed. William Frost. New York: Holt, Rinehart, and Winston, 1953. 73–80.

Dubois, W.E.B. *The Souls of Black Folk.* New York: Penguin, 1989.

Eliade, Mircea. *Shamanism: Archaic Techniques of Ecstasy.* Princeton, NJ: Princeton UP, 1964.

Faris, Wendy B. "Scheherazade's Children: Magical Realism and Postmodern Fiction." *Magical Realism: Theory, History, Community.* Eds. Lois Parkinson Zamora and Wendy B. Faris. Durham, NC: Duke UP, 1995. 163–190.

Fiddes, Nick. *Meat: A Natural Symbol.* London: Routledge, 1991.

Finkelstein, Joanne. *Dining Out: A Sociology of Modern Manners.* New York: New York UP, 1989.

Fishwick, Marshall. *Ronald Revisited: The World of Ronald McDonald.* Bowling Green, OH: Bowling Green University Popular Press, 1983.

Ford, John. *'Tis Pity She's a Whore.* Ed. Brian Morris. New York: W.W. Norton, 1986.

Foucault, Michel. *Discipline and Punish: The Birth of the Prison.* Trans. Alan Sheridan. New York: Vintage, 1977.

_____. "The Eye of Power." *Power/Knowledge: Selected Interviews and Other Writings 1972–1977.* Ed. Colin Gordon. Trans. Colin Gordon, Leo Marshall, John Mepham, and Kate Soper. New York: Pantheon, 1980. 146–165.

_____. *Power/Knowledge: Selected Interviews and Other Writings 1972–1977.* Ed. Colin Gordon. Trans. Colin Gordon, Leo Marshall, John Mepham, and Kate Soper. New York: Pantheon, 1980.

Freidel, David, Linda Schele, and Joy Parker. *Maya Cosmos: Three Thousand Years on the Shaman's Path.* New York: Quill, 1993.

Fussell, Betty. *The Story of Corn.* New York: North Point, 1992.

Gillet, Sue. "Just Women: Marlene Gorris's *Antonia's Line.*" *Senses of Cinema* 17 (2001). <http://www.sensesofcinema.com/contents/cteq/01/17/antonia.html>.

Gillette, Douglas. *The Shaman's Secret: The Lost Resurrection Teachings of the Ancient Maya.* New York: Bantam, 1998.

Goody, Jack. *Cooking, Cuisine, and Class: A Study in Comparative Sociology.* Cambridge, UK: Cambridge UP, 1982.

Gras, Vernon. "Dramatizing the Failure to Jump the Culture/Nature Gap: The Films of Peter Greenaway." *New Literary History* 26 (19995): 123–143.

Greenaway, Peter. *The Cook, the Thief, His Wife, and Her Lover.* Paris: Dis Voir, 1989.

Harris, Joanne. *Chocolat.* New York: Penguin, 2000.

Harris, Marvin. *Good to Eat: Riddles of Food and Culture.* New York: Simon and Schuster, 1985.

Harte, Liam and Lance Pettitt. "States of Dislocation: William Trevor's *Felicia's Journey* and Maurice Leitch's *Gilchrist.*" *Comparing Postcolonial Literatures: Dislocations.* Eds. Ashok Bery and Patricia Murray. New York: St. Martin's, 2000. 70–80.

Hogas, Tore. "'A Destiny We Never Asked For': Gender and Gifts, Property and Power in Jane Smiley's *A Thousand Acres.*" *American Studies in Scandinavia* 33 (2001): 65–73.

Horrocks, Roger. *Masculinity in Crisis.* New York: St. Martin's, 1994.

Iammarino, Sarah. "A Celebration of the Italian Culture: Stanley Tucci and Campbell Scott's *Big Night.*" *VIA: Voices in Italian Americana* 8 (1997): 183–88.

Iles, Timothy. "The Lazy Gaze: The Aesthetics of Consumerism in Itami Juzo's *Tampopo.*" *Asian Cinema* 15 (2004): 225–233.

Inouye, Charles Shiro. "In the Show House of Modernity: Exhaustive Listing in Itami Juzo's *Tampopo.*" *Word and Image in Japanese Cinema.* Eds. Dennis Washburn and Carole Cavanaugh. Cambridge, UK: Cambridge UP, 2001. 126–146.

Iordanova, Dina. "Film Review: Chef in Love." *Russian Review* 57 (1998): 618–619.

Keller, James R. "Excess and Defect: Spenser and Medieval Cosmology in *A Thousand Acres.*" *The Year's Work in Medievalism* 14 (1999): 81–92.

Kellman, Steven G. "Food Fights in Iowa: The Vegetarian Stranger in Recent Midwest Fiction." *Virginia Quarterly Review* 71 (1995): 435–447.

Keppel, Tim. "Goneril's Version: *A Thousand Acres* and *King Lear.*" *South Dakota Review* 33 (1995): 105–117.

Kilb, Andreas. "I Am the Cook: A Conversation with Peter Greenaway." *Peter Greenaway Interviews.* Eds. Vernon Gras and Marguerite Gras. Jackson, MS: U of Mississippi P, 2000. 60–65.

Lanier, Douglas. *Shakespeare and Modern Popular Culture.* New York: Oxford UP, 2002.

Lawrence, Amy. *The Films of Peter Greenaway.* Cambridge, UK: Cambridge UP, 1997.

Leitch, Vincent B. *Deconstructive Criticism: An Advanced Introduction.* New York, Columbia UP, 1983.

Levenstein, Harvey A. *Revolution at the Table: The Transformation of the American Diet.* New York: Oxford UP, 1988.

Ma, Sheng-mei. "Ang Lee's Domestic Tragicomedy: Immagrant Nostalgia, Exotic/Ethnic Tour, Global Market." *Journal of Popular Culture* 30 (1996): 191–202.

Marquez, Gabriel Garcia. *One Hundred Years of Solitude.* Trans. Gregory Rabassa. New York: HarperPerennial, 1991.

Mathieson, Barbara. "The Polluted Quarry: Nature and the Body in *A Thousand Acres.*" *Transforming Shakespeare: Contemporary Women's Re-Visions in Literature and Performance.* Ed. Marianne Novy. New York: St. Martin's, 1999. 127–158.

McDonagh, Melanie. "The Church That Loves Chocolate." *New Statesman* 5 Mar. 2001. 23–24.

McFadden, Margaret H. "Gendering the Feast: Women, Spirituality, and Grace in Three Food Films." *Reel Food: Essays on Food and Film.* Ed. Anne L. Bower. New York: Routledge, 2004. 17–26.

Messner, Michael A. *Power at Play: Sports and the Problem of Masculinity.* Boston: Beacon, 1992.

Mickelsen, David J. "After-Dinner Speakers in *Babette's Feast:* The End Was the Word." *Edda* 1 (2001): 33–47.

Milton, John. *Paradise Lost. John Milton: Complete Poems and Major Prose.* Ed. Merritt Y. Hughes. Indianapolis, IN: Bobbs-Merrill, 1957. 211–469.

Moore, Harriett Bruce. "The Meaning of Food." *American Journal of Clinical Nutrition* 5 (1957): 77–82.

Mulvey, Laura. "Visual Pleasure and Narrative Cinema." *Screen* 16 (1975): 6–18.

Nelson, William. *The Poetry of Spenser: A Study.* New York: Columbia UP, 1963.

"NY Man Sues, Claiming Fast Food Ruined His Health." *New York* 26 July 2002 <http://www.ablewise.com/article/article_130.shtml>

O'Dair, Sharon. "Horror or Realism? Filming 'Toxic Discourse' in Jane Smiley's *A Thousand Acres.*" *Textual Practice* 19 (205): 263–282.

Ogier, James M. "Babette's Verbal Feast: Therapeutic Orality in Text, Translation, and Film." *Scandinavia* 32 (1993): 177–189.

Olson, Catherine Cowen. "You Are What You Eat: Food and Power in Jane Smiley's *A Thousand Acres.*" *Midwest Quarterly* 40 (1998): 21–33.

Pagan, Nicholas O. "*The Cook, the Thief, His Wife, and Her Lover:* Making Sense of Postmodernism." *South Atlantic Review* 60 (1995): 43–55.

Pascoe, David. *Peter Greenaway: Museums and Moving Images.* London: Reakton, 1997.

Petersson, Kerstin. "The Role of Music in Gabriel Axel's Film *Babette's Feast.*" *Essays in Memory of Michael Parkinson and Janine Dakyns.* Ed. Christopher Smith. Norwich: School of Mod. Lang. & European Studies, 1996. 283–289.

Phillips, John. "Sadean Savouries in Peter Greenaway's *The Cook, the Thief, His Wife and Her Lover.*" *Paragraph* 23 (2000): 98–118.

Podles, Mary Elizabeth. "*Babette's Feast:* Feasting with the Lutherans." *Antioch Review* 50 (1992): 551–567.

Popol Vuh. Trans. Dennis Tedlock. New York: Simon and Schuster, 1985.

Pope, Alexander. *Essay on Criticism. The Norton Anthology of English Literature.* Ed. M.H. Abrams et al. Sixth Ed. New York: W.W. Norton, 1993. 2217–2233.

Porton, Richard. *"Felicia's Journey." Cineaste* 25 (1999): 42–43.

_____. "The Politics of Denial: An Interview with Atom Egoyan." *Cineaste* 25 (1999): 39–41.

Rashkin, Esther. "A Recipe for Mourning: Isak Dinesen's *Babette's Feast." Style* 29 (1995): 356–374.

Renner, H.D. *The Origin of Food Habits.* London: Faber and Faber, 1944.

Schele, Linda, and David Freidel. *A Forest of Kings: The Untold Story of the Ancient Maya.* New York: Quill, 1990.

Schiff, James A. "Contemporary Retellings: *A Thousand Acres* as the Latest Lear." *Critique* 39 (1998): 367–382.

Schlosser, Eric. *Fast Food Nation.* New York: Perennial, 2002.

Sedgwick, Eve Kosofsky. *Between Men: English Literature and Male Homosocial Desire.* New York: Columbia UP, 1985.

Sellery, J'Nan Morse. "Women's Communities and the Magical Realist Gaze of Antonia's Line." *Philological Papers* 48 (2001/02): 115–124.

Siegel, Joel. "Greenaway by the Numbers." *Peter Greenaway Interviews.* Eds. Vernon Gras and Marguerite Gras. Jackson, MS: U of Mississippi P, 2000. 67–90.

Simpkins, Scott. "Magical Strategies: The Supplement of Realism." *TCL* 34 (1988): 140–153.

Simpson, Mark. *Male Impersonators: Men Performing Masculinity.* New York: Routledge, 1994.

Sklar, Robert. "The Lighter Side of Feminism: An Interview with Marlene Gorris." *Cineaste* 22 (1996): 26–28.

Spenser, Edmund. *The Faerie Queene.* Ed. A.C. Hamilton. London: Longman, 1977.

Stetco, Dayana. "The Crisis of Commentary: Tilting at Windmills in Peter Greenaway's *The Cook, the Thief, His Wife, and Her Lover." Peter Greenaway's Postmodern/Poststructuralist Cinema.* Eds. Paula Willoquet-Maricondi and Mary Alemany-Galway. Lanham, MD: Scarecrow, 2001. 203–222.

Stevens, Wallace. "Sunday Morning." *The Collected Poems of Wallace Stevens.* New York: Vintage, 1982. 66–70.

Strehle, Susan. "The Daughters' Subversion in Jane Smiley's *A Thousand Acres." Critique* 41 (2000): 211–227.

Tannahill, Reay. *Food in History.* New York: Three Rivers, 1988.

Trevor, William. *Felicia's Journey.* New York: Penguin, 1996.

Ty, Eleanor. "Exoticism Repositioned: Old and New World Pleasures in Wang's *Joy Luck Club* and Lee's *Eat Drink Man Woman. Changing Representations of Minorities East and West.* Eds. Larry E. Smith and John Reider. Honolulu, HI: College of Languages, Linguistics and Literature, University of Hawaii, with East-West Center; 1996. 50–73.

Visser, Margaret. *The Rituals of Dinner: The Origins, Evolution, Eccentricities, and Meaning of Table Manners.* New York: Grove Weidenfeld, 1991.

Waith, Eugene. "Manhood and Valor in Two Shakespearean Tragedies." *ELH* 30 (1950): 265–68.

Wagner, Philip M. "Food as Ritual." *Food and Civilization.* Eds. Seymour M. Farber, Nancy L. Wilson, and Roger H.L. Wilson. Springfield, IL: Charles C. Thomas, 1966. 60–73.

William, Raymond. *Problems in Materialism and Culture.* London: New Left Books, 1980.

Wilson, Bee. "Choc-Full" (editorial). *New Statesman* 11 Dec. 2000: 48–49.

Zamora, Lois Parkinson, and Wendy B. Faris. "Introduction: Daiquiri Birds and Flaubertian Parrot[ie]s." *Magical Realism: Theory, History, Community.* Eds. Lois Parkinson Zamora and Wendy B. Faris. Durham, NC: Duke UP, 1995. 1–14.

Zlotnick-Woldenberg, Carrie. "Felicia's Journey: An Object-Relational Study of Psychopathy." *American Journal of Psychotherapy* 57 (2003): 101–108.

Index